Critical
Issues
in
History

The Eve of the Modern World, 1250-1648

Critical
Issues
in History

UNDER THE EDITORIAL DIRECTION OF *RICHARD E. SULLIVAN*

SIX-VOLUME EDITION

1 *The Ancient World to A.D. 400*
THOMAS W. AFRICA, *University of Southern California*

2 *The Middle Ages, 400-1250*
RICHARD E. SULLIVAN, *Michigan State University*

3 *The Eve of the Modern World, 1250-1648*
J. K. SOWARDS, *Wichita State University*

4 *The Early Modern Era, 1648-1770*
JOHN C. RULE, *Ohio State University*

5 *The Age of Revolution, 1770-1870*
DAVID L. DOWD, *University of Kentucky*

6 *War and Totalitarianism, 1870 to the Present*
JOHN L. SNELL, *University of Pennsylvania*

TWO-VOLUME EDITION

VOLUME I   *Ancient Times to 1648*

VOLUME II   *1648 to the Present*

Critical Issues in History

The Eve of the Modern World

1250-1648

EDITED WITH INTRODUCTIONS BY

J. K. SOWARDS

Wichita State University

D. C. HEATH *and Company, Boston*

ILLUSTRATION CREDITS

Cover and page 223: Section of chapel, Château D'Anet; C. T. Mathews, *The Renaissance Under the Valois,* New York, 1893.

Library of Congress Catalog Card Number: 67-13486
Copyright © 1967 by D. C. Heath and Company
No part of the material covered by this copyright
may be reproduced in any form without written permission
of the publisher.
Printed in the United States of America.

Printed December 1966

Boston
Englewood
Indianapolis
Dallas
San Francisco
Atlanta

PREFACE

This volume, one of a six-volume set, is intended to engage students in *problem-resolving situations* as a technique for enriching their study of European history. The editors who collaborated in preparing these six volumes are convinced that this approach has great value in stimulating interest, encouraging critical thinking, and enhancing historical-mindedness, especially when it is used to supplement the more conventional techniques employed in teaching the general introductory course in European history.

The volume opens with an interpretive essay aimed at placing the five "problems" which follow in the perspective of the period. While all of the problems follow the same structure, the topics they treat are highly diverse: in one, a single man's role in history is debated, while the next examines an ideological issue; in one problem causes are sought, while the next weighs effects.

Each of the five problems is introduced by a short statement defining the issue and directing the student to the crucial questions involved. For the most part selections have been taken from the works of modern historians, with occasional use of the observations of contemporary witnesses. In choosing the selections, the editor has tried to avoid generating conflict for conflict's sake. Rather, he has sought to show how honest divergencies emerge among historians as a result of the complexities of history, varying initial assumptions, different approaches to evidence, and all the other factors that enter into interpretation of the past. The student's efforts to understand how differing interpretations arise and to resolve these differences should increase his ability to manipulate historical data and concepts and deepen his understanding of the historian's craft.

CONTENTS

INTRODUCTION

Modern historians have largely abandoned the old and familiar notion that history is a series of well-defined periods such as "classical antiquity" or "the Middle Ages," connected by transitional epochs. While retaining the conventional labels, they have replaced the static, orderly, and artificial idea of structure with the idea of continuum—what we might call the continuity of change. It is a Heraclitean view which sees every age as an age of transition and great historical changes as the products of accumulation of forces rather than dramatic, cataclysmic happenings.

Yet, even within the concept of the historical continuum there are some ages in which the tempo of change is so marked and the product of change so significant that they can only be properly described as transitional ages. Such a one is the period with which the following problems are concerned—Western Europe in the four crowded centuries between 1250 and 1648. There was not a major facet of the life of Western Europe that did not, in this period, experience change so fundamental that the Europe of the seventeenth century was more like the Europe of every age that followed than it was like any time that had gone before.

The church which, in the thirteenth century, had been a formative force in European politics had, by 1648, been virtually excluded from the councils of political decision. Religion was still a political force to be contended with but it was no longer the unitary religion of medieval Catholicism. The Reformation had brought an end to that and, while the evangelical sects still multiplied and wrangled among themselves, by 1648 a broad belt had been drawn across the European continent to divide Catholic Europe from Protestant Europe. And the division it represented was irrevocable. The last great effort of the Catholic Hapsburg monarchy to turn back the clock of religion and politics had failed and religious division was to remain a permanent part of the European cultural and political scene.

The political frontiers which had marked the Europe of the thirteenth century were gone. For the diplomats who redrew the map of Europe at the Peace of Westphalia (1648) and at the Peace of the Pyrenees (1659) had created the essential shape of modern Europe. A handful of the major powers with which Innocent III had dealt remained but under the rule of constitutional forms and royal dynasties unknown to the thirteenth century. On the periphery of the medieval Europe the barbaric kingdoms of Scandinavia had taken form and intruded into the affairs of the older powers. Gustavus Adolphus, the king of Sweden and "Lion of the North," had played as major a role in the conflicts of central Europe in the seventeenth century as had the German emperor. On the open eastern frontier a major new power had shouldered its way into the family of European nations: the Duchy of Muscovy had become Russia. The menace of the Turks which had threatened and frightened the Europe of the Middle Ages and generated that series of quixotic adventures we call the Crusades was fading into insignificance; the Ottoman Empire was becoming the "sick man of Europe," the object no longer of the fear of the European powers and shortly to be an object of their cupidity. Beyond Europe itself a new world had opened to the enterprise of Europeans. To those remote places of which thirteenth-century men had only been able to speculate, the men of the seventeenth century sailed their ships, planted colonies, founded charter companies, began to carve out overseas empires, and undertook the translation of the ethos of Western Europe to the wider world.

Much of the motivation which had driven men to open that wider world was economic. Indeed, the economic forces which had flourished in the thirteenth century had come to the maturity of their medieval form and had evolved into their modern counterparts. The European money market had long since shifted to the north Atlantic seaboard. The Flemish towns had enjoyed their late medieval prosperity and decayed. The great chartered mercantile companies of Holland and England had appeared with such capital assets and annual volume of trade and profits as to shame the wealth of even the greatest medieval monarchies. Their syndics wielded a power greater than the great Khan and the long arm of their naval policy reached to the other side of the world.

The social structure of medieval Europe had been similarly transformed. The concept of privilege was still dominant and few men even theorized yet about the broad-based democracy that we know in our time. In many parts of Europe the social forms of medieval feudalism still persisted. But, by the mid-seventeenth century, those forms were rapidly becoming moribund under the pressure of two formative forces of the modern world, the nation state and the middle class. Both these forces had existed in embryo in the High Middle Ages and had come to maturity in the four centuries with which we are here concerned. The stubborn barons who could still defy the kings of the thirteenth century had become the self-seeking *frondeurs* or captive courtiers of the seventeenth. The middle class, which had come into precarious existence in the medieval towns, had by the seventeenth century become the most important social class of Western Europe. The men of this class had re-built the European economic machinery. They had in some nations redrawn the charts of government and even in those nations where royal absolutism prevailed they were the men and the class closest the throne. The parliaments and assemblies and political parties which these men dominate in Western Europe today were already forming in the seventeenth century.

The intellectual preoccupation of the thirteenth century was scholasticism. It was the century of Albertus Magnus, St. Thomas Aquinas, and Duns Scotus. But by 1648 even the frame of reference within which scholasticism had meaning was fundamentally changed. Men were still concerned with the state of their souls, whether Catholic or Protestant. The vocabulary of religion was still familiar to the man in the street after more than a century of Reformation and Counterreformation. But Europe was weary of religious wars and of the causes that spawned them. The vision of eternity was being replaced by the vision of the here and now. Not only was there a physical world to be explored and exploited but a new world of the mind was opening, the world of science, that most modern characteristic of the modern world. By 1648 Leibnitz and Newton were already born; Robert Boyle was about to start his revolutionary experiments in chemistry; and Blaise Pascal had already published one of the landmark works in spatial mathematics.

In nearly every sense the four centuries from the mid-thirteenth to the mid-seventeenth were the seed time of our world. The "new Europe" which the Middle Ages had created was rapidly becoming modern Europe.

It is to be expected that an age of such significance as this should have attracted the curious attention of historians for they are perennially concerned to search for cause and to probe for the origins of things. It is equally to be expected that their attention should have led to controversy. This is in the nature of the historiographic process no matter what the period under consideration. But when the period is significant, as this one is, and complex, as it is also, major (and often acrimonious) differences of interpretation are nearly inevitable. They abound in the critical literature of this transitional age between medieval and modern history.

It is the purpose of the five problems that follow to illuminate some of the most important of these controversies. Some of the problems represent flat differences of opinion. Others represent shades of opinion within a broad area of general agreement. Some represent the evolution of a critical position through two or three generations of historical revision. But altogether they give to the interested student some insight into both the multiplicity and subtlety of historical forces and the continually vital process of restudying the past. The student must realize that there is really no such thing as "the dead past"; that no moment of past time is ever completely known; and that no historical controversy is ever conclusively solved.

1

THE DECLINE AND FALL OF THE MEDIEVAL PAPACY

The century and a half before the great jubilee year 1300 had been a time of accelerating growth and accomplishment in the history of Western Europe. Towns had sprung up and prospered; a flourishing network of trade had knit these together and quickened material life; the formless chaos of feudalism seemed to be giving way before the wealth and power and order of the national monarchies. The century and a half after 1300 presents almost exactly the opposite picture. It was a time of general war and devastation, of revolutions and upheaval, of famine and pestilence, and a pervasive attitude of despair and resignation. And it was a time of such crisis in the history of the papacy that this "greatest of medieval institutions" was fundamentally altered.

The striking success of the popes in asserting their primacy in the church in the course of the twelfth and thirteenth centuries had made the history of the papacy almost synonymous with the history of the church. Thus the series of shocks, both external and internal, which battered the papacy in the centuries between the High Middle Ages and the eve of the Reformation was of basic importance in the history of the church and of Western Europe. For the troubles of the papacy must be set within a generally troubled time. The changes that overtook that institution were not so alien to nor so distinct from the changes, equally drastic and painful, to which other institutions were being subjected.

For reasons that are still not entirely clear, the curve of European economic prosperity which had climbed steadily upward for some two centuries dropped sharply downward in the early fourteenth century and general economic recovery did not begin until well after the middle of the fifteenth century. War and pestilence complicated the economic troubles and contributed to them. Agricultural productivity declined and land which had been reclaimed and settled in the thirteenth century expansion reverted to forest and waste. Settled agricultural villages disappeared and Europe seemed to be retreating. In the mid-fourteenth century came the Black Death, the most devastating of medieval plagues. But even before the Black Death there is evidence of a sharp decline in population which was accelerated by the pestilence. Labor shortages resulted and, of course, aggravated the problem of agricultural production. The towns and cities as well as the countryside were declining in population. The effects of the plague were especially bad in the crowded and unsanitary cities. But trade and exchange, the life blood of the cities, was declining also. The volume of trade in northern Europe in 1400 may actually have been less than it was a century before.

Such conditions as these spread alarm in every direction and triggered savage social revolts and equally savage reprisals. At the same time that economic conditions had their effects in other spheres, military, political, and social events contributed heavily to the pattern of economic troubles. Germany and the Empire were in chronic disorder. Kings and antikings fought for a title which had become almost meaningless and, on a lesser scale, the sovereign territorial lords of Germany fought bitterly with each other. Before the middle of the fourteenth century the Hundred Years' War had broken out between England and France, and within a generation had come to involve most of the powers of Western Europe. It was a particularly destructive war, not only because of the tactic of wholesale devastation which was widely employed, but because of the long periods of nominal peace between major engagements which set loose upon the helpless countryside of western France rapacious bands of soldiers to live off the land. Thus the Hundred Years' War, like the chronic military disorder of Germany, was really a series of small and destructive local wars. Moreover, for long periods of time, the government of France — which had been the most stable and centralized power in Europe — was in collapse, and the institutions which had so painfully built over the centuries seemed to be dissolving.

In these desperate times men could see no rhyme nor reason to their problems. They could not fathom the changes that were destroying their lives and fortunes. They rebelled savagely and senselessly. The records of the age are filled with the accounts of peasant revolts and, in the cities, uprisings among the working people. Men were angry, frustrated, and in despair. And they turned, in their desperation, to the most extreme and neurotic expressions of religious fervor. Had the church been able to seize and direct this blind and desperate religious fervor the history of this period might have been very different. But the church as an institution was too deeply involved in the very forces from which men turned. It was too much of the world to take leadership of an otherworldly reaction. And it is against this general background of what Wallace K. Ferguson has called "a changing world" that we must consider the changes that affected the papacy and contributed to its precipitate decline.

The chain of events was triggered by the pontificate of Boniface VIII (1294–1303).

This ambitious and intemperate pope chose to test his exalted notions of papal sovereignty against the power of the French monarchy and that shrewd and able monarch Philip IV: and he lost. But he lost more than a skirmish, for he had failed to realize that the concept of an international spiritual and temporal kingdom of the church, under the rule of the monarchical papacy, was no longer compatible with the rising spirit of the national monarchy. He had set himself and the papacy against the wave of the future.

The victory of the French king overshadowed the selection of Boniface's successor, and the cardinals, fearful of French reprisal, elected a French cleric as Clement V. Shortly Clement took up residence, not at Rome, but at the French city of Avignon obviously within the reach of the French king and apparently subservient to him. For more than seventy years—until 1378—and through seven popes, the papacy remained in exile at Avignon, the so-called Babylonian Captivity of the Church. French popes preferred French clerics to important church positions, and the interests of France seemed to predominate in papal policy. Criticism mounted from every quarter, criticism not only of the scandalous partisanship of the popes, but of their even more scandalous worldliness. And they had no defense. It is probable that this period was the most crucial in the decline of papal prestige in the later Middle Ages.

In 1378 the papacy was restored to Rome but was immediately divided by a disputed election. The result was the Great Schism. An Italian pope reigned in Rome; a French pope returned to Avignon. And their successors perpetuated the condition for forty years. The nations of Europe, already divided on a dozen secular issues, were now divided in religious obedience. The abuses which had been the scandal of the "Babylonian" papacy became even more flagrant, and the criticism and popular hostility to the church more strident.

In their desperation to heal the schism, well intentioned men in both papal camps sought a solution in the summoning of general councils. The first of these was called at Pisa in 1409 to begin the Conciliar Movement. It lasted through the fifteenth century and it must be counted a failure. The schism was finally healed, but the need for reform which was an issue of more pressing importance was not met. The popes chose to fight the councils rather than the problems the councils raised. The monarchical sovereignty of the popes was chosen as the prize to be preserved. And the popes preserved it; but at the cost of their prestige, their spiritual authority and the general condition of the church. On the eve of the Reformation, the traditional church was as ill-prepared as it had ever been to face a major challenge.

In the selections that follow, a number of scholars look at different aspects of this history of the papacy in the fourteenth and fifteenth centuries. The general account of events is not in dispute among them any more than whether the Reformation or the French Revolution actually happened. Nor is the overall significance of the events in dispute. Their significance, indeed, is what makes them well worth repeated study. The scholars whose work is represented here are in disagreement but on matters of emphasis, balance, proportion, causes, and the relative weight of evidence. These differences are in the best tradition of historical revision to which this whole work is directed.

LUDWIG PASTOR

THE CONVENTIONAL VIEW

Ludwig Pastor (1854–1928) devoted most of his long life to the writing of his massive, documentary *The History of the Popes, from the Close of the Middle Ages*. The first volume appeared in 1886. The sixteenth was published posthumously in 1933. He is the greatest representative in modern scholarship of what may be called the "conventional view" of the causes and consequences of the decline of the medieval papacy, the view from which later revisionist scholars must dissent. While there is no one place in the first few books of his history where Pastor "capsulizes" a thesis, the excerpts which make up the following selection clearly reflect his view.

As the earlier historian Edward Gibbon had surveyed the melancholy course of the decline of Rome from the perspective of the high empire, so Pastor—who resembles Gibbon in many ways—surveyed what was to him the equally melancholy decline of the medieval papacy from the perspective of the thirteenth century and the eminence to which Innocent III had raised the papacy above both church and state. But there is a basic difference between Gibbon and Pastor. Gibbon was a harsh and unrelenting judge of his subject: Pastor was a sympathetic witness for his. He was a devoted Catholic, a pupil and disciple of the Catholic apologist-historian Johannes Janssen, a professor of history in the traditionally Catholic University of Innsbruck, and a scholar loaded with the honors of his church in recognition of his scholarship. Yet, despite his religious commitment, Pastor should not be regarded as a narrow, sectarian advocate. He based his work solidly upon documents and relentlessly followed wherever those documents led his argument. Indeed, he was more severe in his judgments than many of his less orthodox predecessors had been for the simple reason that he cared more and thus he responded more heatedly when he discovered evidence of misconduct, gross errors of policy, and personal venality which detracted from the exalted theory of the papacy to which he subscribed.

As the student studies this selection, he should look for the major tenets of Pastor's interpretation and seek to answer such questions as: What were the consequences of the papacy's removal to Avignon? What was the reason for the Great Schism?

What were its consequences? Did the papacy have any realistic alternative to the actions and policies it actually pursued during this period? Perhaps even more important, the student should compare this selection closely with those that follow in this section with an eye to the question: To what extent, despite his careful scholarship, did Pastor's Catholic orthodoxy distort his narrative?

The disastrous struggle between the highest powers of Christendom, which began in the eleventh century and reached its climax in the thirteenth, was decided, apparently to the advantage of the Papacy, by the tragical downfall of the house of Hohenstaufen. But the overthrow of the Empire also shook the temporal position of the Popes, who were now more and more compelled to ally themselves closely with France. In the warfare with the Emperors, the Papacy had already sought protection and had found refuge in that kingdom in critical times. The sojourn of the Popes in France had, however, been only transitory. The most sacred traditions, and a history going back for more than a thousand years, seemed to have bound the highest ecclesiastical dignity so closely to Italy and to Rome that, in the eleventh, twelfth, and thirteenth centuries, the idea that a Pope could be crowned anywhere but in the Eternal City, or could fix his residence for the whole duration of his Pontificate out of Italy, would have been looked upon as an impossibility.

A change came over this state of things in the time of Clement V. (1305–1314), a native of Gascony. Fearing for the independence of the Ecclesiastical power amid the party struggles by which Italy was torn, and yielding to the influence of Philip the Fair, the strong-handed oppressor of Boniface VIII., he remained in France and never set foot in Rome. His successor, John XXII., also a Gascon, was elected, after prolonged and stormy discussions, in 1316, when the Holy See had been for two years vacant. He took up his permanent abode at Avignon, where he was only separated by the Rhone from the territory of the French King. Clement V. had lived as a guest in the Dominican Monastery at Avignon, but John XXII. set up a magnificent establishment there. The essential character of that new epoch in the history of the Papacy, which begins with Clement V. and John XXII., consists in the lasting separation from the traditional home of the Holy See and from the Italian soil, which brought the Popes into such pernicious dependence on France and seriously endangered the universal nature of their position.

O good beginning!
To what a vile conclusion must Thou stoop.[1]

The words of the great Italian poet are not exaggerated, for the Avignon Popes, without exception, were all more or less dependent on France. Frenchmen themselves, and surrounded by a College of Cardinals in which the French element predominated, they gave a French character to the government of the Church. This character was at variance with the principle of universality inherent in it and in the Papacy. The Church had always been the representative of this principle in contradistinction to that of isolated nationalities, and it was the high office of the Pope, as her Supreme Head, to be the common Father of all nations. This universality was in a great degree the secret of the power and influence of the Mediaeval Popes.

The migration to France, the creation of a preponderance of French Cardinals, and the consequent election of seven French Popes in succession, necessarily compromised the position of the Papacy in the eyes of the world, creating a suspicion that the highest spiritual power had become the tool of France. This suspicion, though in many cases unfounded, weakened the general confidence in the Head of the Church, and awakened in the other nations a feeling of antagonism to the ecclesiastical authority which had become French. The bonds which united the States of the Church to the Apostolic See were gradually loosened, and the arbitrary proceedings of the Court at Avignon, which was too often swayed by personal and family interests, accelerated the process of dissolution. The worst apprehensions for the future were entertained.

The dark points of the Avignon period have certainly been greatly exaggerated. The assertion that the

[1] Dante, *Parad.*, xxvii, 59, 60.

From Ludwig Pastor, *The History of the Popes, from the Close of the Middle Ages*, ed., tr. F. I. Antrobus, 6th ed. (London: Kegan Paul, Trench, Trubner & Co. Ltd., 1938), Vol. I, pp. 57–174 with deletions. The elaborate documentation is not reproduced here; the reader is referred to the edition cited. Reprinted by permission of Routledge & Kegan Paul Ltd.

Government of the Avignon Popes was wholly ruled by the "will and pleasure of the Kings of France," is, in this general sense, unjust. The Popes of those days were not all so weak as Clement V., who submitted the draft of the Bull, by which he called on the Princes of Europe to imprison the Templars,[2] to the French King. Moreover, even this Pope, the least independent of the fourteenth century Pontiffs, for many years offered a passive resistance to the wishes of France, and a writer, who has thoroughly studied the period, emphatically asserts that only for a few years of the Pontificate of Clement V. was the idea so long associated with the "Babylonian Captivity" of the Popes fully realized. The extension of this epithet to the whole of the Avignon sojourn is an unfair exaggeration. The eager censors of the dependence into which the Avignon Popes sank, draw attention to the political action of the Holy See during this period so exclusively, that hardly any place is left for its labours in the cause of religion. A very partial picture is thus drawn, wherein the noble efforts of these much-abused Pontiffs for the conversion of heathen nations become almost imperceptible in the dim background. . . .

With the most ample recognition of the worldwide activity of the French Popes, it cannot be denied that the effects of the transfer of the Holy See from its natural and historical home were disastrous. Torn from its proper abode, the Papacy, notwithstanding the individual greatness of some of the Avignon Pontiffs, could not maintain its former dignity. The freedom and independence of the highest tribunal in Christendom, which, according to Innocent III., was bound to protect all rights, was endangered, now that the supreme direction of the Church was so much under the influence of a nation so deeply imbued with its own spirit, and possessing so little of the universal. That France should obtain exclusive possession of the highest spiritual authority was a thing contrary both to the office of the Papacy and the very being of the Church.

This dependence on the power of a Prince, who in former times had often been rebuked by Rome, was in strange contradiction with the supremacy claimed by the Popes. By this subjection and by its worldliness, the Avignon Papacy aroused an opposition which, though it might for a moment be overborne

while it leant on the crumbling power of the Empire, yet moved men's minds so deeply that its effects were not effaced for several centuries. Its downfall is most closely connected with this opposition, which was manifested, not only in the bitter accusations of its political and clerical enemies, but even also in the letters of its devoted friend St. Catherine, which are full of entreaties, complaints, and denunciations. The Papal Government, founded as it was on the principle of authority, built up in independence of the Empire, and gaining strength in proportion to the decay of that power, was unable to offer any adequate resistance to this twofold stream of political and religious antagonism. The catastrophe of the great Schism was the immediate consequence of the false position now occupied by the Papacy. . . .

The disastrous effects produced by the residence of the Popes at Avignon were at first chiefly felt in Italy. Hardly ever has a country fallen into such anarchy as did the Italian peninsula, when bereft of her principle of unity by the unfortunate decision of Clement V. to fix his abode in France. Torn to pieces by irreconcilable parties, the land, which had been fitly termed the garden of Europe, was now a scene of desolation. It will easily be understood that all Italian hearts were filled with bitter longings, a regret which found voice in continual protests against the Gallicized Papacy. . . .

The unmitigated condemnation of the Avignon Popes must have been based in great measure on Petrarch's unjust representations, to which, in later times and without examination, an undue historical importance has been attached. He is often supposed to be a determined adversary of the Papacy; but this is a complete mistake. He never for a moment questioned its divine institution. We have already said that he was outwardly on the best terms with almost all the Popes of his time, and received from them many favours. They took his frequent and earnest exhortations to leave Avignon and return to desolate Rome as mere poetical rhapsodies, and in fact they were nothing more. If Petrarch himself, though a Roman citizen, kept aloof from Rome; if, though nominally an Italian patriot, he fixed his abode for many years, from motives of convenience, or in quest of preferment, in that very Avignon which he had bitterly reproached the Popes for choosing, and which he had called the most loathsome place in the world, must not the Babylonish poison have eaten deeply into his heart? How much easier it would have been for Petrarch to have re-

---

[2] The reference here is to the pope's assistance in Philip IV's attack on the Order of Knights Templar.

turned to Rome than it was for the Popes, fettered as they were by so many political considerations!

But however much we may question Petrarch's right to find fault with the moral delinquencies of the Court at Avignon; however much we may, in many respects, modify the picture he paints of it, no impartial inquirer can deny that it was pervaded by a deplorable worldliness. For this melancholy fact we have testimony more trustworthy than the rhetorical descriptions of the Italian poet. Yet it must in justice be borne in mind that the influx of thousands of strangers into the little French provincial town, so suddenly raised to the position of capital of the world, had produced all the evils which appertain to densely populated places. Moreover, even if we are to believe all the angry assertions of contemporaries as to the corruption prevailing in Avignon, evidence is not wanting, on the other hand, of ardent yearnings for a life conformable to the precepts of the Gospel. . . .

[*The pontificate of John XXII, in almost every sense the apogee of the Avignonese papacy, was followed by those of Benedict XII (1334–1342), Clement VI (1342–1352), Innocent VI (1352–1362), Urban V (1362–1370), and Gregory XI (1370–1378). All these popes were French prelates and all—except Gregory XI—continued their residence at Avignon. But they were not unaware of the bitter criticism their continued exile generated nor certainly of the many political and financial, as well as spiritual, disadvantages they suffered. There was mounting pressure for them to return to Rome. Some halting gestures were made in that direction: Urban V visited Rome briefly. Then Gregory XI did return and in 1378, died in Rome. Editor's note.*]

After an interval of seventy-five years a Conclave again met in Rome, and on its decision depended the question whether or not the injurious predominance of France in the management of the affairs of the Church should continue. Severe struggles were to be expected, for no slight disunion existed in the Sacred College.

Of the sixteen Cardinals then present in Rome, four only were of Italian nationality. Francesco Tibaldeschi and Giacomo Orsini were Romans, Simone da Borsano and Pietro Corsini, natives respectively of Milan and Florence. These Princes of the Church were naturally desirous that an Italian should occupy the Chair of St. Peter. The twelve foreign or "Ultra-montane" Cardinals, of whom one was a Spaniard and the others French, were sub-divided into two parties. The Limousin Cardinals strove for the elevation of a native of their province, the birthplace of the last four Popes. Of the six remaining members of the Sacred College, two were undecided, and the four others, of whom the Cardinal of Geneva was the leader, formed what was called the Gallican faction.

No party accordingly had the preponderance, and a protracted Conclave was to be anticipated. External circumstances, however, led to a different result. Before the Cardinals entered on their deliberations, the Municipal authorities of Rome had besought them to elect a Roman, or at any rate an Italian, and while the Conclave was proceeding, the governors of the districts appeared, and presented the same petition. The populace gathered round the Vatican in the greatest excitement, demanding, with shouts and uproar, the election of a Roman. The Cardinals were compelled to make haste, and as no one of the three parties was sufficiently powerful to carry the day, all united in favour of Bartolomeo Prignano, Archbishop of Bari, a candidate who belonged to no party and seemed in many respects the individual best fitted to rule the Church in this period of peculiar difficulty. He was the worthiest and most capable among the Italian prelates. As a native of Naples, he was the subject of Queen Joanna, whose protection at this crisis was of the greatest importance. A long residence in Avignon had given him the opportunity of acquiring French manners, and ties of equal strength bound him to Italy and to France. On the 8th April, 1378, he was elevated to the supreme dignity, taking the name of Urban VI.

Great confusion was occasioned by a misunderstanding which occurred after the election. The crowd forcibly broke into the Conclave to see the new Pope, and the Cardinals, dreading to inform them of the election of Prignano, who was not a Roman, persuaded the aged Cardinal Tibaldeschi to put on the Papal Insignia and allow the populace to greet him. Hardly had this been done, when, apprehensive of what might happen when the deception was discovered, most of the Cardinals sought safety in flight. Finally, confidence was restored by the assurance of the City authorities that Prignano's election would find favour with the people. It is plain then that the election itself was not the result of compulsion on the part of the Roman populace. If, however, the least suspicion of constraint could be attached to it, the subsequent bearing of the Cardinals was sufficient to completely counteract it. As soon as tranquillity was restored Prignano's election was announced to the people and was followed by his Coronation. All the Cardinals then present in Rome took part in the ceremony, and thereby publicly acknowledged Urban VI. as the rightful Pope. They assisted him in his ecclesiastical functions and asked him for spiritual favours. They announced his election and Coronation to the Emperor and to Christendom in general by letters signed with their own hands, and homage was universally rendered to the new Head of the Church. No member of the Sacred College thought of calling the election in question; on the contrary, in official documents, as well as in private conversations, they all maintained its undoubted validity. . . .

The new Pope was adorned by great and rare qualities; almost all his contemporaries are unanimous in praise of his purity of life, his simplicity and temperance. He was also esteemed for his learning, and yet more for the conscientious zeal with which he discharged his ecclesiastical duties. . . .

But Urban VI. had one great fault, a fault fraught with evil consequences to himself, and yet more to the Church; he lacked Christian gentleness and charity. He was naturally arbitrary and extremely violent and imprudent, and when he came to deal with the burning ecclesiastical question of the day, that of reform, the consequences were disastrous.

The melancholy condition of the affairs of the Church at this period is clear from the letters of St. Catherine of Siena. The suggestions of reform which she had made repeatedly and with unexampled courage had unfortunately not been carried out. Gregory XI. was far too irresolute to adopt energetic measures, and he also attached undue weight to the opinions of his relations, and of the French Cardinals, by whom he was surrounded; moreover, he was fully occupied by the war with Florence, and this was perhaps the chief cause of his inaction. Whether, if longer life had been granted to him, he would really have undertaken the amendment of the clergy, it is impossible to say. One thing is certain, that at the date of the new Pope's accession the work had still to be done. . . .

The plans of reform entertained by Urban VI. filled the French King, Charles V., with wrath. The free and independent position, which the new Pope had

from the first assumed was a thorn in the side of the King, who wished to bring back the Avignon days. Were Urban now to succeed in creating an Italian majority in the Sacred College, the return of the Holy See to its dependence on France would be greatly deferred, if not indeed altogether prevented. Charles V therefore secretly encouraged the Cardinals, promising them armed assistance, even at the cost of a cessation of hostilities with England, if they would take the final step, before which they still hesitated. Confident in his powerful support, the thirteen Cardinals assembled at Anagni, on the 9th August, 1378, published a manifesto, declaring Urban's election to have been invalid, as resulting from the constraint exercised by the Roman populace, who had risen in insurrection, and proclaiming as a consequence the vacancy of the Holy See.

On the 20th September they informed the astonished world that the true Pope had been chosen in the person of Robert of Geneva, now Clement VII. The great Papal Schism (1378–1417), the most terrible of all imaginable calamities, thus burst upon Christendom, and the very centre of its unity became the occasion of the division of the Church. . . .

Christendom had never yet witnessed such a Schism; all timid souls were cast into a sea of doubt, and even courageous men like Abbot Ludolf of Sagan, its historian, bewailed it day and night.

Anti-popes, indeed, had already arisen on several occasions, but in most cases they had very soon passed away, for, owing their elevation to the secular power, it bore more or less clearly on its very face the stamp of violence and injustice. But in the present instance all was different; unlike the Schisms caused by the Hohenstaufens or Louis of Bavaria, that of 1378 was the work of the Cardinals, the highest of the clergy. And, moreover, the election of Urban VI. had taken place under circumstances so peculiar that it was easy to call it in question. It was impossible for those not on the spot to investigate it in all its details, and the fact, that all who had taken part in it subsequently renounced their allegiance, was well calculated to inspire doubt and perplexity. It is extremely difficult for those who study the question in the present day with countless documents before them, and the power of contemplating the further development of the Schism, to estimate the difficulties of contemporaries who sought to know which of the two Popes had a right to their obedience. The extreme confusion is evidenced by the fact that canonized Saints are found amongst the adherents of each of the rivals. St. Catherine of Siena, and her namesake of Sweden, stand opposed to St. Vincent Ferrer and the Blessed Peter of Luxemburg, who acknowledged the French Pope. All the writings of the period give more or less evidence of the conflicting opinions which prevailed; and upright men afterwards confessed, that they had been unable to find out which was the true Pope.

To add to the complications, the obedience of Germany to Urban VI. and that of France to Clement VII. was far from complete, for individuals in both countries attached themselves to the Pope, from whom they expected to gain most. The allegiance of the Holy Roman Empire to Urban was evidently of an unstable character, since ecclesiastics in Augsburg fearlessly, and without hindrance, accepted charges and benefices from the hands of the Antipope and his partisans, and itinerant preachers publicly asserted the validity of his claim. Peter Suchenwirt, in a poem written at this period, describes the distress, which the growing anarchy within the Church was causing in men's minds, and earnestly beseeches God to end it. "There are two Popes," he says; "which is the right one? . . ."

It has been well observed that we can scarcely form an idea of the deplorable condition to which Europe was reduced by the schism. Uncertainty as to the title of its ruler is ruinous to a nation; this schism affected the whole of Christendom, and called the very existence of the Church in question. The discord touching its Head necessarily permeated the whole body of the Church; in many Dioceses two Bishops were in arms for the possession of the Episcopal throne, two Abbots in conflict for an abbey. The consequent confusion was indescribable. We cannot wonder that the Christian religion became the derision of Jews and Mahometans.

The amount of evil wrought by the schism of 1378, the longest known in the history of the Papacy, can only be estimated, when we reflect that it occurred at a moment, when thorough reform in ecclesiastical affairs was a most urgent need. This was now utterly out of the question, and, indeed, all evils which had crept into ecclesiastical life were infinitely increased. Respect for the Holy See was also greatly impaired, and the Popes became more than ever dependent on the temporal power, for the schism allowed each Prince to choose which Pope he would acknowledge. In the eyes of the people, the simple fact of a double Papacy must have shaken the authority of the Holy See to its very foundations. It may truly be said that these fifty years of schism prepared the way for the great Apostacy of the sixteenth century.

It is not within the scope of the present work to recount all the vicissitudes of the warfare between the claimants of the Papal throne—for Urban VI. received immediately a successor. Neither side would yield, and the confusion of Christendom daily increased and pervaded all classes of society. The Cardinals of the rival Popes were at open variance, and in many dioceses there were two Bishops. This was the case in Breslau, Mayence, Liege, Basle, Metz Constance, Coire, Lubeck, Dorpat, and other places, and even the Religious and Military Orders were drawn into the schism.

The conflict was carried on with unexampled violence. While the adherents of the Roman Pope reprobated the Mass offered by the "Clementines," the "Clementines" in their turn looked on that of the "Urbanists" as a blasphemy; in many cases public worship was altogether discontinued. "The depths of calamity," as St. Catherine of Siena said, "overwhelmed the Church." "Mutual hatred," writes a biographer of the Saint, "lust of power, the worst intrigues flourished amidst clergy and laity alike, and who could suppress these crimes? God alone could help, and He led the Church through great and long-continued tribulation back to unity, and made it plain to all that men may indeed in their wickedness wound her, but they cannot destroy her, for she bears within a divine principle of life." Therefore, even amid the direst storm of discord, St. Catherine could write, "I saw how the Bride of Christ was giving forth life, for she contains such living power that no one can kill her; I saw that she was dispensing strength and light, and that no one can take them from her, and I saw that her fruit never diminishes, but always increases." . . .

The literature of this period, a field as yet but little explored, testifies to the general distress caused by the Schism. Touching lamentations in both prose and verse portray the desolation and confusion of the time, and this was aggravated by epidemics. "Whose heart," cries Heinrich von Langenstein, "is so hardened as not to be moved by the unspeakable sufferings of his Mother, the Church?" . . .

From these complaints it is evident how keenly

the need of a Supreme Judge, Guardian, and Guide in ecclesiastical affairs was felt.

Naturally, men did not stop at mere expressions of sorrow, but went on to inquire into the origin of the evil which was bringing such dishonour on the Church. The most clear-sighted contemporary writers point to the corruption of the clergy, to their inordinate desire for money and possessions—in short, to their selfishness—as the root of all the misery. This is the key note of Nicolas de Clémangis' celebrated book, "On the Ruin of the Church" (written in 1401); and in a sermon delivered before the Council of Constance, the preacher insisted that "money was the origin of the Schism, and the root of all the confusion."

It cannot, however, be too often repeated that the ecclesiastical corruption was in great measure a consequence of the Avignon period, and of the influence which State politics had acquired in matters of Church government. The rupture, produced by the recreant French Cardinals, was, in reality, nothing but the conflict of two nations for the possession of the Papacy; the Italians wished to recover it, and the French would not let it be wrested from them.

Those who raised their voices to complain of the corruption and confusion of Christendom were not always men of real piety or moral worth. In many cases they might with advantage have begun by reforming their own lives. Some of them went so far as to charge all the evils of the day upon the ecclesiastical authorities, and stirred up laity and clergy against each other; such persons only destroyed that which was still standing. Others, again, clamoured for reform, while themselves doing nothing to promote it. But at this time, as at all periods in the history of the Church, men were found who, without making much noise or lamentation, laboured in the right way—that is, within the limits laid down by the Church—for the thorough amendment of all that was amiss. . . .

The crisis which the Church passed through at this juncture, is the most grievous recorded in her history. Just when the desperate struggle between the rival Popes had thrown everything into utter confusion, when ecclesiastical revenues and favours served almost exclusively as the reward of partisans, and when worldliness had reached its climax, heretical movements arose in England, France, Italy, Germany, and, above all, in Bohemia, and threatened the very constitution of the Church. This was most natural; the smaller the chance of reform being effected by the Church, the more popular and active became the reform movement not directed by her; the higher the region that needed, but resisted reform, the more popular did this movement become. . . .

The appearance of John Wyclif in England was a matter of far greater moment than heresies of this kind, which were forcibly repressed by the Inquisition. The errors of the Apocalyptics and the Waldenses, of Marsiglio, Occam, and others, were all concentrated in his sect, which prepared the transition to a new heretical system of a universal character, namely, Protestantism. His teaching is gross pantheistic realism, involving a Predestinarianism which annihilates moral freedom. Everything is God. An absolute necessity governs all, even the action of God Himself. Evil happens by necessity; God constrains every creature that acts, to the performance of each action. Some are predestined to glory, others to damnation. The prayer of the reprobate is of no avail, and the predestined are none the worse for the sins which God compels them to commit. Wyclif builds his church on this theory of predestination. It is, in his view, the society of the elect. As an external institution, accordingly, it disappears, to become merely an inward association of souls, and no one can know who does or does not belong to it. The only thing certain is that it always exists on earth, although it may be sometimes only composed of a few poor laymen, scattered in different countries. Wyclif began by a conditional recognition of the Pope, but afterwards came to regard him, not as the Vicar of Christ, but as Anti-Christ. He taught that honour paid to the Pope was idolatry, of a character all the more hideous and blasphemous, inasmuch as divine honour was given to a member of Lucifer, an idol, worse than a painted log of wood, because of the great wickedness he contains. Wyclif further teaches that the Church ought to be without property, and to return to the simplicity of Apostolic times. The Bible alone, without tradition, is the sole source of faith. No temporal or ecclesiastical superior has authority, when he is in a state of mortal sin. Indulgences, confession, extreme unction and orders, are all rejected by Wyclif, who even attacks the very centre of all Christian worship, the Most Holy Sacrament of the Altar.

These doctrines, which involved a revolution, not only in the Church, but also in politics and society, made their way rapidly in England. Countless disciples,—poor clergy whom Wyclif sent forth in opposition to the "rich Church which had fallen away to the devil,"—propagated them through the length and breadth of the land. These itinerant preachers, in a comparatively short time, aroused a most formidable movement against the property of the Church, the Pope, and the Bishops. But a change suddenly took place. King Richard the Second's marriage with Anne, the daughter of the King of Bohemia, was a great blow to the cause of Wyclif in England. The Courts of Westminster and of Prague were of one mind in regard to the affairs of the Church and other important political questions, and would have done anything rather than show favour to Wyclif and his companions, or to France and her anti-Pope, Clement VII.

On the other hand, as this marriage led to an increase of intercourse between England and Bohemia, Wyclif's ideas found entrance into the latter country. English students frequented the University of Prague, and Bohemians that of Oxford; and Wyclif's treatises were widely spread in Bohemia. John Huss, the leader of the Bohemian movement, was not merely much influenced, but absolutely dominated by these ideas. Recent investigations have furnished incontestable evidence that, in the matter of doctrine, Huss owed everything to Wyclif, whose works he often plagiarized with astonishing simplicity.

The opinions of the Bohemian leader, like those of Wyclif, must necessarily have led in practice to a social revolution, and one of which the end could not be foreseen, since the right to possess property was made dependent on religious opinion. Only "Believers," that is to say, the followers of Huss, could hold it, and this right lasted as long as their convictions accorded with those that prevailed in the country. Argument is needless to show that such a theory destroys all private rights, and the attempt to make these principles—so plausibly deduced from the doctrines of the Christian religion—serve as the rule for the foundation of a new social order, must lead to the most terrible consequences. The subsequent wars of the Hussites evidently owed their peculiarly sanguinary character in great part to these views. If Huss declared war against social order, he also called in question all civil authority, when he espoused Wyclif's principle, that no man who had committed a mortal sin could be a temporal ruler, a bishop, or a prelate, "because his tem-

poral or spiritual authority, his office and his dignity would not be approved by God."

Whether Huss realized the consequences of such doctrines, or merely followed his master, may remain an open question; one thing, however, the most enthusiastic admirer of the Czech reformer cannot dispute—namely, that doctrines which must have rendered anarchy permanent in Church and State imperatively required to be met by some action on the part of the civil and ecclesiastical authorities. The results of the opinions promulgated by Huss soon became apparent in the Bohemian Revolution in which the idea of a democratic Republic and of a social system based on communistic principles took practical form. . . .

During the earlier years of the Schism, efforts had been made to establish the legality of the one, and the illegality of the other Pope, by means of arguments founded on history and on Canon Law, but in consequence of French intrigues the question had only become more and more obscured. As time went on, conscientious men, who anxiously strove to understand the rights of the case, were unable to decide between claims which seemed to be so equally balanced, while in other cases passion took no account of proofs, and power trampled them under foot. Despair took possession of many upright minds. The Schism seemed an evil from which there was no escape, a labyrinth from which no outlet could be found. The path of investigation which, by the lapse of time and in consequence of the prevailing excitement, had necessarily become more and more difficult, seemed to lead no further. The University of Paris, which suffered much from the discord of Christendom, now sought to assume the leadership of the great movement towards unity. In 1394 her members were invited to send in written opinions as to the means of putting an end to the Schism. In order that all might express their opinions with perfect freedom it was decided that the documents should be placed in a locked chest in the Church of St. Mathurin. The general feeling on the subject is manifested by their number, which amounted to ten thousand. Their examination was to be the work of a Commission formed of members from all the Faculties of the University. Three propositions emerged from this mass of documents. The first was the voluntary retirement of the two Popes (Cessio). The second the decision of the point of law by a commission selected by the two Popes (Compromissio). The third, an appeal to a General

The Eve of the Modern World

Council. The University recommended the voluntary retirement of both Popes as the simplest and safest course, and as rendering a fresh election of one whom both parties would acknowledge, possible. The endeavours to restore unity by this means were carried to their further point under Gregory XII., after the failure of the French scheme of forcibly imposing peace on the Church by the common action of all the western powers. They seemed at first in Gregory's case to promise success, but all hopes of the kind soon proved delusive.

[*And there was left open to the church only the appeal to a General Council. It was this impasse which produced the Conciliar Movement and extended it on through most of the fifteenth century with further damage to the universal authority and prestige of the papacy. The way was thus prepared for the coming of the Reformation, in Pastor's phrase, "the great Apostacy of the sixteenth century." Editor's note.*]

GUILLAUME MOLLAT

A MAJOR REVISIONIST VIEW

Guillaume Mollat, the French cleric and church historian, was one of the major figures of the first generation of modern scholars to undertake a revision of views of this period in the history of the papacy. The first edition of his *The Popes at Avignon* appeared in 1912, while Pastor's magisterial volumes were still issuing from the press. The ninth French edition, published in 1950, was much enlarged and substantially revised in light of recent scholarship, much of it Mollat's own. He had worked the archives as assiduously as Pastor, devoting his attention almost exclusively to the Avignonese popes and to the papal "system" which emerged under their hands. He had written on papal fiscal measures in Brittany, on the civil and canon law, and starting in 1950 he published a series of studies, based on his long archival research, dealing with the letters patent and the private and public papers of the Avignonese popes Benedict XII, Urban V, Gregory XI, and Clement V. But his major interpretive work was *The Popes at Avignon*, from which the following selection is taken.

Mollat deals in this book with only a portion of the problem with which we saw Pastor concerned in the previous selection, but it is a crucial portion of the general problem if the student will recall the position that Pastor took on the Avignonese popes and their "pernicious dependence on France," the beginning, as he saw it, of a string of causation leading to the undoing of the medieval papacy.

In *The Popes at Avignon*, Mollat undertakes to reassess the "general opinion" to which, he claims, Pastor had yielded with regard to the Babylonian Captivity. From this reassessment emerges a very different estimation of the popes' motives in not returning to Rome, a very different view of the papacy's relations with the French kings, and a very different explanation of the papal fiscal policies, usually explained in terms of moral lapse, weakness, or avarice. The student should observe carefully the "case" Mollat makes in each instance. He should determine whether the almost clinical refusal of the author to take a moral position—in spite of his being a member of the Catholic clergy—works to distort his narrative in the same way that the advocacy of Pastor might have distorted his. He should consider that Mollat, while a churchman, was also a Frenchman and what effect this might have had upon his point of view. And finally, he should reflect a bit on the basic critical problem of historical revision: not so much the patient study and restudy of the documents as the patient "rethinking of the past."

Between 1305 and 1378 seven popes succeeded one another on the throne of St Peter and lived, more or less continuously, in Avignon, on the banks of the Rhône.

Was it an unheard-of occurrence and in fact a "scandal" in the annals of the Church for them to reside outside Rome? The majority of non-French writers . . . seem to suggest it. Yet, for all they were bishops of Rome, a large number of the popes were elected and crowned elsewhere than at Rome and governed the world from some place other than Rome. During the latter half of the thirteenth century their subjects' unrest made it impossible for the popes to reside in the Eternal City and they were obliged to emigrate, to such an extent that it became exceptional for them to live in Rome.

Nothing is more enlightening in this respect than the itinerary followed by the popes throughout the half-century preceding their installation at Avignon. After a stay of five months and a few days in Rome, where he suffered the greatest restriction of his liberty and had his authority impeded by the noble families, Benedict XI (1303–04) left for Perugia where he died. According to Ferreto Ferreti of Vicenza, he was thinking of making an indefinite stay in Lombardy. His predecessor, Boniface VIII (1294–1303), was much less frequently to be found at the Lateran palace than at Anagni, Orvieto or Velletri. Celestine V (1294), the holy hermit, never saw Rome; elected at Perugia and crowned at Aquila, he proceeded to Sulmona, Capua and Naples, where he renounced his title. Nicholas IV (1288–92) was elected at Rome and sometimes resided at Santa Maria Maggiore; but he lived as a rule at Rieti and Orvieto. Honorius IV (1285–7), after his election at Perugia, liked to live at Santa

Sabina; only in the extreme heat of summer did he retreat to Tivoli or Palombara. Martin IV (1281–5), a Frenchman, elected at Viterbo, *ubi tunc residebat Romana Curia*,[1] never went outside Tuscany and Umbria. Also elected at Viterbo, Nicholas III (1277–80) was unusual in being crowned at Rome; he divided his time between that city, Sutri, Vetralla and Viterbo. John XXI (1276–7) never left Viterbo, where he had been elected and where he died and was buried beneath the walls of his own palace. Innocent V and Adrian V occupied the pontifical throne for brief periods only, during the first six months of the year 1276. After two months' stay in Rome, Gregory X (1271–6) went to Orvieto and then to France, where he summoned the fourteenth oecumenical council at Lyons. His return journey to Italy was made in short stages, with many halts in "the sweet land of Provence." He went to Orange, Beaucaire and Valence and back to Vienne, in order to return to Italy by way of Switzerland and he died at Arezzo. The French Pope Clement IV (1265–8) did not issue a single document from Rome. He went to Perugia, Assisi, Orvieto, Montefiascone and Viterbo. Urban IV (1261–4), another Frenchman, had only three residences, Viterbo, Montefiascone and Orvieto; he died in his litter on the way from Orvieto to Perugia. Alexander IV (1254–61) was elected and crowned at Naples, and had a liking for Anagni and Viterbo; at the beginning and end of his pontificate, he spent a few months at the Lateran Palace, and died at Viterbo. Innocent IV (1243–54), who was elected and consecrated at Anagni, spent only a very short time at Rome; he was obliged to flee from Frederick II and to take refuge at Lyons from 1244 until 1251. When he returned to Italy, he settled in the peaceful

[1] "Where the Roman Curia resided at that time. [Editor's note].

From G. Mollat, *The Popes at Avignon, 1305–1378*, tr. Janet Love from the 9th French edition (New York and London, 1963), pp. xiii–xxii, 343–44. Reprinted by permission of Thomas Nelson & Sons Ltd., London; a paperback edition is published by Harper & Row, Inc., New York.

country of Umbria and then went to Naples, where he died. . . .

The establishment of the papacy outside Rome in the fourteenth century, then, does not constitute an unheard-of revolution in history; it was brought about and prepared by a long series of circumstances and events. The really extraordinary and unprecedented circumstance is the prolonged residence of the popes outside Italy. Moreover the Italians, once they were deprived of the considerable advantages provided by the presence of the papacy, did not fail to follow Petrarch and St Catherine of Siena in copious expressions of blame and complaint. Ughelli—to quote only one of the best known—goes so far as to assert that the transference of the Holy See to Avignon was a greater disaster for his country than the barbarian invasions. German scholarship has echoed these sentiments. Gregorovius declares that the Avignon popes were the "slaves" of the kings of France; Hase refers to them as "bishops of the French court"; Martens maintains that they would not have dared to exercise any sovereign authority without the approval of the French kings. Pastor yields to the general opinion: he reproaches the papacy with having caused the Church to lose its universality by becoming French and thus arousing popular suspicion and feelings of hostility; he alleges that this move precipitated the decline of religious feeling. Other writers, both in France and elsewhere, have bitterly denounced the excessive concern of the court at Avignon with finance, the looseness of its morals, its extravagant tastes, its nepotism and absolutism. In a word, according to the majority of historians, the Avignon papacy was the source of the greatest evils for the Church and, in the last analysis, the chief cause of the great schism of the West. Whatever may have been claimed in its defence, the judgment of history remains unfavourable towards it. Is this judgment confirmed or invalidated by the publication of the Papal Registers and the studies that have appeared since the opening of the Vatican Archives? A statement of the facts will make a reply possible.

We shall endeavour, in the following pages, to study in detail and with reference to the texts of the Archives, the pontificates of Clement V, John XXII, Benedict XII, Clement VI, Innocent VI, Urban V and Gregory XI. These have usually been the victims of prejudice caused by a chauvinism which is not, on this occasion, French. We are not writing a defence, but an historical account, sketching biographies, clarifying policy and describing institutions without any preconceived notion save that of stating what the texts imply.

THE ESTABLISHMENT OF THE HOLY SEE AT AVIGNON

The chronicler Ptolemy of Lucca reports that as soon as Bertrand de Got was elected pope, "he determined to fix his residence in the Comtat-Venaissin and never to cross the Alps." This is a misstatement. It is true that the cardinals' letters, giving notice of the election, were expressed in such a way as to deter Clement V from going to Italy. They depicted that country as given over to anarchy and the Papal States as devastated by war. Nevertheless, the pope announced his intention of going to Italy as soon as peace was made between the kings of England and France, and the crusade organised. He chose the place for his coronation on imperial soil, at Vienne in Dauphiné, a town on the main road to Italy. He invited only a limited number of cardinals to his coronation: two bishops, two priests and two deacons.

Although Clement V subsequently changed his plans, he still had every intention of leaving France, where circumstances had detained him. In 1306 the ambassador of Aragon wrote to James II: "The pope signified [to the cardinals] that it was his intention to stay here until the coming month of March. For then he will give leave to the court to cross the Alps and will meet with the king of France at Poitiers, that he may persuade him to receive the cross and ratify the peace between himself and the king of England. And from that time forward, without tarrying in any other place, my said lord the pope will go to Italy." According to the same ambassador, during the meeting at Poitiers in 1308, the supreme pontiff expressed his joy at encountering Philip the Fair, for it was his intention to go to Rome but to entertain the king before his departure. On 11 April 1308, Clement was considering the restoration of the ciborium to the high altar of St John Lateran and said: "By the grace of God we propose to put back with our own hands the most famous wooden altar in the place where it formerly was." Moreover, in the next year he was promising that within the space of two years he would himself crown the Emperor Henry VII at Rome. Why did Clement V not carry out these intentions that he had so often expressed?

The pope's object in choosing to hold his coronation at Vienne and not on Italian soil was to attract the kings of France and England to the ceremony and to take advantage of their presence to work for the conclusion of a lasting peace between them. In this he was carrying out a cherished plan of the late Boniface VIII, who had dreamt of going to France to settle the Anglo-French differences. Like his predecessor, Clement V considered that the crusade would be impossible without the effective co-operation of France and England. Such co-operation could not properly be sought until the day when the two countries had signed the peace. Clement V worked untiringly to reconcile them. He arranged the marriage of Isabella of France with the future Edward II. Despite his efforts, final reconciliation was not achieved until 1312.

On 28 November 1306, however, Clement V declared that peace negotiations, which by that date were well advanced, could have been completed by the intervention of nuncios alone. But other causes hindered his departure for Rome. Chief among these was the pressure exercised by the French court. As early as July and August 1305, French ambassadors sought Clement V and reminded him that the action brought against the deceased Boniface VIII was not yet finished. The pope, anxious to avoid a renewal of this action, made a concession that was to have considerable consequences: he decreed that his coronation should now take place not at Vienne but at Lyons. On 14 November 1305 this ceremony was performed in that city in the presence of Philip the Fair. It was followed by very important negotiations. The king of France was insistent that the trial of Boniface VIII should be renewed. It was agreed that this should be discussed at a future meeting; with the result that Clement V was obliged to put off until a more favourable time his departure for Italy.

The pope made his way from Lyons to Mâcon and Cluny and then reached Languedoc by way of Nevers, Bourges, Limoges and Périgueux. An illness which almost proved fatal helped to keep him for nearly a year in the Bordeaux area (May 1306 –March 1307) and prevented the proposed meeting with Philip the Fair from taking place at Michaelmas 1306. After a partial recovery, Clement V once more set out on his journeyings and reached Poitiers in April 1307. Here he could come to no understanding with the king of France, who refused to agree to all the proposed compromises to end the lawsuit against Boniface VIII, which was still hanging fire. They parted without coming to any decision. On 13 October 1307 a sensational event took place: the mass arrest of the Templars. A further interview with Philip the Fair became necessary. This, too, took place at Poitiers (May–July 1308). The king's demands on this occasion were such that Clement V resolved not to proceed with his enterprise. He could not contemplate going to Rome. It would have been madness to leave Philip the Fair master of the situation on the eve of the opening of the Council of Vienne, where decisions would be taken gravely affecting the interests of the Church, and where in particular the scandalous trial of the Templars would be debated. In complete agreement with the cardinals, Clement V decided to transfer the court to Avignon (August 1308).

This city possessed valuable assets. Rapid and frequent communication with Italy was ensured by both land and water routes. It was near France but not dependent upon her. There was nothing to fear from the suzerains of Avignon, the Angevin princes of Naples; their energies were largely absorbed in defending the integrity of their kingdom of the Two Sicilies against the encroachments of the ambitious house of Aragon, and in the promotion of Guelph interests in the rest of the peninsula; moreover, were they not vassals of the Church? Lastly, the city of Avignon formed an enclave in the Comtat-Venaissin, a possession of the Holy See. No town could provide the papacy with a more peaceful refuge and more powerful guarantees of independence and security.

Once he had taken this decision, Clement V made his way by short stages across the south of France. In March 1309 he entered Avignon and so inaugurated the papacy's long exile which was to last for more than seventy years and which, through ill-justified comparison with the sojourn of the Chosen People in a strange land, has come to be known as "the Babylonian captivity."

The pope's establishment at Avignon still remained provisional in character. Clement V lived unpretentiously in the convent of the Dominicans. He caused only the registers of letters of his two predecessors to be brought from Italy, and left the greater part of the pontifical treasure at the church of St Francis of Assisi. He stayed for only a very short time in Avignon itself, preferring the towns and castles of the Comtat-Venaissin.

The lawsuit brought against Boniface VIII caused the supreme pontiff the gravest anxiety between 1309 and 1311. Clement V was skilful enough to succeed in delaying the proceedings as much as possible and ultimately in silencing the worst accusers of the dead pope. As for the trial of the Templars, this was settled at the Council of Vienne (16 October 1311–6 May 1312). At the very moment when Clement might have gone to Italy, his health, never very robust, took a turn for the worse. According to the chronicler Ptolemy of Lucca, who had his information from the lips of the pope's confessor, it declined rapidly after the promulgation, at the Council of Vienne, of the Constitution *Exivi de Paradiso*. The pope, feeling that his end was near, dictated his will on 9 June 1312. His sickness grew worse in the course of the years 1313 and 1314 and finally overcame him on 20 April 1314.

Even if Clement V had enjoyed better health, he could not have crossed the Alps in 1312 or 1313. Henry VII's entry into Italy had set the whole country in revolt. From 7 May 1312, Rome served only as a battlefield where Guelphs and Ghibellines attacked each other brutally. Henry VII lost no time in treating the papacy as an enemy and in defying the threat of excommunication against anyone attacking the king of Naples. In such circumstances who can blame Clement V for staying in the Comtat-Venaissin? Where else could he have found so safe a refuge?

Under the successors of Clement V, Rome and Italy, despite their peoples' protestations and repeated appeals, remained inhospitable to the papacy. "Ah! Italy, abode of sorrow," wrote Dante, "vessel without a helmsman amidst a dreadful storm, no longer art thou mistress of thy peoples, but a place of prostitution. Now, those who live in thy dominions wage implacable war amongst themselves; those protected by the same wall and the same ramparts rend each other. Search, unhappy country, around thy shores and see if in thy bosom a single one of thy provinces enjoys peace." Italy was indeed incessantly laid waste by war in the reign of John XXII. In 1332 the pope contemplated crossing the Alps, after Bertrand du Poujet's victories over the Ghibellines. He conceived the plan of pacifying Lombardy and Tuscany, and then proceeding to Rome. Bologna, which had yielded to the Church, was provisionally chosen as a place of residence. Preparations for the pope's reception were made: a citadel was built at the Galliera gate; an order even reached Rome itself for the pontifical dwellings to be restored and the gardens

cultivated afresh. The rebellion of Bologna and the completion of arrangements for the crusade put a speedy end to the pope's plans. In 1333 the king of France was appointed captain-general of the Christian army. That year and the next negotiations were more active than ever between the courts of Paris and Avignon. The departure of the Holy See for Italy would have displeased Philip VI—who had been much angered by the intentions of John XXII—and would have hindered the preparations for the expedition which seemed definitely arranged; undoubtedly it would have gravely compromised the ultimate success of the crusade.

At the beginning of his pontificate, Benedict XII listened to the grievances of the ambassadors sent him by the Romans. In a Consistory held in July 1335, he decided, with the unanimous consent of his cardinals, that the court would leave Avignon about the first of the following October and transfer provisionally to Bologna. The cardinals changed their minds in a second Consistory. They considered it best to postpone the departure for Italy, for, in addition to the many difficulties of the journey itself, they thought that a move on the part of the Holy See would interfere with the plans for the crusade and the settling of urgent business. Moreover, an investigation made on the spot gave ample evidence that sedition at Bologna was still causing too much unrest to justify the transfer of the Holy See within its walls. The cardinals' foresight was justified. Bologna speedily revolted once more against the Church; elsewhere, in Romagna and in the Marches, the nobles were planning to become independent; while at Rome revolution reigned from 1347 until 1354.

Under Clement VI war became inevitable. It was to devastate Italy until the day when the fierce sword of Albornoz conquered the various tyrants, great and small, who were disturbing the peace. Urban V thought this a favourable moment to re-establish the papacy in Rome. As is well known, the hostility of his own subjects forced him to return to Avignon. The pope's fears were not illusory. Under Gregory XI the Roman factions were once more aroused. They plotted to massacre the foreigners who made up the papal court and the non-Italian cardinals, so as to compel the pope to settle forever in the Eternal City. What is worse, a Roman cardinal, in order to seize the triple crown for himself, is alleged to have had the dire thought of making an attempt on the life of Gregory XI. According to other contemporaries, if Gregory XI had left Italy again, as he had shown that he intended to do, the Romans would have created an antipope in opposition to him. In any event, the precautions taken by the supreme pontiff on 19 March 1378 show clearly how much he feared serious trouble after his death.

To sum up, the fact that for many years the popes did not live in Italy is explained by that country's persistent hostility. The popes of the fourteenth century were bound to have fresh in their minds the memory of the attempt on the life of Boniface VIII perpetrated at Anagni; this attack had only been made possible by the connivance of the Romans.

The continued residence of the popes on the banks of the Rhône is thus adequately explained and even justified by the need to put an end to the suit brought against Boniface VIII and to wind up the trial of the Templars, by the imminence of the crusade, by the attempts at conciliation between France and England, and above all by the unsettled state of Italy. To these primary causes must be added some secondary ones: the preponderance of French cardinals in the Sacred College and their marked distaste for Italian soil; the construction by Benedict XII of the Palace of the Popes, at once an admirable work of art and a fortress which for long guaranteed the most complete security; the purchase of Avignon from Joanna I, queen of Naples, in 1348; Clement VI's devotion to his country; the age and infirmity of Innocent VI; the manoeuvres and intrigues of the kings of France, who wished to keep the papal court within their sphere of influence; and the popes' anxiety to preserve friendly relations with the only genuine allies on whom they could count in the bitter conflict with Louis of Bavaria.

CONCLUSION

It was for long customary to judge the Avignon popes only in the light of the malevolent accounts of contemporary chroniclers, and the tendentious writings of Petrarch, St Catherine of Siena and St Bridget of Sweden. All these used to be accepted quite uncritically and without question.

Since, however, documents from the archives were published, though only in an abridged form some seventy or eighty years ago, it has become possible to modify the judgment of history which had hitherto remained uniformly unfavourable to the Avignon papacy.

In the first place, the Avignon popes have frequently been criticised for being too humble in their attitude towards France, and too willing to modify their general policy to suit the particular convenience of the French royal house. In certain instances, such as the trial of the Templars, and in the case of certain popes, such as Clement V and Benedict XII, this criticism still seems justified. But to take a more general view, the diplomatic activities of the Avignon popes were carried on with a real independence both in the East and in the West, and in their foreign policy they unremittingly pursued a threefold aim: to bring peace to Europe, to conquer the Holy Land and to recapture the Papal States.

It must be admitted that the Avignon popes failed to realise their plans for a Crusade. It is difficult to decide how Utopian such plans were, in view of the political situation in fourteenth-century Europe. The popes may well have thought that their influence over the princes of Christendom was still sufficient to justify a hope of success in the noble enterprise. Indeed, throughout the century, their arbitration and intervention were constantly requested, or at least accepted, except in the case of the imperial election, which was now beyond the Roman pontiff's sphere of influence.

The most commonly held grievance against the Avignon popes is that they continued to stay on the bank of the Rhône, far from the Eternal City, which seemed abandoned "without hope of return." On this particular point, the results of our historical investigations are quite unambiguous. Italy was plunged into political anarchy and could not guarantee safe shelter to the papacy. Throughout the fourteenth century the popes tried, with varying success, to restore peace in the peninsula and to take their place once more among the small states that were in process of formation. The victories of Cardinal Albornoz and his skilful policy, which was carried on by Gregory XI, eventually made Rome once more a fitting habitation for the pope.

The Italian policy of the Avignon popes provides at least an explanation and to a certain extent an excuse for their financial system, which was in many ways a new one, and which was eventually to cause serious harm to Christian countries. This discontent was to come into the full light of day at the time of the Great Schism of the West.

The financial policy of the Avignon popes was

closely linked with the increasing tendency to centralise the administration of the Roman Church. This tendency received a lively impetus from, and was very similar to, the corresponding centralisation which was going on in the various European states during the fourteenth and fifteenth centuries as a result of the constitution of national monarchies. It was to give rise to the dangerous forces of reaction which almost carried the day at the Council of Basle.

In conclusion, the religious activities of the Avignon popes stand out in the zeal with which they put down heresy, reformed the religious orders and brought the knowledge of the Gospel to distant lands.

PETER PARTNER

ANOTHER VIEW OF PAPAL FISCALITY

In the following selection, the British scholar Peter Partner limits the focus of our larger problem still further to the question of "Papal Finance and the Papal States." But again, as in the case of the selection from Mollat, this is an extremely important aspect of the problem. Most of the charges that the "general opinion" has leveled against the popes of the later Middle Ages and early modern times go back ultimately to the "secularization of the papacy" and its concern for temporalities at the expense of its ancient spiritual functions. The most often cited evidence of papal temporality is, moreover, the concern of the popes with finance: the historical record reveals a tissue of complaints and charges against the financial policies of the papacy going back from modern scholarship through the Reformation to the strident critics of the fourteenth and fifteenth centuries. It is to these two causally related issues—the secularization of the papacy and papal finance—that Partner addresses himself in this article.

The base of Partner's argument is the well-accepted fact that from the eighth century the papacy played a double role as an international spiritual power on the one hand and as an Italian secular state on the other. He goes on to argue that the maintenance and successful operation of the papal state in Italy was essential to the success of the papacy in its international dimension. But the very bureaucratic practices which were necessary to the successful operation of the papal state were precisely those that brought down upon the papacy the storm of criticism for its secularism. He traces the course of the popes' recovery of the papal state and the increasingly successful administration of it through the opening years of the Reformation and observes the paradox that when the Reformation did break, it was at the moment when the popes were less guilty of the "money-grabbing" with which they were charged than they had been for centuries.

The student should "test" this paradox the author presents. He should note the modern pragmatic defense Partner presents for the papal bureaucracy and for the widely criticized practices of nepotism and the sale of church offices. And he should note the role of the various secular powers in forcing upon the papacy those very secular practices which they then took occasion to criticize.

Machiavelli never missed a chance to bait the Church, and the Papal State does not escape his irony. He taunts the Popes as old and ailing men, unfit for war and dogged by approaching death. The inefficiency of their rule was proverbial; few of them could stand up to the fearful physical and mental gymnastics required of a Renaissance prince. Of all rulers, only they "possess states and do not defend them, have subjects and do not govern them."

This is savage and penetrating, but it is far from being the whole truth. Machiavelli, who considered persons rather than bureaucracies, forgot that the Papal State was managed by the Roman curia, which was probably the most efficient, tenacious and conservative bureaucracy in Europe. Most officers of the Papal court were lawyers, and the claims of the Papacy, which was itself the fount of Canon Law in the West, were pressed by them inexorably from one pontificate to another. They were ambitious and competent men, whose integrity tended to be that of the good civil servant rather than that of the good priest, and to their legal minds the enforcement of the financial rights of the Papacy was of the first importance. And when it is considered how often temporal princes had seized, corrupted and misused the Papacy in its moments of political impotence, their view seems neither nonsensical nor necessarily self-interested.

Papal revenues arose from both "spiritual" and "temporal" sources—that is, in part from a great variety of taxes concerned with the conferment of benefices and the spiritual primacy of the Papacy, in part from the money tribute paid by certain kingdoms, and in part from the government of the lands that the Papacy directly controlled. It was this last, the "Patrimony of St. Peter" of the Middle Ages, the "temporal power" of modern times, that aroused Machiavelli's scorn.

The Pope had since the early Middle Ages been a political ruler as well as a landlord; his worldly rule was based on the so-called "donations" of the Frankish kings in the eighth century. After many vicissitudes, he found himself in the thirteenth century in control of a loosely-knit state, which in the west included Rome and its district, the ancient Latium as far south as Terracina and Ceprano, and as far north as the river Pescia, running inland along the Sienese border into Umbria, to Città della Pieve, Perugia and Città di Castello. On the Adriatic it extended from Ravenna and Bologna in the north (with suzerainty over Ferrara and some neighbouring areas), south down the coast to Ascoli Piceno, and eastwards into the mountainous interior to the Duchy of Spoleto. The two richest areas of this territory were the great town of Bologna, and the southeastern area known as the March of Ancona, which had a flourishing sea trade, and an agriculture of the open countryside, which did not, as elsewhere in central Italy, cling round the walls of the cities. But in the earlier Middle Ages the Papal hand lay lightly on the March, where the communes were as independent as they were prosperous, and lighter still on Romagna, the area in all Italy most prolific of tyrants, of semi-autonomous *signori* whose profession was arms and who, whenever not rigorously coerced, denied all but the nominal suzerainty of the Pope. The country south of Rome was sterile, dominated by the Roman baronage, disorderly, and usually administered at a loss. To the north of Rome, in that part of northern Latium and Umbria known as the Patrimony of St. Peter in Tuscia, Papal rule was strongest. The whole State was one of the five great powers of Italy, an equal to Milan, Venice and the Kingdom of Naples, had it not been worked on by such powerful centrifugal forces, and governed by such short-lived rulers. But the Papal lands tended to be thought a mere source of income rather than a State to be governed. They were ruled through the same bureau, the Apostolic Chamber, that collected the spiritual taxes, and the Pope sometimes appeared in his dominions to be more a tax-collector than a prince.

When the reform of the Church was discussed in the fifteenth century it was recognized by all but the extreme radicals that the Pope and Cardinals should have a substantial income, to pay for the central administration of the Church and for that expensive pageantry which the Middle Ages associated with princely power. Reformers at the great Council of Constance in 1414–1418 tended to say that the

From Peter Partner, "Papal Finance and the Papal State," *History Today*, VII (1957), pp. 766–74. Reprinted by permission of Peter Partner.

The Eve of the Modern World

Papacy should maintain itself from its worldly revenues, and cut the spiritual ones, whose collection fostered corruption and worldliness, to a minimum. But here they ignored the most tragic part of the problem facing the later medieval Papacy. The Popes might indeed have sacrificed a large part of their spiritual revenues, had they been certain of their power to collect the temporal ones. But the disorders of Italy, rebellion within the Papal State and aggression without, constantly forced them to impose heavy spiritual taxes in order to deal with political rebellions, or even to prevent the Papal State from crumbling away altogether. The abolition of spiritual taxes, and the democratic constitution which the extreme "conciliar" party wanted to force on the Papacy, would have meant the destruction of the Papal State.

These problems changed little in essence for centuries, and, if the situation is viewed from the point of view of the Papal curia, the "periods" in which Papal history has been marked out by modern historians appear rather artificial. We are accustomed to think of the Renaissance as the epoch when the Papacy was an Italian principate, with the Borgia in the forefront of the scene. But although it was exercised only with difficulty, the effective rule of the Popes over their temporal state dates at the latest from the second half of the thirteenth century. This is rather more than a century after the consolidation of the powers of the kings of England and France, but Papal rule lacked a score of the advantages enjoyed by the developing national state. From the thirteenth century, however, the Papal State possessed a complex system of government, a network of provincial rectors, a system of law, a developed central administration. But the role of the temporal power was much complicated by its Janus face—the spiritual primacy of St. Peter; from the time of the Carolingian donations of the eighth century one face of the Papacy was turned inward to Italy and the other outward to Europe, with important consequences for the history of Italy and of the Church. The two aspects of policy are interlocked: the "universal" policy of the Papacy led to a bitter struggle with the Emperors, which led in turn to the seizure by the Empire of whole provinces of the State of the Church. On the other hand, the European prestige of the Papacy afforded many political advantages to the temporal power, and from the spiritual power the Popes drew the money that made possible the decisive conquest of their own patrimony.

This conquest was not easy, and its methods were complex. When Boniface VIII died miserably in 1303, after his bitter humiliation at Anagni at the hands of the agents of Philip the Fair of France and of the Roman family of Colonna, one of the oldest techniques for furthering the temporal power seemed to have ended in defeat and discredit. We have the habit of judging those Popes who enriched their own families at the expense of the Church rather hardly, and of automatically calling a "nepotistic" Pope a bad one. But this is a somewhat prim and anachronistic view of a practice that to contemporaries was not essentially immoral; and it also underrates the practical effectiveness of a realistic policy. The Pope had few troops at his command; and in central Italy the disruptive forces of communes, tyrants and barons were too self-seeking and too sophisticated to be coerced into political obedience by purely spiritual fulminations. If a Pope were to reduce the temporal power to order, he would be best elected from one of the great Roman baronial families—a Conti, a Savelli, an Orsini—so that he might use the military and political force of his family in the service of the Roman Church. This policy was adopted throughout the thirteenth century, and the rise of the temporal authority from impotence to power is convincing proof of its effectiveness; but it had its dangers. The Church paid a heavy price in grants of money and land, and in a certain decline of moral stability. Quarrels and civil war often followed the death of a Pope, when the jealous and perhaps despoiled nobles of one family would fall upon another, which under the rule of their dead kinsman had been enjoying the fruits of office. A further peril was the Pope who pressed the claims of his family with such indiscretion as to attack the whole basis of temporal government. Such a Pope was Boniface VIII, such another was Alexander Borgia, a pair disparate in their moral outlook, but similar in having plans for their families of such grandiosity as to threaten to secularize the whole temporal power. Boniface gave the Caetani family an enormous quantity of money and land, and—encouraged, it is true, by motives unconnected with family—mercilessly expropriated their Colonna enemies. He thus drew down a vengeance that caused disorder and ruin in the Papal State for a good many years, and was a contributory cause of the transfer of the Holy See to Avignon in 1309, where for almost seventy years the Popes remained in the so-called "Babylonian Exile."

It has long been usual to reprove the Avignonese

Popes for their rapacity and for a certain degree of moral turpitude, and to allege the entire decadence of the authority of the Holy See in Italy to be a result of their refusal to desert the pleasant wines of Provence for the bitter beverage of rebellion and danger that would be forced on them in Rome. It is doubtful if the first branch of this charge can be proved; and the second is certainly unjust. The fourteenth century was the epoch of the universal financial domination of the Papacy, which, using its Italian bankers as a European credit system, enforced its taxes and its system of distributing clerical office in every corner of the Church, and enjoyed thereby an immense revenue. But the Papacy at Avignon was not, for this reason, a different entity from the Papacy at Rome. Its system was a development of the already highly articulated organization in use at Rome: the methods of Boniface VIII were not in this respect very different from those of his Avignonese successors, nor was his income so very much less than theirs. And, similarly, the Avignonese Popes were far from forgetting their responsibilities to the temporal power; not only were they anxious for peace so that they might return to Italy, but they wanted to rule with a firmer hand in the Papal State, to suppress tyrants and rebellious barons, to limit the independence of the towns. To this end legates and commissioners were sent from Avignon to Italy charged with commissions of reform, to combat the corruption of the rectors and the intrusion of local interests into Papal government. It was a hard struggle; and, as is common in medieval government, each wave of war and unrest seems to present a picture of irreparable chaos, only to recede and to leave the central authority in a slightly stronger position than before. The times demanded a combination of subtlety and brutal strength. The old hegemony of the free cities, which had been glad to accept Papal protection on limited terms, was ending, and everywhere was being succeeded by the rule of the tyrant, the *signore*. The Papacy did its best to play off one *signore* against another, and, where it could, to assert the *signoria* of the Church against any city which gave it the opportunity. Thus the city of Rome, which in the thirteenth century had much increased its independence vis-à-vis the Popes, in the succeeding century lost ground; in 1347 the dictatorship of Cola di Rienzo, that exotic propagandist of a united Italy under a reborn classical Rome, marks one of the last effective stands of the commune of Rome against Papal authority.

The great agent of the Avignonese Popes in their reconquest of the temporal power was the Spanish Cardinal Gil Albornoz, who between 1353 and 1367 re-established the authority of the Church in every part of the State, and enacted a legal code that was to remain in force in the Papal State until 1817. What other legates had attempted piecemeal, Albornoz achieved in gross. Without finally crushing the tyrants of Romagna, he forced them at least to pay tribute; he built or repaired a network of fortresses, and enjoyed an immense personal prestige from which Papal government as a whole benefited. It proved beyond his power to break the influence of the Visconti, the tyrants of Milan, and the mediocre support he received in this enterprise from the curia assured its failure. Thirty years before John XXII had conducted a comparable war against the Visconti, designed perhaps to impose the influence of the Church over the whole of North Italy, and this policy also had failed. The Papacy at its strongest was able to arbitrate but not to dominate in Italy—a fact repugnant to Machiavelli and to those Italian patriots who disliked the balance of power, and wished one of the Italian states to become strong enough to unite the peninsula.

The military effort to re-establish the temporal power needed money; and most of this was supplied from the "spiritual" revenues of the Church. The Avignonese Popes did not spend all their revenues on clothes and on the construction of their admirable palace; John XXII spent over three-fifths of his income on the Italian wars, and some of his successors spent a similar amount. The temporal princes, many of whom were far on the way toward the creation of the national state, blackmailed the Popes into giving them a substantial share of the clerical taxes nominally due to the Papacy. But the Church groaned under the weight of taxes, the more so because, as time advanced, the princely middlemen took a larger percentage, forcing an increase to be made in gross taxes to maintain the same net income. This state of affairs, which involved a cure of souls being treated principally as the object of legal rights, aroused increasing protest from the truly pious, who saw spiritual things being treated as earthly chattels, from the impoverished clergy and, ironically enough, from many of the princes, who used the pietistic outcry as a lever to get themselves better terms from the Papacy. Denunciations of these Papal exactions was to become a Protestant commonplace, although the part played by the princes was discreetly omitted and has been dragged back to the light only by the labours of modern scholarship.

The Papacy finally returned to Rome in 1377. It was at once afflicted in the following year by the longest and most pernicious schism of the Middle Ages. Until 1417, the Church was without a certain head, and the allegiance of Europe was divided between two and sometimes three claimants to the tiara. The consequences were in every way disastrous. Christendom almost lost its nerve; clerical taxes were collected with more and more difficulty; the power of temporal rulers in Church affairs and their share in clerical taxation both increased sharply. But in one respect the influence of the Schism on Papal power was less deadly than is often thought. Losing many of their spiritual taxes, the Popes were thrown back upon the temporalities. The Cardinals, who had had the right to enjoy half the temporal income, could no longer enforce their claim. The turbulence of the times favoured the Popes, in that the communes could no longer easily maintain themselves outside the larger political units, and the decay of their political and financial privileges was accelerated. Boniface IX, by the time of his death in 1404, was as complete a master of the Papal State as any Pope before him; and, although in the latter part of the Schism the temporal power drifted into utter ruin, the effects of his work were not entirely lost.

The Schism was the great crisis of Papal finance, a crisis more severe and decisive than the Reformation. Early in 1417, the income of the Holy See (then vacant) was nil. It was no longer practical for the Popes to impose arbitrary taxes, or even to collect ordinary ones, without making terms with the temporal rulers, who did not thereby neglect their own interests. The "tenth," the direct tax for the extraordinary needs of the Papacy, became extremely difficult to impose outside Italy. Some taxes were entirely abolished at the Council of Constance. The income of Martin V, the Pope elected at Constance in 1417, was at first between a quarter and a third of that of the Avignonese Popes. Ways out were found; but the decay of the whole tax-collecting system meant that a steep moral price had to be paid in order to maintain even this modest income. The chancery taxes, imposed on anyone who had to seek an official document from the Papal court, were very much increased. Dispensations and compositions of various kinds were charged at a high rate; the indulgence became financially important. No one of these measures brought in a huge sum,

but together they kept the curia from bankruptcy. The newly discovered alum mines at Tolfa were a windfall for the Popes. The sale of offices, an institution more respectable in the Middle Ages than now, but even then rather shocking in a clerical context, had begun seriously in the Papal court during the Schism. At the start providing a real additional income, this practice had the effect of multiplying the number of offices held; and when, late in the fifteenth century, whole colleges of new offices were created at a stroke, it turned into a system of State life-annuities. The salaries of the venal offices were on the average about eleven per cent of the purchase price; percentage charges were made when an office was sold by one holder to another. The capital invested grew by 1520 to between two and a half and three million ducats, and the annual interest absorbed a huge sum. Thus there grew up a kind of privileged stock exchange, to which entry was reserved for the officials of the Roman curia—a fact that had disastrous results for the many attempts made by the Popes to reform the curia.

These expedients were insufficient to cure the basic malaise of Papal finances, which were saved from disaster only by a large increase of the income from the temporal power. From being negligible at the beginning of the Avignonese period, this grew steadily with the spread of effective Papal suzerainty, so that by the third quarter of the fifteenth century Papal budgets estimate that over half Papal income was derived from the Papal State. Perhaps the revenues actually due were not increased a great deal; what was decisive was the regularity of their collection, a factor depending entirely on firmness of government. This was achieved in the same intermittent, wasteful but effective fashion as before. Martin V (Pope from 1417–1431) proved to be the refounder of the temporal power in Italy. A Colonna, he used the system of nepotism with great success, and, having found central Italy in chaos and the lands of the Church in the hands of tyrants, at his death he left the Papal State swollen in wealth and extent, and governed with a firm hand. The power of the Pope in the more distant provinces, Romagna and the March of Ancona, increased steadily as the tyrants there were brought to order. The most effective repression in these provinces since Albornoz' time was conducted by Cesare Borgia, who had his father lived would have tried to turn the whole of central Italy into a duchy or a kingdom of his own. But Julius II turned Borgia's work to the service of the Church—the observation is Machiavelli's. By the time of that fierce pontiff's death in 1513, the Papal State had little more to fear from internal enemies; and, although it led to the sack of Rome in 1527, the Spanish domination in Italy protected the Popes from external foes. The last serious communal rebellion was that of Perugia in 1539; and from this period until the French Revolution the Papal State led a relatively tranquil existence.

The effect of this seems to have been that, from the pontificate of Julius II, Papal revenues rose steeply, and for the first time regained the level they had in their heyday in the fourteenth century—but with the difference that, instead of being drawn from the clerical estate all over Europe, they were provided mainly by the inhabitants of the Papal State. In the medieval phrase, the Pope was "living of his own." The Reformation period, in which criticism of Papal "bloodsucking" reached its peak, was thus a period in which the "spiritual" taxes in fact sank to a low proportion—perhaps a quarter—of Papal revenue. Taxation for the benefit of the Church was still not lacking in Europe; but the naïve criticism of the reformers overlooked the long line of middlemen who stood between the tax-payer and Rome.

Once the Papal budget had been balanced, it was, in theory, at last possible to plan a drastic reform of the Roman court, which would iron out its complex and irritating bureaucratic anomalies, and disperse the tribe of clerical hangers-on. But for a long time no such reform was attempted, partly because of the spendthrift dilettantism of Popes like Leo X (Pope from 1513–1521), partly because of political crises, but perhaps most of all because a hoary and conservative bureaucracy would not permit its leader to encroach on ancient privilege. Papal income continued to rise. But not until the Council of Trent was a root-and-branch reform of the Roman curia attempted. By that time Papal finances were predominantly the finances of the Papal State; the losses occasioned by the Tridentine reforms were met by increases in the salt tax.

From a financial point of view the Reformation is therefore a paradox; the final outburst against Papal money-grabbing came at the moment when the Popes were less guilty under this charge than they had been for many centuries. If the reformers had turned their attention to the growing share of Church revenues which was enjoyed by the temporal princes, they might have had a more realistic view of the situation.

WALLACE K. FERGUSON

A MODERN SYNTHESIS

The following selection is taken from an article, "The Church in a Changing World: A Contribution to the Interpretation of the Renaissance," by the eminent American historian of the Renaissance, Wallace K. Ferguson. In it he presents a new interpretation of this period in the history of the church which he states more elaborately in his recently published book, *Europe in Transition 1300–1520*. Despite its small compass, this article takes a broader view even than the selection from the much more comprehensive work of Pastor. The result is to present this segment of the history of the church and the papacy as a distinct period in church history, a major period of transition between the high Middle Ages and modern times. It is part of the author's general argument in favor of the Renaissance as a distinct historical period.

In this article Ferguson's argument is that the church and the papacy were able to dominate the Christian world in the age of Innocent III because that world was still

The Eve of the Modern World

predominantly feudal; that, with the crisis of Boniface VIII, the church and papacy began to lose ground as feudalism gave way before the rising national monarchies and the general changes in society marking the passing of feudalism; that the changes for which the late medieval popes have been criticized were actually awkward and ill-contrived accommodations to these changed material conditions of institutional life; and that, after the upheaval of the Reformation, the church regained its strength and the papacy its integrity not by counterreformation but by a return to fundamental spirituality.

The student should compare the treatment of the Avignonese papacy in this selection with its treatment in the preceding ones. He should note Ferguson's argument that the popes of the fifteenth century turned to the consolidation of their secular power in Italy and behaved like other contemporary Italian princes; and he should note the difference between this argument and the one advanced by Partner in the previous selection. He should note how Ferguson explains the Conciliar Movement in terms not of the reform of abuses but in terms of a fundamental conflict of constitutional theory. And finally, the student should attempt to follow the systematic development of the author's "thesis."

The historical interpretation of that phase in the development of European civilization represented by the fourteenth, fifteenth, and sixteenth centuries poses a problem that has aroused much interest and no little controversy among scholars in the ninety-odd years since Burckhardt first treated these centuries as a period in the history of Italian civilization and labeled it the Renaissance. Since then, scholars who did not share Burckhardt's preconceptions, or who were interested primarily in other countries or in some particular aspect of culture, have presented widely divergent views of the spirit, content, and chronological limits of the Renaissance,[1] with the result that the value of the concept for purposes of periodization has been greatly vitiated. Much of the confusion concerning the Renaissance arises, I think, from the fact that it has been used indiscriminately as a style concept or to denote an intellectual movement, and that, when considered as a historical period, it has commonly been regarded from the point of view of one country or one particular cultural or religious interest, so that its interpretation has been constructed upon too narrow a foundation. It seems to me that, if we consider the economic, social, and political, as well as the intellectual, aesthetic, and religious life of the centuries from 1300 to 1600, we shall find a certain unity of development in all the countries of western Europe. It seems to me, too, that, if the various aspects of their civilization are related to one another in a reasonably well co-ordinated synthesis, these three centuries may be treated as a period in the history of western European civilization as a whole, and that such a periodic concept may have sufficient validity to serve as a useful, if not indispensable, instrument of historical thought. For this period the term Renaissance may not be well chosen, but it is still the only commonly accepted term we have for a crucially important historical period, and one that cannot be treated satisfactorily by the simple device of attaching it to either the medieval or the modern age, or by dividing it between them.

It is, indeed, the distinguishing characteristic of these centuries that they are neither medieval nor modern, but represent a transitional stage which has a character of its own. In a paper read at the meeting of the Modern Language Association in December, 1950,[2] I defined the Renaissance as a period characterized by the gradual shift from one fairly

---

[1] For review of the major trends in the interpretation of the Renaissance, see W. K. Ferguson, *The Renaissance in Historical Thought* (Boston, 1948).

[2] W. K. Ferguson, "The Interpretation of the Renaissance: Suggestions for a Synthesis," *Journal of the History of Ideas*, XII (1951), 483–95.

From Wallace K. Ferguson, "The Church in a Changing World: A Contribution to the Interpretation of the Renaissance," *American Historical Review*, LIX (1953), pp. 1–18. Reprinted by permission of the American Historical Association and the author.

well co-ordinated and clearly defined type of civilization to another, yet at the same time possessing in its own right certain distinctive traits and a high degree of cultural vitality. As a more precise hypothesis I suggested that it was a transition from a civilization that was predominantly feudal and ecclesiastical in its social, political, and cultural manifestations and agrarian in its economic foundations, to one that was predominantly national, urban, secular, and laic, in which the economic center of gravity had shifted from agriculture to commerce and industry and in which a simple money economy had evolved into capitalism. What I want to consider here is the problem of the Church and the papacy in this synthesis. To what extent do they fit? And to what extent does this approach to the interpretation of the Renaissance serve to illuminate a crucial segment in the history of the Church?

The conception of this period as peculiarly an age of transition makes it necessary to establish first of all a fairly definite idea of the nature of the civilizations that preceded and followed it. But, since historical thought tends naturally toward a genetic treatment and, indeed, cannot avoid the problem of causation, the interpretation of a transitional age is necessarily bound up more closely with the age out of which it grew than with that into which it later developed. By far the greater part of the controversy over the character of the Renaissance has concentrated attention upon its relation to the Middle Ages. This is the essential problem of the Renaissance scholar. The question of the relation of the Renaissance to the following period belongs rather to scholars whose field of interest is the early modern period. That is their genetic headache; let us leave it to them. This may seem an irresponsible attitude, and I may be following too closely the example of that little bird, the prototype of all historians, who always liked to fly backwards, because he didn't care where he was going but liked to see where he had been. I think, however, that in so far as our interest is concentrated upon the transitional age itself, we must consider of first importance the question of what were the causes, nature, and extent of change. And that leads us back inevitably to the Middle Ages. As Carl Becker once remarked, a historian can describe anything only by first describing what it successively was before it became that which it will presently cease to be.

The origins of the Church, of course, carry us back to a period before the Middle Ages. From that early period it inherited not only its basic doctrine but also the concept of universality and the hierarchical organization that have remained constant throughout its history. In considering what was peculiarly medieval in the Church, however, and therefore likely to change with the passing of medieval civilization, we need go no further back than the centuries in which feudalism was taking shape, that is, roughly the eighth, ninth, and tenth centuries. In these centuries, if we accept Pirenne's thesis, western Europe had been reduced to an almost purely agricultural economy. And I think we might describe feudalism as fundamentally the adaptation of social and political organization to an economy in which land was almost the only form of wealth. Under these circumstances, central governments lacked the financial resources to govern effectively, so that legal jurisdiction and governmental authority were parceled out among the great landholders. Under these circumstances, too, the clergy, as one of the two classes that did not work the land yet had a very important function to perform, became a landholding class. Even earlier, in the Merovingian period, bishops had become administrative officers with secular rule over their cities. Now, as feudal lords, the bishops and abbots became the rulers of fiefs, barons ecclesiastical with sovereign rights in their baronies. From this period on, the Church was committed to the exercise of temporal authority and to great possessions. But, by the nature of feudal tenure, a lord was also a vassal. And the barons ecclesiastical were at the same time vassals of secular lords: kings or emperors. From this arose much interference by laymen in the election of church officials, and the ill-omened figure of Simon Magus cast its shadow across the Church. This was the period in which the Church was most completely feudalized. In their dual capacity as feudal vassals and church officers, prelates were forced to divide their services, often somewhat unequally, between God and Mammon, but they also exercised a great deal of independent authority. The utter inadequacy of fiscal income made effective central government almost impossible for either the papacy or the monarchies, so that the conflict of secular and spiritual interests operated on the level of diocese and fief rather than of Church and state in the broader sense.

The eleventh century marked the beginning of a tremendous revival in every branch of medieval civilization. Regular commercial relations were reestablished between Italy and the Levant. From the seacoasts trade spread inland until the whole of western Europe was covered with a network of trade routes along which traveled not only merchants but also pilgrims, crusaders, students, and churchmen on official business. At intervals along these trade routes old cities revived or new ones sprang up. They became centers of local trade and skilled industry and, at the same time, furnished a market for surplus agricultural products. The twelfth and thirteenth centuries were characterized by a steadily growing prosperity in both country and city. The population of western Europe probably doubled during this period. Money economy, reintroduced through commerce and industry in the cities, spread to the countryside and made possible the partial conversion of landed wealth into fluid wealth that could be mobilized and concentrated. But, though this economic revival received its initial impetus from trade and depended for its continuing growth on the growth of cities, European society still retained in main outlines the structure which had been given it by the feudal system and the Church. The vigorous culture which made the twelfth and thirteenth centuries the classic period of medieval civilization was preeminently the culture of the feudal nobility and the clergy.

Feudalism, indeed, lasted long after the passing of that condition of almost exclusive agricultural economy in which it had been formed and which had justified its existence. The rights and privileges of the dominant feudal classes were protected by their monopoly of military force, by long-established jurisdictional authority, and by custom so ingrained that no other form of social and political organization could be imagined. As Joseph Calmette has observed, feudalism had become a kind of Kantian category, in terms of which the medieval mind perceived the social world.[3] Nevertheless, the growth of a money economy made possible, even in this period, the gradual recovery by central governments of some of the powers that had been lost in practice, if not in theory, during the early feudal era. In the early stages of this development, however, the government of the Church was in a position to take advantage of the new situation to better effect than were the feudal monarchies. Though partially feudalized in practice, the Church had never been as feudalized in theory as were the secular states. Its hierarchical principle was deeply rooted in both tradition and dogma. The feudal system, it is true, was also in theory hierarchical; but the feudal hierarchy consisted of a fortuitous network of personal relations which changed its form with each generation and which the accidents of marriage and inheritance rendered increasingly chaotic. The hierarchy of the Church, on the other hand, was a rationally organized administrative system, modeled upon that of the Roman Empire. Whereas the secular monarchies could establish effective state government only by destroying the feudal hierarchy as a political reality, the ecclesiastical monarchy had only to tighten its control of the hierarchy to make it an effective instrument of central government.

Even so, this was no easy task, for the officers of the Church were also vassals of emperors or kings. Bishops resisted the extension of papal authority not only because it infringed upon their independent diocesan jurisdiction but also because, in many cases, they felt a prior loyalty to the king or emperor who had nominated and enfeoffed them. This was the most serious obstacle to the growth of a strong centralized government in the Church. The vigorous assertion of the papal monarchy by Gregory VII led inevitably to the Investiture Controversy with the emperors and to less overt conflicts with other kings and princes. It also led to an unprecedented expansion of the claims of papal supremacy from the ecclesiastical into the temporal sphere. For, so long as the officers of the Church were also temporal lords, whose support was essential to secular rulers, the government of the Church could not be disassociated from that of the state. An effective papal monarchy within the Church could, therefore, be achieved only by establishing papal supremacy over the secular states. In this the popes were never entirely successful, but in the age of Innocent III they came very close to the fulfillment of their ambition. In their contest with the powers of this world the popes could count on the immense spiritual authority conferred upon them by unchallenged faith in the saving power of the Church. Their spiritual weapons were not yet blunted by overuse. They enjoyed the prestige of leading the military might of Christendom against the infidel; and they were actively supported by all the reforming elements in the monastic orders, by the doctors of the new scholastic learning, and by the development of canon law in the new universities. It must not be forgotten that the assertion of papal supremacy began as a reform movement at a time when reform of the Church was sadly needed. There is something, too, in Heinrich von Eicken's theory that the supremacy of the Church over temporal governments was the logical

[3]Joseph Calmette, Le Monde féodal (Paris, 1946), p. 169.

extension into practice of the ascetic conviction of the worthlessness of all things worldly.[4] At any rate, the concern with temporal affairs, which threatened eventually to secularize the Church, had in the twelfth century the full support of St. Bernard and all the most ascetic elements in both the secular and regular clergy.

Despite all these advantages, it is doubtful whether the papacy or the Church as an institution could have achieved the dominant position they held in the age of Innocent III if political and social life had not still been cast in the feudal mold—and that not only because secular governments were still too much weakened by feudal particularism to resist the encroachments of the spiritual authority upon the temporal sphere. The privileged legal status of the clergy fitted naturally into a society in which all legal status depended upon social status. The immunity of the clergy from secular jurisdiction was only one of many immunities, akin to that of the burghers or any other corporate body. The ecclesiastical courts and the canon law competed not with state courts and state law but with a bewildering variety of feudal and urban courts and laws. Everywhere the Church had the advantage that its institutions were universal, while those of the secular world were local and particular. The universality of the Church, indeed, found its perfect complement in the particularism and localism of feudal society. There could be little real conflict between a knight's loyalty to his immediate lord and the Christian's loyalty to the head of the *Respublica Christiana*. Seldom did these centruies witness any type of warfare between the extremes of the localized feudal brawl and the crusade against the infidel. Finally, it was largely due to the conditions of life in a feudal society that the clergy were able to maintain a practical monopoly of education. As the only class in society which had a felt need for these things, the clergy became the principal protagonists of learning, music, and art. They were thus able to give them a direction consonant with their own interests, and to place upon them the stamp of a universal uniformity that did much to impede the growth of national sentiment or national cultures. The feudal nobilty had their vernacular literatures—troubadour lyric, chanson, romance, or Minnesang—but serious thought served the Church. The best brains of Europe functioned below a tonsure. And what medieval men had of visual beauty or the concourse of sweet sounds they owed to the universal Church.

The conditions so uniquely favorable to papal supremacy and to the dominant position of the Church in European society lasted until about the end of the thirteenth century. Even before that time, however, there were signs, though the cloud was no larger than a man's hand, that the halcyon days were passing. The conflict between the thirteenth-century popes and the viper brood of the Hohenstaufen ended in the practical destruction of the Empire. But, in the process, the papacy lost something of the moral prestige that had been its greatest asset in the days of the Investiture Controversy. A moral conflict had degenerated into a squabble over territorial sovereignty in Italy. The spiritual weapons of the Apostolic See had been used too freely in defense of the material patrimony of St. Peter, and popes had too often cried crusade when there was no crusade. So far as any contemporary could observe, however, the papacy was stronger than ever. The Empire was shattered, and, during the greater part of the thirteenth century, France was ruled by a saint and England by a pious fool, neither of whom would offer effective resistance to the spiritual ruler of Christendom. When in 1300 Boniface VIII proclaimed the first Jubilee Year, it seemed as though all Europe had come to Rome to pour its varied coinage into the papal coffers. Two years later, in the bull *Unam Sanctam*, Boniface proclaimed in uncompromising terms the subjection of the temporal to the spiritual authority and concluded by declaring that, for all human creatures, obedience to the Roman pontiff is altogether necessary to salvation. The storm that broke immediately thereafter indicated the extent to which conditions had changed. Philip the Fair was no saint, and Edward I no pious fool. Nor were these sovereigns content to act as mere feudal suzerains within their kingdoms. The reigns of these two kings mark the first decisive stage in the transition from feudal to national monarchy, and a national monarch, determined to be master in his own state, could scarcely tolerate either the papal claims to supremacy or the immunity of the clergy from royal jurisdiction and royal taxation. In the rising national monarchies the papacy met for the first time a secular power too strong for it. The arrest of the aged pope at Anagni marked the end of a period which had opened with an emperor standing barefoot in the snow before the gates of Canossa.

[4] Heinrich von Eicken, *Geschichte und System der mittelalterlichen Weltanschauung* (Stuttgart, 1923), pp. 325 ff.

The Eve of the Modern World

The crisis precipitated by the conflict between Boniface VIII and Philip the Fair led to a series of events which seriously undermined the authority and prestige of the papacy; the long exile at Avignon under the shadow of the French monarchy, the scandal of the Great Schism, the conciliar movement, and the anarchy in the Papal States. All of these events aggravated the difficulties inherent in the position of the Church in a changing world. Yet their significance may easily be exaggerated. The anarchy in the Papal States which made Rome unsafe was not new. There had been schisms before the Great Schism, and antipopes before Clement VII. As Guillaume Mollat has recently pointed out, the absence of the popes from Rome was not unprecedented nor necessarily disastrous.[5] It has been calculated, indeed, that "between the years 1100 and 1304, that is, two hundred and four years, the popes lived one hundred and twenty-two outside Rome and eighty-two in Rome: a difference of forty years in favor of absence."[6]

What seems to me more significant than these external events in the history of the papacy is the profound though gradual change which took place in the whole civilization of western Europe in the three centuries following 1300. It was a change caused by the interaction of political and social factors, complicated by shifts in the social balance and by the imponderable element of a changing *Weltanschauung*. But one factor at least was, I think, of basic importance: the expansion within feudal society of a money economy during the preceding two or three hundred years. By the end of the thirteenth century it had begun to disintegrate a system never intended for it. Even before that time, the manorial system, with its exchange of labor and produce for the use of land and its closely integrated relation of landholders to dependent workers, had begun to be replaced by a system of cash payments—of rents, leases, and wages. The result was a fundamental change in the economic and social foundations of feudalism. The disrupting effect of this change was aggravated by widespread famines in the early years of the fourteenth century, by the depopulation of Europe resulting from the Black Death and the succession of only relatively less fatal epidemics that followed, by the devastation of France during the Hundred Years' War, by the cessation of coloniza-

[5] Guillaume Mollat, *Les Papes d'Avignon* (Paris, 1949), pp. 9 ff.

[6] Louis Gayet, *Le Grand Schisme d'Occident* (Florence, 1889), p. 3.

tion and of the assarting of waste land, in short by a series of economic crises and depressions which bred intense social unrest and seriously undermined the economic stability of the feudal classes, including the landholding clergy, and loosened their hold upon the land and its people.

At the same time that the economic and social foundations of feudalism were crumbling, the political and jurisdictional powers of the feudal nobles were being absorbed by the central governments in the great national states and in the smaller principalities of Germany and the Netherlands, as they had been already in the city-states of Italy. The money economy which undermined the independence of the feudal classes served to increase the powers of central government. Money furnished the sinews of administration as of war, and though the total wealth of the European states may not have increased materially during the period of economic crisis from 1300 to about 1450, governments everywhere were learning to utilize the available wealth to better effect by levying new taxes, by imposing import, export, and excise duties, by borrowing from the great Italian banking houses, and, in general, by evolving a more efficient fiscal system. The change in military technique from the feudal array to the royal armies and mercenary companies of the Hundred Years' War is but one symptom of a process which, by the end of the fifteenth century, had subordinated feudal particularism to royal absolutism and had transformed the feudal vassal of the Middle Ages into the courtier of the early modern period.

Meanwhile, in the urban centers of commerce and industry an equally fundamental change was taking place. Even before 1300, in Italy and the Netherlands, a simple money economy had begun to develop into an embryonic capitalist system. That development continued steadily during the following centuries and spread to all parts of western Europe. The first hundred and fifty years or so of this period, it is true, lacked the steadily expanding prosperity of the preceding centuries. There were periods of acute depression and social unrest in all the great commercial and industrial cities during the fourteenth century. Some cities declined, while others grew. It is difficult to estimate how much the wealth of the cities actually increased during this period. There is, however, ample evidence of an increasing concentration of wealth and of a revolutionary development in the techniques of capitalist business enterprise.

One result, the cultural and religious implications of which I shall return to later, was the spread of lay education in the cities; another, the growth of an urban patriciate composed of laymen who had the wealth, leisure, and cultivated taste to fit them for active participation in any form of intellectual or aesthetic culture. Still another result, the implications of which are more germane to my present argument, was the evolution by merchants, bankers, and financiers of new and more efficient methods of book-keeping and accounting, as well as of more efficient techniques for the mobilization and transportation of money in large quantities. The development of state fiscal systems, the more rational accounting introduced into state chanceries, the hard-headed calculation behind the pious façade of royal policies, even the national bankruptcies that mark this period, are all evidence of the application to public finance of techniques and attitudes first worked out in the domain of private capitalist enterprise.

All of these changes operated, directly or indirectly, to alter the character of medieval society; and, inasmuch as the Church had adapted itself with remarkable success to medieval conditions, any change was almost certain to be prejudicial to it. And, in fact, it did become increasingly difficult for the Church to maintain its dominant position in society and for the papacy to maintain the temporal supremacy it had won in the feudal era. At the same time, the papacy could not conceivably abandon without a struggle powers and privileges which the Church had possessed for centuries and had exercised for the good of the Christian community and for the salvation of souls. Not only would the abandonment of its traditional policy have involved encroachment upon too many vested interests; it would also have involved a grave dereliction of duty, the abdication of a responsibility for the moral government of Christendom that had been asserted by saints and popes and rationalized by centuries of canon law and scholastic argument. But to maintain its position under the new conditions, the government of the Church would have to fight with new weapons. It would have to meet the growing centralization of state administration with an increased centralization in the administration of the Church; and, as money became more and more the essential source of power, it would have to rival the fiscal system of state governments by establishing a more efficient fiscal system of its own. Or so it must have seemed to anyone likely to achieve high office in the Church. There were mystics, like the spiritual Franciscans, who felt differently, and reformers, like John Wycliffe, whose conviction that wealth and power were a hindrance rather than a help to the Church drove them into heresy. But mystics are seldom successful politicians, even ecclesiastical politicians, and spiritually-minded reformers who advocated a return to apostolic poverty or the abandonment to Caesar of the things that were Caesar's were not likely to rise to positions of great authority in an institution committed to great possessions and to the exercise of temporal power. Yet the fiscal system and the concentration of administrative authority in the papal curia, both of which were developed with such skill by the fourteenth- and fifteenth-century popes, should not be considered simply the result of official will to power or avarice in high places. To the hierarchical mind there must have seemed no alternative. The changing policy of the Church as it strove to meet changing conditions must have seemed merely the continuation through new methods of the traditional policy of the preceding centuries. No Biblical injunction warned of the danger of putting old wine into new bottles.

Nevertheless, the development within the Church of a highly organized and centralized fiscal system implied more than the mere adaptation to old ends of a new means. Hitherto, the papal supremacy had been founded largely upon moral authority. The wealth of the Church had remained, even after the reintroduction of money economy, to a great extent decentralized. It was wealth drawn largely from land and held by the officers of the local church organization. By the end of the thirteenth century, however, the increased circulation of money, together with the growth of new techniques of bookkeeping, banking, and exchange, had made possible an effective system of taxation in both Church and state. Thereafter, the centralization of governmental authority and the elaboration of a fiscal system went hand in hand. In this the papacy was simply keeping pace with the secular governments. But the results were different, for the Church was not a secular institution devoted solely to secular ends, though its officers may occasionally have lost sight of this fact in their preoccupation with *Realpolitik*. The possession of wealth had always carried with it the threat of a materialism that might sap the spiritual vigor of the Church. Since the days of Peter Damiani preachers had complained that men were inspired to seek office in the Church by avarice and ambition. So long as the wealth of the Church remained decentralized, however, its central government had remained relatively uncontaminated. Under the new conditions not only the wealth but the materialism that went with it, seemed to be concentrated in an unprecedented degree in the papal curia. Contemporary wits noticed that the word Roma furnished an acrostic base for the apothegm *radix omnium malorum avaritia*.

Nor did the danger end there, for the blight of fiscality spread throughout the Church. The increasing demands of the papal curia forced preoccupation with finance upon all the officers of the Church down to the parish level. And the effort of the papal chancery to introduce a fiscal system into an institution that had never been designed for it led inevitably to the systematization of simony and to traffic in spiritual goods. The fourteenth-century popes, it is true, were very largely successful in gaining that control of the nomination of prelates for which the medieval popes had labored in vain. But, as Dean Inge once remarked, in matters of religion nothing fails like success. The reservation to the papal curia of the right of nomination to vacant benefices throughout Christendom did not achieve a reform of the Church. On the contrary, fiscal pressures, diplomatic negotiations with secular princes, and nepotism in the curia made papal provisions the source of new abuses: absenteeism, duplication of offices, traffic in expectancies, the outright sale of benefices, and close calculation of the financial value of every office. Through the imposition of annates and *servitia* the system also imposed a crushing tax upon benefices, so that many of the charitable and other services expected of the local clergy were left undone. I need not describe here the fiscal expedients to which that financial genius, John XXII, and the other popes of this period resorted. Nor need I emphasize their deleterious effects upon clerical morality. These things are well enough known. Conditions were doubtless never as bad as the reforming preachers would have us believe. One cannot, however, entirely ignore the evidence of a cloud of witnesses to the effect that secular and material interests had done much to corrupt the spiritual character of the clergy, high and low. The pamphlet literature of the conciliar movement furnishes ample evidence of a widespread demand for reform of the Church in head and members, and of a growing conviction that reform could be achieved only by depriving the papal monarchy of some of its sovereign powers.

The conciliar movement, however, was by its very nature doomed to failure. Its constitutional theory ran counter to the trend of growing absolutism in the state as well as in the Church. The position of the bishops had been weakened by many of the same political and economic factors as had undermined the independence of the feudal nobles. The principle of free canonical election, for which the councils strove, had for centuries been no more than partially realized, and it was now a lost cause. It served the interest of the kings no more than of the popes. Finally, the whole conception of the ecumenical council as an international body governing a universal Church had become partially anachronistic. In practice, at any rate, it was vitiated by the intrusion of national governments, national interests, and national sentiments, which divided the councils and frustrated the attempt to impose a permanent control upon the papal executive.

The popes were thus able to weather the storm of the conciliar movement, and they emerged with their theoretical sovereignty intact and with a stronger hold than ever upon the administration of the Church. If so much was won, however, much also was lost. During the crisis years of the Captivity and the Schism the popes had gradually abandoned in practice their claims to supremacy over secular rulers. The fifteenth-century popes made their peace with kings and princes through a series of tacit agreements or formal concordats, by which they shared the nomination of church officers and the taxation of the clergy with the secular rulers. In England, the Statute of Provisors, which the fourteenth-century parliaments had used as an instrument to check papal provisions to English benefices, was allowed to become a dead letter. The English kings were content to leave to the popes the right of provision, and incidentally the annates or *servitia* paid by those who received their benefices by papal collation, on the tacit understanding that a certain number of royal ministers or favorites would be nominated. A similar tacit agreement to share some of the fruits of the papal right of provision in Germany with the emperor and the electors underlay the formal Concordat of Vienna of 1448, by means of which Nicholas V won the emperor Frederick III away from the Council of Basel. The French monarchy, long accustomed to special consideration by the Avignonese popes, proved more difficult to deal with. The Pragmatic Sanction of Bourges in 1438 was a unilateral assertion of the liberties of the Gallican Church, and for more than half a century it remained a threat to the principle of papal sovereignty. The theory of papal authority was finally saved by the Concordat of Bologna in 1516, but only at the cost of surrendering to Francis I the most profitable fruits of control of the national church.

In the system of concordats the papacy made its first adjustment to a world of strong secular states. The popes made such practical concessions as were necessary, without apparent impairment of their own *plenitudo potestatis*. For an estimate of the results we can scarcely do better than quote Professor McIlwain's masterly summary:

They were concessions only. But they were concessions guaranteed by a bilateral document in the nature of a treaty, which implies two treaty-making powers. The concordats were in fact the price the Papacy paid for its victory over the councils and it was a price heavier than appeared at the time. They were a tacit acknowledgement of the sovereignty of national states and they mark the virtual end of the medieval theory that Christendom in its secular aspect is one great state as in its spiritual it is a single Church. From such an admission the logical inference must come sooner or later that the Church is *in* every nation instead of embracing all nations, and this can ultimately mean only that its functions are primarily spiritual and that its participation in secular matters is never justifiable except for a spiritual end—*ad finem spiritualem.*[7]

That was undoubtedly the ultimate result; but it was not the moral immediately drawn from the situation by the popes in the century between the Council of Basel and the Council of Trent. Having failed to maintain the universal sovereignty that had been possible in the feudal age, they concentrated their attention upon restoring their temporal sovereignty in their own states. In this transitional stage, the popes became Italian princes. They suppressed the independent despotisms in the Papal States by force; they employed armies of mercenaries, waged wars, made and broke alliances, and in general took their place as one of the powers in the state system of Europe. In this period political expediency dominated papal policy, though fiscal considerations were not neglected. The College of Cardinals now included members of the ruling families of Italy and the chief ministers of the great European states. Never before had the papacy seemed so securely established as a temporal power, but never before had its power seemed so purely temporal as it did in the age of Alexander VI and Julius II. This was its period of greatest peril. On the one hand the pope, as

[7] C. H. McIlwain, *The Growth of Political Thought in the West* (New York, 1932), p. 352.

temporal ruler of the states of the Church, was no more than a third-rate power, on the level more or less of Milan or Florence. In the game of power politics he was no match for France or Spain. In 1527 the papacy that had chosen to live by the sword came very close to perishing by the sword, and thereafter the popes, as temporal rulers, were drawn into the Spanish sphere of influence, becoming satellites whose foreign policy was dominated by Spanish kings. On the other hand, the preoccupation of the papal curia with temporal politics during these crisis years made it peculiarly unfitted to combat the spiritual revolution that broke out in Germany and that, within two generations, separated half of northern Europe permanently from the Church of Rome. The papacy survived this crisis too, with its sovereignty over what remained of the Church strengthened rather than weakened; but it did so only by ceasing to compete with secular states upon their own terms, by withdrawing into the spiritual sphere in which its authority was unchallenged, by restating the doctrines of the Church in the spirit of the great scholastic age, by employing the militia of the Society of Jesus rather than hired mercenaries, and by leaving coercive jurisdiction to the secular arm of state governments. Not that the temporal power of the papacy, the privileged status of the clergy, and the great possessions of the Church were completely abandoned in the Counter-Reformation. Much remained that would be whittled away only very gradually in the following centuries. But, by the end of the sixteenth century, the main lines which were to be followed in the Church's adjustment to the modern world were already clearly indicated. The transition from medieval to modern forms was nearly complete.

So far I have concentrated attention primarily upon the papacy and the Church in their relation to the secular states. That, however, is only a part of the problem of assessing the position of the Church in the changing civilization of the Renaissance. The relation of the Church to contemporary changes in culture, religious sentiment, and general *Weltanschauung* is of equal if not greater importance, but it is less easy to summarize in a brief paper. Here I can do no more than make a few general observations.

One factor of primary importance for the whole cultural evolution of the Renaissance period, it seems to me, was the growth of lay education. This was not an entirely unknown phenomenon in the Middle Ages. As James Westfall Thompson and oth-

The Eve of the Modern World

ers have demonstrated, there was more literacy, at least, among medieval laymen then historians used to suppose, though that is not saying very much.[8] Nevertheless, the magnificent intellectual and aesthetic achievements of the twelfth and thirteenth centuries, if we exclude the vernacular literature of chivalry, was almost entirely the work of clerics and was patronized, organized, and directed by the Church *ad majorem Dei gloriam*. Under feudal conditions the nobles had little use for learning and less for art, while the burghers had not yet acquired the wealth, social security, or independent cultural tradition that would enable them to compete with the clergy in this sphere. In Italy, however, before the end of the thirteenth century, and in other countries of western Europe somewhat later, the social and economic development of the cities had reached a point where literacy was a necessity, and higher education a possibility, for the middle and upper classes of the urban population. To this end the growth of communal governments staffed by lay administrators, increasing prosperity, and the gradual evolution of a more self-confident burgher tradition all contributed. But on a purely material level the major factor, I think, was the expansion of business enterprise which accompanied the transition from itinerant to sedentary commerce, and the growth of capitalist forms of business organization. This involved, on the one hand, bookkeeping, written instruments of credit and exchange, accurate calculation of profit and loss, complicated negotiations with distant agents or partners, and a much more precise definition of civil law, all of which made literacy indispensable for everyone connected with business in any managerial capacity and also called into being a numerous learned class of lay lawyers, scribes, and notaries. On the other hand, it resulted in the concentration of wealth and the accumulation of surplus capital which furnished the means for lay patronage of literature, learning, and the arts. It also created a new class of leisured *rentiers*, who lived on inherited wealth and were free to devote themselves to intellectual or aesthetic interests. The concentration of both wealth and political power in royal or princely courts served the same purpose in slightly different ways. Such courts became centers for the patronage and dissemination of lay culture, and so exposed the courtly nobility to a wider range of cultural interests than had been available in the isolated baronial castles of the feu-

[8]J. W. Thompson, *The Literacy of the Laity in the Middle Ages* (Berkeley, 1939).

dal era. After 1450 the invention of printing vastly increased the lay reading public and tipped the scale decisively in favor of lay participation in all forms of literary culture; but that epoch-making invention was itself the answer to a demand already large enough to ensure its being a profitable venture.

The spread of lay education and lay patronage and the growth of a distinct class of lay men of letters greatly expanded the secular content of Renaissance culture. This does not imply any necessary decline in religious sentiment. On the contrary, it was accompanied in many places by a pronounced growth in lay piety. Nevertheless, it was detrimental in many ways to the dominant position which the Church had acquired in medieval society. It deprived the Church of its exclusive control of higher education and the clergy of their monopoly of learning and serious thought. And it created a rival, if not an antagonist, to the ecclesiastical culture of the preceding centuries. Evidence of this may be found everywhere in Renaissance music and art, as well as in literature and learning. The revival of antiquity is but one aspect, if the most prominent, of this general trend. Humanism grew up largely as a lay interest, the offspring of lay education, though many humanists were technically clerics. It was, at any rate, not controlled and directed by the Church as scholasticism had been, and it may even be said to have imposed itself upon the Church in the person of such popes as Nicholas V and Pius II and the scores of humanists highly placed in the ecclesiastical hierarchy. In the long run, humanism of the Erasmian variety inspired the most telling attacks upon the temporal power, wealth, and materialism of the Church in the period just preceding the Protestant Reformation.

The reforming Christian humanism of the Erasmian circle represents another aspect of the danger to the medieval Church inherent in the spread of lay education. As I noted in passing, this was accompanied in many places by a distinct revival of lay piety. But the lay piety inspired by mystical preachers like Eckhart and Tauler, and represented by such movements as that of the Friends of God in the Rhineland or the *Devotio Moderna* in the Netherlands, was in large part a reaction against the sacerdotalism of the Church, its mechanization of the means of salvation and the materialism of the contemporary clergy. It is clear that in these years of crisis the Church was not satisfying the spiritual needs of many thoughtful and pious laymen. Left to find their own way toward a sense of personal communion with Christ, they read the New Testament and devotional works which, while entirely orthodox, still had the effect of shifting the emphasis in religious thought from the services of the Church to the inner life of faith and a loving devotion to the person of Christ. It was this peculiarly lay piety that Erasmus, who had been taught in his early years by the Brethren of the Common Life, introduced to a wide circle of educated readers in the *Enchiridion Militis Christiani* and a score of other works less ostensibly devotional.

It may be, too, that the growing bourgeois ethic, if I know what I mean, was in these centuries drifting away from the moral teaching and ascetic ideals of the medieval Church. The pious burgher, sober and hard-working, may well have resented the attitude of the doctors of the Church who barely tolerated commercial activity; and he may also have been tempted to regard the monks, especially such monks as he saw about him, as men who had not so much fled the pleasures and temptations of the world as escaped from its responsibilities. Finally, the intellectual independence which education gave to laymen, together with the individualism fostered by a complex and changing society, might well have made men less ready to accept without question the absolute authority of the Church in matters of doctrine or the claim of the clergy to be the indispensable purveyors of the means of salvation. There has, I think, been a good deal of confused thinking concerning the relationship of capitalism to Protestantism. Nevertheless, I think there can be little doubt that the economic and social conditions which made possible a widespread lay literacy and stimulated a growing sense of self-confident individualism did, at the same time, create an intellectual and moral atmosphere favorable to the reception of Luther's doctrine of the freedom of a Christian man and the priesthood of all believers.

Consideration of the Protestant Reformation, however, except as it affected the Catholic Church, lies beyond the scope of the present discussion. The Church survived this crisis also, with its membership sadly diminished but with its divinely inspired authority strongly reaffirmed. Though papal infallibility was not yet a dogma, the popes after Trent enjoyed an absolute authority in matters of faith and morals greater than that of even their most authoritative medieval predecessors. In the cultural and religious, as well as in the political and administrative fields, the Counter-Reformation completed the Church's

adjustment to the modern world. Since then it has changed but relatively little. Yet, if I have assessed aright the predominant characteristics of modern civilization, it was no more than a partial adjustment, and was in some respects a reaction. It was certainly no surrender to the new elements that had grown up within Western civilization since the High Middle Ages. It was rather an orderly retreat to a previously prepared position. The withdrawal of the Church into the spiritual sphere in which its authority could still be exercised in absolute fashion involved not only the abdication of temporal supremacy but also the partial rejection of the secular philosophies, the natural sciences, and large areas of the autonomous lay culture that grew out of the Renaissance. While making concessions where concessions were unavoidable, and abandoning such claims to authority in secular matters as changing conditions had made untenable, the Church returned after the Counter-Reformation, though in a more purely spiritual sense, to the conception of its nature and function that had been formulated in the twelfth and thirteenth centuries. What it could not dominate it rejected, and so maintained, in an ever-shrinking sphere, the authoritative direction of human activity that, in the Middle Ages, had approached a universal domination of the temporal as well as the spiritual life of the Christian community.

But if the Church thus finally succeeded in adapting the medieval ideal to the realities of the modern world, it did so only after a series of well-nigh disastrous crises, which lend to its history during the transitional period a special character. If we consider the events and the changes in ecclesiastical polity that fill the years between the death of Boniface VIII and the period of reconstruction after the Council of Trent, and if we take as the common factor in all of them the efforts, often misguided or self-defeating, of the Church and the papacy to maintain the position they had achieved during the Middle Ages in the midst of a social complex that was being radically altered by new economic, political, and cultural forces, we may, I think, safely conclude that the three centuries of the Renaissance constitute a distinct period in Church history, and that to treat them as such will serve to clarify much that might otherwise remain obscure. The Renaissance Church and the Renaissance papacy were neither medieval nor modern; rather they were caught in a state of uneasy maladjustment between two worlds. It is the distinguishing mark of a genuinely transitional period that the unresolved conflict between traditional institutions and ways of thinking on the one hand, and, on the other, changing economic, political, and social conditions creates a state of acute crisis. The Renaissance was such a period, and the effects of the conflict, as well as the fundamental causes, are, I believe, nowhere more clearly evident than in the history of the Church.

2

RENAISSANCE HUMANISM: CHRISTIAN OR PAGAN?

The men, events, and movements we study today under the term, "The Renaissance" have been studied since their own times and their importance has been continuously recognized. The Renaissance popes, the wealth of Venice or Florence, the speculations of Machiavelli, the poetry of Petrarch, the scholarship of Erasmus, the saintliness of Thomas More were not discovered "only yesterday." But the containing concept of the Renaissance as an historical period with its own distinctive characteristics, its own form, and its own limits is a comparatively new concept in historical scholarship, scarcely more than a century old. And it has been a strife-torn century. For there is almost no aspect of the concept of the Renaissance that has not been called into question, including the concept itself. Medievalists have contended that the vaunted newness of the Renaissance was not new at all and that the whole movement was an inseparable extension of the Middle Ages. They have claimed that the salient characteristic of individualism was by no means unique with the Renaissance and that medieval scholars, politicians, and entrepreneurs were fully as individualistic as Petrarch, Ludovico Sforza, or Cosimo de' Medici. Critics have probed and questioned every major figure and work identified with the Renaissance. They have disputed the primacy of Italy within the Renaissance framework and recently they have raised the question of whether the florescence of the Renaissance was related to the traditional economic factor of surplus or was a response to severe economic depression. But virtually all critics of the Renaissance except the most unregenerate, have recognized that humanism was the most characteristic movement of the age. Indeed, if the Renaissance culture is to be set off at all from that of the preceding age, it is because it was a humanistic culture.

Much has been written on "The Age of Humanism" and "The World of Humanism." The term has been defined so narrowly that it becomes little more than the enthusiastic study of Latin and Greek and so broadly that it becomes a universal philosophy. Yet the basic character of the movement, fundamental and important as it is to the whole concept of the Renaissance, remains obscure. Scholars can agree that this writer was a humanist and that one was not. There is even reasonable agreement as to what constitutes humanistic influence in the plastic arts, in the music, the drama, and the literature of the period. But fundamental agreement on the definition of humanism itself remains to be found. Part of the problem is a confusion of terms and definitions, as the student will see in the selections that follow. Part of it is the divergence of points of view among the critics themselves.

Part of it is simply the scope and complexity of the movement. But since humanism is so crucial to the concept of the Renaissance the questions about the nature of humanism are correspondingly crucial. Among them one of the most important is the extent to which humanism was a pagan revival.

This problem has been implicit from the beginning of the systematic study of the Renaissance, as we see in the first selection that follows from Jacob Burckhardt. This is natural enough because of the close identification of humanism with classical antiquity—which is to say pagan antiquity—and the enthusiasm with which the humanists embraced all things classical possibly, it has been suggested, even classical paganism. The problem was complicated and judgment prejudiced by the behavior of many of the humanists themselves, on the one hand, in their open adulation of everything ancient and, on the other, in their flaunting of the commonly accepted canons of Christian behavior. In a few dramatic instances they rejected those canons; some even did so on the philosophic grounds of preferring the ancient systems. Thus the double charges of paganism and libertinism have each lent credence to the other and the result has been a kind of stereotype of corrupt "pagan-tinged" Italian humanism.

Another stereotype has contributed to this tradition by contrast, the stereotype of Christian humanism. This stereotype describes the humanism that flourished in those "more Christian" lands north of the Alps as sharply opposed to the pagan or pagan-tinged humanism of Italy. Men had no trouble identifying Erasmus or Thomas More, John Colet or LeFevre d'Etaples as Christians. Their writings were persistently concerned with the Christian tradition, the texts of the Church fathers, and with scripture. And the libertine element, which was so damaging to the reputation of Italian humanism, was largely lacking in their personal lives. While this stereotype is as dangerous and limiting as any other stereotype, the concept of Christian human-ism as such still occurs, even in the respected modern critical literature of the Renaissance, as the student will see in the selection from Harbison.

But, nonetheless, this double tradition has made a basis for the pagan thesis in interpreting Renaissance humanism. Scholars have begun, however, to reexamine the roots of the charge. They have begun to restudy the individual humanists themselves, their specific works, and their contemporary reputations. They have begun to frame new definitions. And, in all, this revisionist movement has begun to raise some of the questions which are dealt with in the selections to follow from Walser and Kristeller.

JAKOB BURCKHARDT

THE PAGAN THESIS

With the publication in 1860 of Jacob Burckhardt's *The Civilization of the Renaissance in Italy* the modern study of the Renaissance as an historical period began. This pioneering work was a brief essay rather than an exhaustive, multivolume treatise but in it Burckhardt raised most of the fundamental questions of Renaissance scholarship. Much of subsequent scholarship has been devoted to proving or disproving the Burckhardtian position on one or another of these questions; to filling in the skeletal outlines of his work with more detailed enquiry; and to following out the implications of his thought.

Burckhardt identified the humanists as those who had fashioned the new intellectual framework of the Renaissance and pointed out that the source of their inspiration was the revival of antiquity. As they sought to identify with their beloved antiquity they turned their backs upon the Christian tradition that was their medieval heritage with the result that Burckhardt bluntly declared, "This humanism was in fact pagan." Thus the problem with which the following selection from *The Civilization of the Renaissance in Italy* deals is close to the center of the complex "Burckhardt Thesis."

Some of the leading elements of this thesis are the protean individualism that Burckhardt ascribed to Renaissance men, the essential worldliness he saw in their outlook, and the importance of classicism and the revival of antiquity in promoting that worldliness. All these parts of the larger general argument are to be found in the present selection. The student should observe how they are related to Burckhardt's position on the question of Renaissance paganism. But, most basically, the student should be aware that Burckhardt's position in this regard is actually a point of view and that many of the same "facts" which he uses to prove Renaissance humanism pagan, later writers will use to rescue it from precisely that indictment.

These modern men, the representatives of the culture of Italy, were born with the same religious instincts as other mediaeval Europeans. But their powerful individuality made them in religion, as in other matters, altogether subjective, and the intense charm which the discovery of the inner and outer universe exercised upon them rendered them markedly worldly. In the rest of Europe religion remained, till a much later period, something given from without, and in practical life egotism and sensuality alternated with devotion and repentance. The latter had no spiritual competitors, as in Italy, or only to a far smaller extent.

Further, the close and frequent relations of Italy with Byzantium and the Mohammedan peoples had produced a dispassionate tolerance which weakened the ethnographical conception of a privileged

From Jakob Burckhardt, *The Civilisation of the Period of the Renaissance in Italy,* tr. S. G. C. Middlemore, 2 vols. (London: C. Kegan Paul & Co., 1878), Vol. II, pp. 297–320 with deletions.

Christendom. And when classical antiquity with its men and institutions became an ideal of life, as well as the greatest of historical memories, ancient speculation and scepticism obtained in many cases a complete mastery over the minds of Italians.

Since, again, the Italians were the first modern people of Europe who gave themselves boldly to speculations on freedom and necessity, and since they did so under violent and lawless political circumstances, in which evil seemed often to win a splendid and lasting victory, their belief in God began to waver, and their view of the government of the world became fatalistic. And when their passionate natures refused to rest in the sense of uncertainty, they made a shift to help themselves out with ancient, oriental, or mediaeval superstition. They took to astrology and magic.

Finally, these intellectual giants, these representatives of the Renaissance, show, in respect to religion, a quality which is common in youthful natures. Distinguishing keenly between good and evil, they yet are conscious of no sin. Every disturbance of their inward harmony they feel themselves able to make good out of the plastic resources of their own nature, and therefore they feel no repentance. The need of salvation thus becomes felt more and more dimly, while the ambitions and the intellectual activity of the present either shut out altogether every thought of a world to come, or else caused it to assume a poetic instead of a dogmatic form.

When we look on all this as pervaded and often perverted by the all-powerful Italian imagination, we obtain a picture of that time which is certainly more in accordance with truth than are vague declamations against modern paganism. And closer investigation often reveals to us that underneath this outward shell much genuine religion could still survive.

The fuller discussion of these points must be limited to a few of the most essential explanations.

That religion should again become an affair of the individual and of his own personal feeling was inevitable when the Church became corrupt in doctrine and tyrannous in practice, and is a proof that the European mind was still alive. It is true that this showed itself in many different ways. While the mystical and ascetical sects of the North lost no time in creating new outward forms for their new modes of thought and feeling, each individual in Italy went

his own way, and thousands wandered on the sea of life without any religious guidance whatever. All the more must we admire those who attained and held fast to a personal religion. They were not to blame for being unable to have any part or lot in the old Church, as she then was; nor would it be reasonable to expect that they should all of them go through that mighty spiritual labour which was appointed to the German reformers. The form and aim of this personal faith, as it showed itself in the better minds, will be set forth at the close of our work.

The worldliness, through which the Renaissance seems to offer so striking a contrast to the Middle Ages, owed its first origin to the flood of new thoughts, purposes, and views, which transformed the mediaeval conception of nature and man. The spirit is not in itself more hostile to religion than that "culture" which now holds its place, but which can give us only a feeble notion of the universal ferment which the discovery of a new world of greatness then called forth. This worldliness was not frivolous, but earnest, and was ennobled by art and poetry. It is a lofty necessity of the modern spirit that this attitude, once gained, can never again be lost, that an irresistible impulse forces us to the investigation of men and things, and that we must hold this inquiry to be our proper end and work. How soon and by what paths this search will lead us back to God, and in what ways the religious temper of the individual will be affected by it, are questions which cannot be met by any general answer. The Middle Ages, which spared themselves the trouble of induction and free inquiry, can have no right to impose upon us their dogmatical verdict in a matter of such vast importance. . . .

In the course of the fifteenth century the works of antiquity were discovered and diffused with extraordinary rapidity. All the writings of the Greek philosophers which we ourselves possess were now, at least in the form of Latin translations, in everybody's hands. It is a curious fact that some of the most zealous apostles of this new culture were men of the strictest piety, or even ascetics. Fra Ambrogio Camaldolese, as a spiritual dignitary chiefly occupied with ecclesiastical affairs, and as a literary man with the translation of the Greek Fathers of the Church, could not repress the humanistic impulse, and at the request of Cosimo de' Medici, undertook to translate Diogenes Laertius into Latin. His contemporaries, Niccolò Niccoli, Giannozzo Manetti, Donato Acciaiuoli, and Pope Nicholas V, united to a many-sided humanism profound biblical scholarship and deep piety. In Vittorino da Feltre the same temper has been already noticed. The same Maffeo Vegio, who added a thirteenth book to the "AEneid," had an enthusiasm for the memory of St. Augustine and his mother Monica which cannot have been without a deeper influence upon him. The result of all these tendencies was that the Platonic Academy at Florence deliberately chose for its object the reconciliation of the spirit of antiquity with that of Christianity. It was a remarkable oasis in the humanism of the period.

This humanism was in fact pagan, and became more and more so as its sphere widened in the fifteenth century. Its representatives, whom we have already described as the advanced guard of an unbridled individualism, display as a rule such a character that even their religion, which is sometimes professed very definitely, becomes a matter of indifference to us. They easily got the name of atheists, if they showed themselves indifferent to religion, and spoke freely against the Church; but not one of them ever professed, or dared to profess, a formal, philosophical atheism. If they sought for any leading principle, it must have been a kind of superficial rationalism—a careless inference from the many and contradictory opinions of antiquity with which they busied themselves, and from the discredit into which the Church and her doctrines had fallen. This was the sort of reasoning which was near bringing Galeotto Martio to the stake, had not his former pupil, Pope Sixtus IV, perhaps at the request of Lorenzo de' Medici, saved him from the hands of the Inquisition. Galeotto had ventured to write that the man who lived uprightly, and acted according to the natural law born within him, would go to heaven, whatever nation he belonged to.

Let us take, by way of example, the religious attitude of one of the smaller men in the great army. Codrus Urceus was first the tutor of the last Ordelaffo, Prince of Forlì, and afterwards for many years professor at Bologna. Against the Church and the monks his language is as abusive as that of the rest. His tone in general is reckless to the last degree, and he constantly introduces himself in all his local history and gossip. But he knows how to speak to the edification of the true God-Man, Jesus Christ, and to commend himself by letter to the prayers of a saintly priest. On one occasion, after enumerating the follies of the pagan religions, he thus goes on: "Our theologians, too, quarrel about 'the guinea-pig's

tail,' about the Immaculate Conception, Antichrist, Sacraments, Predestination, and other things, which were better let alone than talked of publicly." Once, when he was not at home, his room and manuscripts were burnt. When he heard the news he stood opposite a figure of the Madonna in the street, and cried to it: "Listen to what I tell you; I am not mad, I am saying what I mean. If I ever call upon you in the hour of my death, you need not hear me or take me among your own, for I will go and spend eternity with the devil." After which speech he found it desirable to spend six months in retirement at the home of a wood-cutter. With all this, he was so superstitious that prodigies and omens gave him incessant frights, leaving him no belief to spare for the immortality of the soul. When his hearers questioned him on the matter, he answered that no one knew what became of a man, of his soul or his body, after death, and the talk about another life was only fit to frighten old women. But when he came to die, he commended in his will his soul or his spirit to Almighty God, exhorted his weeping pupils to fear the Lord, and especially to believe in immortality and future retribution, and received the Sacrament with much fervour. We have no guarantee that more famous men in the same calling, however significant their opinions may be, were in practical life any more consistent. It is probable that most of them wavered inwardly between incredulity and a remnant of the faith in which they were brought up, and outwardly held for prudential reasons to the Church.

Through the connexion of rationalism with the newly born science of historical investigation, some timid attempts at biblical criticism may here and there have been made. A saying of Pius II has been recorded, which seems intended to prepare the way for such criticism: "Even if Christianity were not confirmed by miracles, it ought still to be accepted on account of its morality." The legends of the Church, in so far as they contained arbitrary versions of the biblical miracles, were freely ridiculed, and this reacted on the religious sense of the people. Where Judaizing heretics are mentioned, we must understand chiefly those who denied the Divinity of Christ, which was probably the offence for which Giorgio da Novara was burnt at Bologna about the year 1500. But again at Bologna in the year 1497 the Dominican Inquisitor was forced to let the physician Gabriele da Salò, who had powerful patrons, escape with a simple expression of penitence, although he was in the habit of maintaining that Jesus was not God, but son of Joseph and Mary, and conceived in the usual way; that by his cunning he had deceived the world to its ruin; that he may have died on the cross on account of crimes which he had committed; that his religion would soon come to an end; that his body was not really contained in the sacrament, and that he performed his miracles, not through any divine power, but through the influence of the heavenly bodies. This latter statement is most characteristic of the time; Faith is gone, but magic still holds its ground.

With respect to the moral government of the world, the humanists seldom get beyond a cold and resigned consideration of the prevalent violence and misrule. In this mood the many works "On Fate," or whatever name they bear, are written. They tell of the turning of the wheel of Fortune, and of the instability of earthly, especially political, things. Providence is only brought in because the writers would still be ashamed of undisguised fatalism, of the avowal of their ignorance, or of useless complaints. . . .

We cannot on the other hand, read without a kind of awe how men sometimes boasted of their fortune in public inscriptions. Giovanni II Bentivoglio, ruler of Bologna, ventured to carve in stone on the newly built tower by his palace, that his merit and his fortune had given him richly of all that could be desired—and this a few years before his expulsion. The ancients, when they spoke in this tone, had nevertheless a sense of the envy of the gods. In Italy it was probably the Condottieri who first ventured to boast so loudly of their fortune.

But the way in which resuscitated antiquity affected religion most powerfully, was not through any doctrines or philosophical system, but through a general tendency which it fostered. The men, and in some respects the institutions of antiquity were preferred to those of the Middle Ages, and in the eager attempt to imitate and reproduce them, religion was left to take care of itself. All was absorbed in the admiration for historical greatness. To this the philologians added many special follies of their own, by which they became the mark for general attention. How far Paul II was justified in calling his Abbreviators and their friends to account for their paganism, is cer-

tainly a matter of great doubt, as his biographer and chief victim, Platina, has shown a masterly skill in explaining his vindictiveness on other grounds, and especially in making him play a ludicrous figure. The charges of infidelity, paganism, denial of immortality, and so forth, were not made against the accused till the charge of high treason had broken down. Paul, indeed, if we are correctly informed about him, was by no means the man to judge of intellectual things. It was he who exhorted the Romans to teach their children nothing beyond reading and writing. His priestly narrowness of views reminds us of Savonarola, with the difference that Paul might fairly have been told that he and his like were in great part to blame if culture made men hostile to religion. It cannot, nevertheless, be doubted that he felt a real anxiety about the pagan tendencies which surrounded him. And what, in truth, may not the humanists have allowed themselves at the court of the profligate pagan, Sigismondo Malatesta? How far these men, destitute for the most part of fixed principle, ventured to go, depended assuredly on the sort of influences they were exposed to. Nor could they treat of Christianity without paganizing it. It is curious, for instance, to notice how far Gioviano Pontano carried this confusion. He speaks of a saint not only as "divus," but as "deus";[1] the angels he holds to be identical with the genii of antiquity; and his notion of immortality reminds us of the old kingdom of the shades. This spirit occasionally appears in the most extravagant shapes. In 1526, when Siena was attacked by the exiled party, the worthy canon Tizio, who tells us the story himself, rose from his bed on the 22nd July, called to mind what is written in the third book of Macrobius, celebrated Mass, and then pronounced against the enemy the curse with which his author had supplied him, only altering "Telus mater teque Juppiter obtestor" into "Tellus teque Christe Deus obtestor."[2] After he had done this for three days, the enemy retreated. On the one side, these things strike us as an affair of mere style and fashion; on the other, as a symptom of religious decadence.

[1] "Divus" and "deus" were both classical Latin words for God. Apparently Pontano preferred these to the more medieval flavored "sanctus," the usual word for saint. [Editor's note.]

[2] "Mother Earth and thou Jupiter I beseech." "Earth and thou Christ God I beseech." [Editor's note.]

ERNST WALSER

PAGAN FORM: CHRISTIAN SUBSTANCE

Although Ernst Walser was a student of Burckhardt at Basel, his mature scholarship marks a decisive shift away from the position taken by his master on almost every fundamental point. He disputed the most basic of Burckhardt's assumptions, asserting that the Renaissance was not a distinct, integral period. He based his assertion upon the detailed study of the works of the most significant Renaissance humanists from which he concluded that these key figures in the conception of the Renaissance actually represented no more than a continuation of typically medieval modes of thought. The key point in Walser's thesis is his denial that Renaissance humanism was basically pagan and his contrary assertion that the humanists remained fundamentally Christian and orthodox, as their medieval predecessors had been. The following excerpt from Walser's most important book concentrates on this point.

He argues first that most of the instances of alleged humanistic paganism are actually no more than the Renaissance enthusiasm for the "style" of antiquity or evidence merely of the critical philological skepticism and anticlericalism of the age; and that such attitudes did not destroy fundamental Christian belief. He contends that even the most damaging evidence of apparent pagan revival is not to be accepted. He argues that the Florentine Neoplatonists, customarily regarded as the clearest and most consistent example of the revival of a classical philosophic system, "were of the deepest Christian piety" and not essentially different from the earlier medieval Christian thinkers who borrowed bits and pieces of classical thought. He argues that the famous carnival songs and practices associated with Lorenzo de' Medici, and again usually regarded as pagan revivals, are not so much revivals as survivals of the ancient and durable nature magic common to Europe and, in Italy, merely disguised in classical dress, thus becoming another evidence of the "purely external, formal and fashionable" manifestation of Renaissance paganism.

We are confronted by the accusation that the study of antiquity was responsible for the destruction of Christian belief in the Quattrocento or that it was at least certain proof of the irreligiosity of the age. The charge against the humanists for their disbelief is based on their aesthetic paganism, on their critical skepticism, and on their anti-clericalism. Therefore, paganism, criticism, and anti-curialism will be dealt with before we finally take a stand regarding the positive religious elements.

At the outset we are confronted with the accusation of heathenism or paganism. Are we not to consider as completely valid the . . . charge of Erasmus[1] when it is supported by the eloquent lament of preachers like Savonarola or by such an impeccable witness as Machiavelli?

Let us attempt to get hold of the problem at a more

[1] A reference to Erasmus' impatience with rhetorical archaisms in his dialogue *Ciceronianus*. [Editor's note.]

From Ernst Walser, *Studien zur Weltanschauung der Renaissance* in *Gesammelte Studien zur Geistesgeschichte der Renaissance* (Basel, 1932), pp. 102–17. Used by permission of Benno Schwabe & Co. Translated by the editor.

fundamental level: on what basis does that which is new in the Renaissance admiration of antiquity actually rest? The remembrance of the power and splendor of the Roman Empire, after its fall, had never been extinguished in the hearts of mankind; above all not in Italy. In this instance the spectacle of antiquity's continuing survival would be tantamount to a history of its whole cultural development: and Germanic, Greek, and Arabic influences appear as negligible factors in the face of the onflowing continuum of Roman antiquity. Many an administrative institution of antiquity survived through the Middle Ages in Italy; here Roman law continued in effect; Latin continued to be regarded here as a national language so that the newly formed vernacular began to be written only at a time when other peoples of the post-classical world already possessed a real literature in their vernaculars. In Italy ancient heathen religious concepts, barely disguised under a robe of Christianity, continued in constant procession through the dark centuries as well as through those illuminated by art and knowledge. Timorous legends of Nero, Vergil, and Augustus grew up like ivy around the powerful ruins of a lost world.

Thus in Italy Roman antiquity was considered, throughout the Middle Ages, not as a period of foreign domination—as was the case in other countries—but rather as a thoroughly national past. And every attempt at Italian unification, from the Middle Ages down to the present, has had strength, driving force, and the prospect of continuing success only if undertaken in the holy name of ancient Rome. Moreover, antiquity continued to be perpetuated by the schools. In the study of the ancient authors there came to life and exhausted itself the concept of each and every field of knowledge from the fall of Rome until into the twelfth century.

This preoccupation with antiquity, however, did not pass through the centuries as a constantly diminishing force: it was rather as if antiquity were borne to the barren shore of mankind like a powerful, recurring wave. The Irish monks of Charlemagne, the Benedictine abbeys under the Ottonians pored over the classical authors, transcribed their works, and carried on textual criticism which was as good as—or even better than—that of the earlier Renaissance humanists. It was the period of high scholasticism that first made a distinction between ancient and Christian knowledge by accomplishing the co-

lossal task of creating a new and harmoniously constructed Christian world view from a mixture of classical and Christian elements. It was first in high scholasticism that all the branches of knowledge became a solidly joined structure which ascended from the Seven Liberal Arts to philosophy and then to its completely overshadowing discipline, theology. This, however, did not prevent rational and mystic thinkers—even in the Middle Ages—from surrendering themselves to rather bold speculations which remained unmolested by the church as long as they did not give offense to revealed religion. Thus we see a group of individual religious thinkers in whose works all the classical philosophic systems are repeated no less often than will be the case with the humanists.

Thus while the actual Renaissance begins with Petrarch, there is in its involvement with pagan antiquity, the collecting of ancient authors, and the sifting of their texts, nothing essentially different from what was already being done in the purely medieval Carolingian and Ottonian pre-Renaissances. Even the medieval princes had accepted the *Roman de Titus Livius* and the *Prouesses du bon chevalier Jules César* into their curiosity cabinets. But by the mid-fourteenth century we sense that a new era and a new attitude toward antiquity are beginning.

The new decisive factor which Petrarch and his followers add and which rises over mankind like a dawn of understanding is the profoundly sensitive perception not of the content of the classics but rather of their formal beauty. The deepest roots of humanism and the great common bond that ties all humanists together is neither individualism nor politics, philosophy nor common religious ideas (in all these things their opinions were widely different): the great common bond is simply artistic sensitivity. Moreover, there is in it—especially as literature is concerned—a conscious reaction against the overly dry, rational work of scholasticism. Nor can it be said that humanism emanated by any means from one particular caste: neither from the scholars nor the priests nor the laity. Rather its ideas appealed to widely dispersed men of the most varied occupations and positions—school masters, priests, bishops, merchants, lawyers. Generally speaking, at first it was a case of a few isolated individuals who were caught up in the new enthusiasm while the great mass of their professional and social compeers continued to persist in the traditional. It is therefore incorrect when Philippe Monnier,[2] for example, speaks of a fundamental opposition between the Italian humanists and the monks since capable men in orders like Marsilio, Traversari, and Aliotti were among the most enthusiastic partisans of humanism. On the other hand, thoroughgoing humanists like Salutati, Niccoli, and others were friendly in the extreme toward the monks. No, the opposition to the humanists was assembled from all possible class levels and camps, just as was the community of humanists itself. The opponents were in part defenders of the scholastic method: in part, to be sure, they were monks, but only those mystic and ignorant ascetics of the stamp of Jacopone da Todi, who had of old also been deadly enemies of scholasticism along with every other variety of learning.

The new-found aestheticism developed like a pervasive cloud and expressed itself especially well in literature. Its herald was Francesco Petrarca although he was not its inventor, for such deep flowing movements go beyond the energy of a single man.

His poetry found receptive hearts and kindled in them the flame of poetry. The poet of Laura writes in annoyance of the flocks of would-be poets who disturbed him daily in his quiet cell at Vaucluse with the ill-bred children of their muse: it was especially painful to convince poetizing cardinals of the hopelessness of their efforts. Lawyers and physicians, craftsmen of every description flocked to him; and he views with horror the time when not only fishermen, hunters, and peasants will make rhymes but even the oxen before the plow will ruminate verses. Even a dry and matter of fact nature like Salutati began with Latin verses of dubious beauty: fortunately he later tended to restrict himself to the epistle and the treatise. However, this poetical fire was soon extinguished once more and into its place moved that element which became typical of the entire Renaissance: eloquence. Petrarch, even as a boy, upon reading the speeches of Cicero and before he completely understood the meaning of the words, felt himself deeply moved by their soft ring and the quiet, flooding harmony of their rhythm. . . .

Thus the forms of antiquity developed into the outward means of expression—whether the rhetoric was false or genuine—for the whole cultural life of Italy. And from this time on, certain purely medieval heirlooms of knighthood and chivalry wrapped

[2]*Le Quattrocento* (New Edition, 1908), I, 124 ff.

themselves in the stylish little mantle of antiquity, masquerading as "feeling for nature" and Neoplatonism (just as neo-humanist concepts and ideals did). Thus we find a complete ladder of purely outward paganism.

The lowest rung of humanistic study was, beyond a doubt, the passion for citing authorities. Already in the Middle Ages writers were wont to parade their erudition by deploying in rank and file everything (and on every occasion) that might serve as an authority. This was all the more justified since in that time more wrangling went on by citing authorities than by real proofs. A frightening example of this is to be had in the otherwise rather vigorous tracts of the Swiss Felix Hemmerli. The humanists also—especially those of the early period—freely imitated this wretched practice except that from now on are cited not only the great scholastics but classical authors in great profusion. In these classical citations then we see simply the expression of scholarly vanity, ever self-renewing and blooming from a truly eternal rootstock: but there is no unbelief here. Under the same heading are to be placed the classical expletives *Per Jovem, Dii boni, Edepol,* etc. behind which it is foolish to suspect a decrease in Christian belief and thought (although especially zealous and ignorant monks occasionally did so). Thus countless examples of contemporary matters—in both church and state—represented in classical dress present a low level understanding of antiquity and truly deplorable taste. This is the typical form of paganism. And it is precisely on this point that the most exacting examination of the facts is necessary in order to decide whether this is simply a literary fashion (which is the case in the overwhelming majority of cases) or whether there is here a spirit in opposition to Christianity. In the carry-over of classical form and usage to contemporary things the humanist school master was the preeminent performer: as in the case when the rhetorician Porcellius traveled self-importantly between the battle lines of the brawling mercenary captains Piccinino and Sforza in order to sing their deeds in heroic style after the model of the battles of Scipio and Hannibal. Also belonging to purely formal paganism are many expressions which cannot be allowed to deceive us even when they concern matters of Christian religion. The Middle Ages had arrived at similar results from the opposite direction in that the circle of Old Testament prototypes and prophecies (Adam as a symbol of Christ, the Tree of Knowledge as a symbol of the cross, etc.) had also been extended to heathen mythology (Leda as a symbol of the Immaculate Conception). Even though Dante, in purely formal pagan terms, calls the Redeemer *Giove crocifisso*, he was not aware of committing any greater sacrilege than contemporary medieval theologians who had explained Vergil's *Fourth Eclogue* or Aeneas (after the example of Fulgentius) in Christian symbolic terms. In like fashion, in his *Africa*, Petrarch has both the goddesses Rome and Carthage appear before Jupiter at Olympus begging for help before the battle of Zama: the father of the gods explains to them that he himself will descend to earth after ten years of Saturn's rule and will redeem mankind by his own ignominious death. Boccaccio in *Filocolo, Fiammetta,* and *Ameto* presents veritable masterpieces of disguising contemporary things in classical dress.

Similar examples run through the entire Italian Quattrocento and Cinquecento and are found no less often in France. The devout Guillaume Budé calls Christ a two-headed Janus (to explain the unity of divine and human nature), a Mercury (interpreter of heavenly and earthly wisdom), Prometheus (who brought mankind the true fire from heaven), Hercules Alexicacus (destroyer of the monster), and Achilles. Job, on the other hand, is one of the philosophers persecuted by Fortune. Ronsard, in his *Hymne de l'Hercule chrétien,* described the life of Christ by illustrating every phase of the Redeemer's life with a deed of Hercules. I also class with these superficial paganisms the cult of Mercury which the overwrought Ciriaco d'Ancona promoted: his language and personality are here strikingly reminiscent of Rabelais' Limousin pupil! The pious epics of the time of Leo X and Clement VII are also rich in such illustrations. Take, for example, the unspeakable work of Sannazzaro, *De partu virginis:* God the Father after he has instructed the heavenly legions in the mysteries of the redemption—in a meeting at Olympus—inspires them with sympathy for sinful mankind. A delegation of *genii* (Laetitia, Concordia, Right-Love, etc.) tie on their wings and escort scantily clad Horae in their flight down to the shepherds of the field. At this the constellations are enraptured and the moon (with unwitting humor) contemplates the dance of joy already going on among the stars. Then we pass into the depths where the river god Jordan is sitting by the Crystal Urn with his daughter rivers and is relating a prophecy of Proteus which the latter had heard from Apollo and in which the nereids are pictured swimming toward Christ as he walks on the ocean and a trembling Neptune kisses

his foot. Among the small and stupid humanists paganism assumed the ridiculous form of hollow, pedantic Ciceronianism which Erasmus rightly ridiculed. In 1529 a professor at Bologna, Romolo Amaseo, announced in the solemn welcoming address for the Emperor Charles V and Pope Clement VII, that he would rather be the dead servant of Cicero than to have to live in such a grim and miserable present. But in the same manner as the leading humanists of the foregoing century had made fun of such silliness, on this occasion Bembo made no less a fool of the valiant Amaseo.

We note then: the newly awakened aestheticism, with reference to the forms of classical antiquity, expresses itself in a long gradation which runs from the most sensitive taste to the worst fashion fad. However, it would be altogether incorrect to infer a diminished Christianity from these tricks of speech contrived on the model of classical rhetoric. Precisely those examples cited from Erasmus' *Dialogus Ciceronianus* should, one and all, be set under the rubric of the completely harmless and purely external paganisms.

The same comments concerning purely superficial and formal paganism in literature must certainly also be made in art. Classical fruit garlands, putti, and the like become henceforth a part of ornamental accessory just as do the undraped figures in the background of Michelangelo's Holy Family in the Uffizi. And these certainly do not prove the decline of orthodoxy any more than does the fact that Lippi's Madonna in the Annunciation is sitting in a splendidly decorated Renaissance room. And when the classical fashion (or fad) occasions the closest association of pagan mythology and Christian ideas in the pious epics of a Sannazzaro why then should not the same happen in art? When Filarete admits Aesopian fables, classical emperors, virtues and scenes like Ganymede and Leda into the ornamentation of the doors of St. Peter's one no more takes offense at this ornamental paganism than one does at Proteus and Apollo who, in Sannazzaro, prophesy the birth of Christ. These bronze reliefs prove nothing either about the faith of the artist or that of the patron. This latter was none other than Eugenius IV, a foe of liberal humanistic study, who would certainly have been man enough to send the doors and the artist *a casa il diavolo* if the depiction had offended him. People felt all the less injured by this ornamental paganism since church sculpture of the Middle Ages was accustomed to represent much worse things: unedifying *novella* subjects (not just the ribald adventure of the harnessed Aristotle but also the lewd revenge of Virgil the magician on the Roman women); animal and human grotesques; indeed downright phallic images. . . . Moreover, people viewed all things connected with procreation with a beautiful simplicity which is still characteristic of the south European today and of which admirable preachers like St. Bernardino da Siena spoke. The medieval (and earlier south European) concept of the sacred was constituted quite differently from ours: what crude hocus-pocus our clergy performed with the "Fools' Mass" and the "Asses' Mass" not only at carnival but even at the ecclesiastical primitial celebrations! Probably for this reason the church dances of the sixteenth century were held in a holy place in order to insure the recovery of those stricken with the "dancing sickness" through the magical influence of the Lord's house. Therefore, when Savonarola, revered for the ardor of his convictions and for his martyr's death, damns all colorful pomp and thundering music, out of his own gloomy asceticism, as the heathenizing work of the devil and longs for the times (and when were they really?) when the sacramental cup was of wood and the priests of gold, we certainly will not believe every word. It is equally unjustified though to damn his opponent, Fra Mariano da Genazzano, as a hypocrite and aesthetic heathen (as did the romantically naive description of Villari) simply because he spoke out for a reasonable and nonascetic exercise of religion and declined to indulge in hysterical and apocalyptic prophecies in order to teach fear and horror to his listeners!

Much more difficult to judge than the paganism of external form is the paganism of content. It is true that Stoic, Neoplatonic, and Epicurean precepts frequently appear in the writings of the humanists: and in their ultimate consequences all these systems are anti-Christian. But are these mementos of classicism not already to be found in scholasticism? The medieval thinkers borrowed from all these theories just as much as they could use for their own speculations but anything beyond this they completely rejected. Does not the basically scholastic nominalism lead to crass materialism in the final analysis; and, on the other hand, does not its adversary, medieval realism, lead to pantheism of the purest sort? And we see the same thing with the humanists. To be precise, the stoicism of Petrarch and Salutati is tied into a fundamental sympathy with the most severe monastic asceticism.

As early as the first years of the fifteenth century Cardinal Francesco Zabarella (d.1417) departed from the crude medieval popular concept of *porcus Epicuri* (probably stemming from a Horatian source) and condemned the hedonism of Epicurus only where the philosopher considered his goal to be coarse and sensual rather than purely spiritual joy. This latter point of view was represented by Niccoli in the treatise of Lorenzo Valla, *De voluptate*. To be precise, the Neoplatonists such as Marsilio Ficino, Pico della Mirandola and their numerous followers in Italy and France were of the deepest Christian piety. To be sure, there were individual thinkers in the fifteenth and sixteenth centuries who were no longer Christians and who found their comfort in life as in death in the train of thought of heathen philosophers. Their number, however, is no greater than it was in the preceding centuries and the proof of their paganism has a claim to accuracy only when it is verified by numerous unequivocal signs and is not merely reasoned from a few Stoic or Epicurean sentences.

The criticism of the *Canti carnascialeschi* also seems to me rather intricate. It is known that A. F. Grazzini, who lived a generation after Lorenzo de' Medici, ascribed to the Magnifico the innovation in the carnival songs "di variare non solamente il canto ma le invenzioni e il modo di comporre le parole."[3] Pasquale Villari explains this as if Lorenzo had accustomed his fellow citizens to this sort of spectacle in the devilish intention of choking off their sentiments of liberty by such corruption. Popular amusement with parades and songs at carnival time, as at the beginning of May, were an invention neither of the Medici nor the Renaissance. As for the *Calendimaggio* festivals, they go back at least to the battle of Campaldino in 1265. The fifteenth century added to this the greator splendor and mythological ornamentation of *trionfi* such as that of *Bacco ed Arianna*. The greater splendor resulted from the greater prosperity and improved standard of living which is clearly demonstrated by the development of Florentine household furnishings. The classical costumes resulted from the joy in the newly discovered "forms" of antiquity. Not very much can be inferred from such external trappings. For example, even the brave Gessner in the eighteenth century styled his hair in "antique" fashion and, with his upright old Zurich comrades, held idyllic "lamb-pious" fests

[3]Not only of modifying the song but the improvisations and the manner of composing the words. [Editor's note.]

—without consequently becoming a pagan! And furthermore, many earlier Italian dance songs, in word and rhythm, directly recall Lorenzo de' Medici. The old French and old Provençal May and dance tunes admonish young women, as do the *canti,* to enjoy life and to exchange the *jaloux* (the poor stupid husband) for a youthful lover. We need not take this any more literally for the Middle Ages than for the Renaissance. The fact that Florentine women did not actually carry out such foolish advice was assured less by the barbaric laws against adultery than by husbands themselves who always carried their daggers loose in their scabbards. Finally, it would be well to remember the stream of bluntly realistic and erotic love songs which came down, together with the idealistic ones, from the time of the Sicilians—and also the unbelievable mass of crudity that both lords and ladies of the Renaissance faithfully took over from the Middle Ages. All these mitigating factors are still not sufficient to explain the strange fact that the sole object of all the *Canti carnascialeschi* we know (with only negligible exceptions) was the repugnantly graphic description of the crudest love pleasures with a forwardness which makes it barely conceivable how such literal depictions would sound in the streets in the ears of an entire population. Unfortunately nothing is preserved of the women's dance songs prior to the twelfth century: this includes the *obscina et turpea cantica cum choris foemineis*[4] from seventh century France as well as the *cantiunculae* and *naeniae, quarum aliae*

maleficiorum aliae stupri causa[5] of the tenth century which Italian women performed on the calends of January and March and on St. John's Day. But does not this call to *copula* together with the circumstances of the procession open the question whether we might not suspect an ancient custom in these *canti* which, in the final analysis, rests upon a fertility ritual. In all Europe similar symbols were widespread at such carnivals and spring festivals. Even the May King—who was also to be found in Florence and who still appears in the dance songs of Lorenzo de' Medici—belongs to the spring magic for which Mannhardt has assembled a persuasive mass of evidence. This explains by itself the licentious content. Thus Lorenzo il Magnifico is not to be credited with the invention of the whole carnival "carryings-on" but rather with only its more sumptuous setting and classical trappings.

The paganism of the Renaissance, with all its thousandfold forms in literature, art, folk festivals, etc. is a purely external, formal and fashionable element. In the case of very isolated individuals, it can be used as decisive proof of unbelief. But it would be thoroughly wrong to use it in its totality as evidence of a decline in orthodoxy, of the growth of indifference, of the decline of public morality, etc. The few Renaissance men who were actually convinced anti-Christians did not hold this view out of either indifference' or paganism but rather out of a religious disposition or even out of a deep need for other forms of belief.

[4]Filthy and obscene songs with female choruses. [Editor's note.]

[5] Songs and incantations some of which were associated with witchcraft, others with lust. [Editor's note.]

PAUL OSKAR KRISTELLER

A NEW VIEW OF THE PROBLEM

Like Ernst Walser, Paul Oskar Kristeller has spent most of his life dealing in detail with the actual works of individual humanists, studying their writings and editing their texts, especially those of the major humanistic philosophers such as Marsilio Ficino. From the study of these sources he brings, again like Walser, a new point of view to bear upon the question of the alleged paganism of the Renaissance.

He agrees with Walser, calling "the Renaissance a fundamentally Christian age."

He agrees to an extent with one of Walser's principal points, that much of the striking newness an older generation of scholars saw in the Renaissance was actually a continuation of medieval patterns of thought and action. He stresses the vigorous continuity of medieval religious forms and practices right through the Renaissance, as well as the "persistence of church doctrine, institutions, and worship."

But much of the case Kristeller makes for "Christian humanism" is derived from his well known theory about the nature of humanism itself, that it was essentially "neither religious nor antireligious, but a literary and scholarly orientation that could be and, in many cases, was pursued without any explicit discourse on religious topics by individuals who otherwise might be fervent or nominal members of one of the Christian churches." Moreover, he asserts that, within the frame of this concept, the humanists returned to the classical texts of Christianity as they had earlier returned to the texts of pagan antiquity and applied their scholars' tools not in the restoration of paganism but in the salutary work of "sacred philology."

Thus to the extent that he recognizes a traditional conflict at all, Kristeller sees the humanists not as neopagans in conflict with Christianity but as professional scholars, practitioners of the "new learning," in conflict with the professional methodology of scholasticism.

In reading this selection the student should observe whether Kristeller changes the ground or the terms of the traditional argument. And, if he does so, does he produce a more sensible case, does he "define the problem away," or does he make the problem conform to his definition?

Many historians of the last century tended to associate the Italian Renaissance and Italian humanism with some kind of irreligion, and to interpret the Protestant and Catholic Reformations as expressions of a religious revival which challenged and finally defeated the un-Christian culture of the preceding period. The moral ideas and literary allegories in the writings of the humanists were taken to be expressions, real or potential, overt or concealed, of a new paganism incompatible with Christianity. The neat separation between reason and faith advocated by the Aristotelian philosophers was considered as a hypocritical device to cover up a secret atheism, whereas the emphasis on a natural religion common to all men, found in the work of the Platonists and Stoics, was characterized as pantheism. This picture of the supposed paganism of the Renaissance which was drawn by historians with much horror or enthusiasm, depending on the strength of their religious or irreligious convictions, can partly be dismissed as the result of later legends and preconceptions. In part, it may be traced to charges made against the humanists and philosophers by hostile or narrow-minded contemporaries, which should not be accepted at their face value. Most recent historians have taken quite a different view of the matter. There was, to be sure, a good deal of talk about the pagan gods and heroes in the literature of the Renaissance, and it was justified by the familiar device of allegory, and strengthened by the belief in astrology, but there were few, if any, thinkers who seriously thought of reviving ancient pagan cults. The word pantheism had not yet been invented, and although the word atheism was generously used in polemics during the later sixteenth century, there were probably no real atheists and barely a few pantheists during the Renaissance. The best or worst we may say is that there were some thinkers who might be considered, or actually were considered, as forerunners

Reprinted by permission of the publishers from Paul Oskar Kristeller, *The Classics and Renaissance Thought* (Cambridge, Mass.: Harvard University Press), pp. 71–87, with deletions. Copyright, 1955, by the Board of Trustees of Oberlin College.

A New View of the Problem

of eighteenth-century free thought. There was then, of course, as there was before and afterwards, a certain amount of religious indifference and of merely nominal adherence to the doctrines of the Church. There were many cases of conduct in private and public life that were not in accordance with the moral commands of Christianity, and there were plenty of abuses in ecclesiastic practice itself, but I am not inclined to consider this as distinctive of the Renaissance period.

The real core of the tradition concerning Renaissance paganism is something quite different: it is the steady and irresistible growth of nonreligious intellectual interests which were not so much opposed to the content of religious doctrine, as rather competing with it for individual and public attention. This was nothing fundamentally new, but rather a matter of degree and of emphasis. The Middle Ages was certainly a religious epoch, but it would be wrong to assume that men's entire attention was occupied by religious, let alone by theological, preoccupations. Medieval architects built castles and palaces, not only cathedrals and monasteries. Even when the clerics held the monopoly of learning, they cultivated grammar and the other liberal arts besides theology, and during the High Middle Ages, when specialization began to arise, nonreligious literature also expanded. The thirteenth century produced not Thomas Aquinas alone, as some people seem to believe, or other scholastic theologians, but also a vast literature on Roman law, medicine, Aristotelian logic and physics, mathematics and astronomy, letter-writing and rhetoric, and even on classical Latin poetry, not to mention the chronicles and histories, the lyric and epic poetry in Latin and in the vernacular languages. This development made further progress during the Renaissance period, as a glance at the inventory of a manuscript collection or at a bibliography of printed books will easily reveal, and it continued unchecked during and after the Reformation, whatever the theologians of that time or later times may have felt about it. If an age where the nonreligious concerns that had been growing for centuries attained a kind of equilibrium with religious and theological thought, or even began to surpass it in vitality and appeal, must be called pagan, the Renaissance was pagan, at least in certain places and phases. Yet since the religious convictions of Christianity were either retained or transformed but never really challenged, it seems more appropriate to call the Renaissance a fundamentally Christian age.

To prove this point, it would be pertinent in the first place to state that the medieval traditions of religious thought and literature continued without interruption until and after the Reformation, and that Italy was no exception to this rule. The study of theology and canon law, and the literary production resulting from it, tended to increase rather than to decline, a fact that is often overlooked because historians of these subjects have paid less attention to that period than to the earlier ones, except for the material directly connected with the Reformation controversies. German mysticism was succeeded during the very period with which we are concerned by the more practical and less speculative *Devotio Moderna* in the Low Countries, a movement that produced such an important document as the *Imitation of Christ,* contributed to a reform of secondary education all over Northern Europe, and had a formative influence on such thinkers as Cusanus and Erasmus. Effective preachers made a deep impression on the learned and unlearned alike all over fifteenth-century Italy, and sometimes led to revivalist movements and political repercussions, of which Savonarola is the most famous but by no means an isolated instance. In Italy no less than in the rest of Europe, the religious guilds directed the activities of the laity and exercised a tremendous influence upon the visual arts, music, and literature. Partly in connection with these guilds, an extensive religious literature of a popular character was circulated, which was composed either by clerics or by laymen, but always addressed to the latter and usually in the vernacular languages. These facts, along with the persistence of church doctrine, institutions, and worship, would go a long way to prove the religious preoccupations of the Renaissance period.

Yet we are not so much concerned with the undoubted survival of medieval Christianity in the Renaissance as with the changes and transformations which affected religious thought during that period. As a distinguished historian has put it, Christianity is not only medieval, but also ancient and modern, and thus it was possible for Christian thought during the Renaissance to cease being medieval in many respects, and yet to remain Christian. This novelty is apparent in the new doctrines and institutions created by the Protestant and Catholic Reformations, a topic on which I shall not attempt to elaborate. I shall merely show that the humanist movement, as we have tried to describe it in our first lecture, had its share in bringing about those changes in religious thought.

The Eve of the Modern World

The view that the humanist movement was essentially pagan or anti-Christian cannot be sustained. It was successfully refuted by the humanists themselves when they defended their work and program against the charges of unfriendly theologians of their own time. The opposite view, which has had influential defenders in recent years, namely that Renaissance humanism was in its origin a religious movement, or even a religious reaction against certain antireligious tendencies in the Middle Ages, seems to me equally wrong or exaggerated. I am convinced that humanism was in its core neither religious nor antireligious, but a literary and scholarly orientation that could be and, in many cases, was pursued without any explicit discourse on religious topics by individuals who otherwise might be fervent or nominal members of one of the Christian churches. On the other hand, there were many scholars and thinkers with a humanist training who had a genuine concern for religious and theological problems, and it is my contention that the way they brought their humanist training to bear upon the source material and subject matter of Christian theology was one of the factors responsible for the changes which Christianity underwent during that period. The most important elements in the humanist approach to religion and theology were the attack upon the scholastic method and the emphasis upon the return to the classics, which in this case meant the Christian classics, that is, the Bible and the Church Fathers.

In order to understand the significance of these attitudes, we must once more go back to antiquity and the Middle Ages. Christianity originated in a Jewish Palestine which had become politically a part of the Roman Empire, and culturally a part of the Hellenistic world. At the time when the new religion began to spread through the Mediterranean area, its sacred writings which were to form the canon of the New Testament were composed in Greek, that is, in a language which showed the marks of a long literary and philosophical tradition, and in part by authors such as Paul, Luke, and John, who had enjoyed a literary and perhaps a philosophical education. In the following centuries, the early Apologists, the Greek Fathers, and the great Councils were engaged in the task of defining and developing Christian doctrine, and of making it acceptable to the entire Greek-speaking world. Thus the reading and study of the Greek poets and prose writers was finally approved, with some reservations, whereas the teachings of the Greek philosophical schools were subjected to careful examination, rejecting everything that seemed incompatible with Christian doctrine, but using whatever appeared compatible to bolster and to supplement Christian theology. After the precedent of Philo the Jew, Clement of Alexandria and the other Greek Fathers went a long way in adding Greek philosophical methods and notions, especially Stoic and Platonist, to the doctrinal, historical and institutional teachings contained in the Bible, and in creating out of these diverse elements a novel and coherent Christian view of God, the universe, and man. At the same time, a similar synthesis of ancient and Christian elements was achieved by the Latin Fathers of the Western Church. Writers like Arnobius, Cyprian, Lactantius, and Ambrose embody in their writings the best grammatical and rhetorical training, based on the Roman poets and orators, that was available in their time. Jerome added to his consummate Latin literary education that Greek and Hebrew scholarship which enabled him to translate the entire Bible from the original languages into Latin. Augustine, the most important and complex of them all, was not only an excellent and cultured rhetorician according to the standards of his time, but also made use of the allegorical method to justify the study of the ancient Roman poets and prose writers. Furthermore, Augustine was a learned and productive philosophical and theological thinker, who left to posterity a substantial body of writings in which traditional religious doctrine was enriched with novel theological ideas like the City of God, original sin, and predestination, and also with philosophical conceptions of Greek and especially Neoplatonic origin, like the eternal forms in the divine mind, the incorporeality and immortality of the soul, conceptions which appear more prominently in his earlier, philosophical writings, but which he did not completely abandon even in his later years when he was engaged in Church administration and in theological controversies with the heretics of his time. Thus Christianity, during the first six centuries of its existence, which still belong to the period of classical antiquity, absorbed a large amount of Greek philosophical ideas and of Greek and Latin literary traditions, so that some historians have been able to speak, with a certain amount of justification, of the humanism of the Church Fathers. In recent years, it has become customary among theologians and historians to ignore or to minimize the indebtedness of Philo, Augustine, and the other early Christian writers to Greek philosophy. I must leave it to the judgment of present-day theologians and their followers whether they are really serving their cause by trying to eliminate from Christian theology all notions originally derived from Greek philosophy. Certainly those historians who follow a similar tendency and deny the significance of Greek philosophy for early Christian thought can be corrected through an objective study of the sources.

During the early Middle Ages, the Latin West had very limited philosophical and scientific interests, as we have seen, but it continued as best it could the grammatical and theological studies sanctioned by Augustine and the other Latin Fathers; and a number of Spanish, Irish, Anglo-Saxon and Carolingian scholars achieved distinction in this way. In the history of theology, a marked change from the pattern of the patristic period occurred with the rise of scholasticism after the eleventh century. What was involved was not merely the influx of additional philosophical sources and ideas, both Platonist and Aristotelian, of which we have spoken in the preceding lectures. Much more important was the novel tendency to transform the subject matter of Christian theology into a topically arranged and logically coherent system. There was no precedent for this either in the Bible or in Latin patristic literature, although certain Greek writers like Origen and John of Damascus had paved the way. The desire for a topical arrangement found its expression in the collections of sentences and church canons which culminated in the twelfth century in the *Libri Sententiarum* of Peter Lombard and the *Decretum* of Gratian which for many centuries were to serve as the standard textbooks of theology and of canon law. At the same time, the rising interest in Aristotelian logic led to the endeavor, first cultivated in the schools of Bec, Laon, and Paris, to apply the newly refined methods of dialectical argument to the subject matter of theology, which thus became by the standards of the time a real science. It is this method of Anselm, Abelard, and Peter Lombard which dominates the theological tradition of the high and later Middle Ages, including Bonaventura, Aquinas, Duns Scotus, and Ockham, not the older method of Peter Damiani or St. Bernard, who tried in vain to stem the rising tide of scholasticism and whose influence was hence confined to the more popular and practical, less scientific areas of later religious literature.

If we remember these facts concerning the history of theology in the West, we can understand what it meant for a Renaissance humanist with religious convictions to attack scholastic theology and to advocate a return to the Biblical and patristic sources of Christianity. It meant that these sources, which after all were themselves the product of antiquity, were considered as the Christian classics which shared the prestige and authority of classical antiquity and to which the same methods of historical and philological scholarship could be applied. Thus Petrarch shuns the medieval theologians except St. Bernard and quotes only early Christian writers in his religious and theological remarks. Valla laments the harmful influence of logic and philosophy upon theology and advocates an alliance between faith and eloquence. And Erasmus repeatedly attacks the scholastic theologians and emphasizes that the early Christian writers were grammarians, but no dialecticians. In his rejection of scholastic theology and his emphasis on the authority of Scripture and the Fathers, even Luther no less than John Colet is in agreement with the humanists, whereas the attempt to combine the study of theology with an elegant Latin style and a thorough knowledge of the Greek and Latin classics characterizes not only many Italian humanists and Erasmus, but also Melanchthon, Calvin, and the early Jesuits.

If we try to assess the positive contributions of humanist scholarship to Renaissance theology, we must emphasize above all their achievements in what we might call sacred philology. Valla led the way with his notes on the New Testament, in which he criticized several passages of Jerome's Vulgate on the basis of the Greek text. He was followed by Manetti, who made a new translation of the New Testament from Greek into Latin and of the Psalms from Hebrew into Latin, a work which has not yet been sufficiently studied. Erasmus' edition of the Greek New Testament is well known. It is this humanist tradition of biblical philology which provides the background and method for Luther's German version of the entire Bible from the Hebrew and Greek, as well as for the official revision of the Vulgate accomplished by Catholic scholars during the second half of the sixteenth century, and for the official English version completed under King James I. The theological exegesis of the Bible and of its various parts had always been an important branch of Christian literature ever since patristic times. It was temporarily overshadowed, though by no means eliminated, by the predominance of Peter Lombard's *Sentences* in the theological curriculum of the later Middle Ages, but it derived new force in the sixteenth century from the emphasis of Protestant theology upon the original source of Christian doctrine. To what extent the exegesis of that period was affected by the new methods and standards of humanist philology, seems to be a question which has not yet been sufficiently investigated.

An even wider field was offered to humanist scholarship by the large body of Greek Christian literature of the patristic and Byzantine period. Some of this material had been translated into Latin towards the end of antiquity and again during the twelfth century. Yet it is an established fact not sufficiently known or appreciated that a large proportion of Greek patristic literature was for the first time translated into Latin by the humanists and humanistically trained theologians of the fifteenth and sixteenth centuries. This applies to many important writings of Eusebius, Basil, and John Chrysostom, of Gregory of Nazianzus and of Nyssa, not to mention many later or lesser authors, or the writings which had been known before and were now reissued in presumably better Latin versions. Early in the fifteenth century, Leonardo Bruni translated Basil's letter which defended the reading of the pagan poets on the part of Christian students, and this welcome support of the humanist program by a distinguished Church author attained such a wide circulation that we may assume that it was used in the classroom. About the same time, Ambrogio Traversari, a monk with a classical training, dedicated a considerable amount of his energy to the translating of Greek Christian writers, thus setting an example to many later scholars, clerics, and laymen alike. These Latin versions attained great popularity as the numerous manuscript copies and printed editions may prove. They were often followed by vernacular translations, and in the sixteenth century, by editions of the original Greek texts. Thus we must conclude that the Renaissance possessed a much better and more complete knowledge of Greek Christian literature and theology than the preceding age, and it would be an interesting question, which to my knowledge has not yet been explored, whether or to what extent the newly diffused ideas of these Greek authors exercised an influence on the theological discussions and controversies of the Reformation period.

Whereas a considerable proportion of Greek Christian literature was thus made available to the West through the labors of the humanists, the writings of the Latin Church Fathers had been continuously known through the Middle Ages, and never ceased to exercise a strong influence on all theologians and other writers. Yet in this area also humanist scholarship brought about significant changes. The humanists were fully aware of the fact that authors like Ambrose and Lactantius, and especially Jerome and Augustine, belong to the good period of ancient Latin literature, and hence must be considered as "Christian classics." Consequently, some of their works were included in the curriculum of the humanistic school, as in that of Guarino, and regularly listed as recommended readings by humanist educators like Bruni, Valla, Erasmus, and Vives. Thus the Latin Fathers were read in the humanistic period no less than before, but they were grouped with the classical Latin writers rather than with the medieval theologians, and this fact could not fail to bring about a change in the way in which they were read and understood.

Moreover, the new philological methods of editing and commenting which the humanists had developed in their studies of the ancient authors were also applied to the Latin Church Fathers. We know in the case of Augustine that many manuscript copies and printed editions of the fifteenth century were due to the efforts of humanist scholars, and that Vives composed a philological commentary on the City of God, with which he was said in true humanist fashion to have restored St. Augustine to his ancient integrity. The application of humanist scholarship to Latin patristic literature culminated in the work of Erasmus, who prepared for a number of the most important writers critical editions of their collected works. His example was followed by Protestant and Catholic scholars alike, and later in the sixteenth century, the pope appointed a special committee of scholars for the purpose of publishing the writings of the Fathers in new critical editions.

Another field in which humanist scholarship was applied to the problems which concerned the churches and theologians was the study of ecclesiastic history. The critical methods developed by the humanists for the writing of ancient and medieval history on the basis of authentic contemporary documents and evidence were first applied to church history by Valla in his famous attack on the Donation of Constantine. In the sixteenth century, the Magdeburg Centuriatores used this method to rewrite the whole history of the church from the Protestant point of view, and later in the century, Cardinal Baronius and his assistants undertook the same task for the Catholic side.

A New View of the Problem

The humanist interest in early Christian literature was not limited to philological and historical preoccupations, but also had its doctrinal consequences in philosophy and theology. Just as the philological study of the pagan philosophers led the way towards a revival of Platonism and of other ancient philosophies, and more specifically to a new kind of Aristotelianism, so the humanistic study of the Bible and of the Church Fathers led to new interpretations of early Christian thought, that are characteristic of the Renaissance and Reformation period. Thus the attempt to interpret the Epistles of Paul without the context and superstructure of scholastic theology was made by scholars like Ficino, Colet, and Erasmus before it had such powerful and decisive results in the work of Luther. Even more significant and more widespread was the influence exercised during the Renaissance by St. Augustine. . . .

I think we are now at last prepared to offer a meaningful interpretation of the term "Christian humanism" that is so often applied to the Renaissance or to earlier periods. Confining the term humanism, according to the Renaissance meaning of the words humanist and humanities, to the rhetorical, classical, and moral concerns of the Renaissance humanists, regardless of the particular philosophical or theological opinions held by individual humanists, and of the theological, philosophical, scientific, or juristic training which individual scholars may have combined with their humanist education, we might choose to call Christian humanists all those scholars who accepted the teachings of Christianity and were members of one of the churches, without necessarily discussing religious or theological topics in their literary or scholarly writings. By this standard, practically all Renaissance humanists, before and after the Reformation, were Christian humanists, since the alleged cases of openly pagan or atheistic convictions are rare and dubious. But it is probably preferable to use the term Christian humanism in a more specific sense, and to limit it to those scholars with a humanist classical and rhetorical training who explicitly discussed religious or theological problems in all or some of their writings. In this sense, neither Aquinas nor Luther were Christian humanists, for the simple reason that they were theologians, but not humanists as that term was then understood, although Luther presupposes certain scholarly achievements of humanism. On the other hand, we must list among the Christian humanists not only Erasmus, Vives, Budé, and More, but also Calvin, the elegant Latin writer and commentator of Seneca; Melanchthon, the defender of rhetoric against philosophy, who had more influence on many aspects of Lutheran Germany than Luther himself and who was responsible for the humanistic tradition of the German Protestant schools down to the nineteenth century; and finally the Jesuit Fathers, many of whom were excellent classical scholars and Latin writers, and who owed part of their success to the good instruction offered in their schools and colleges in the then fashionable humanistic disciplines. For the tradition of humanist learning by no means came to an end with the Protestant or Catholic Reformations, as might appear if we look only for the headlines of the historical development. It survived as vigorously as did the tradition of Aristotelian scholasticism, cutting across all religious and national divisions, flourishing at Leiden and Oxford no less than at Padua and Salamanca, and exercising as formative an influence upon the minds of the philosophers and scientists trained in the schools and universities of the seventeenth and eighteenth centuries.

E. HARRIS HARBISON

NEW THESIS OR OLD?

The following selection is from a series of essays by the late E. Harris Harbison entitled *The Christian Scholar in the Age of the Reformation*. The very title of the work betrays the author's underlying assumption with reference to the neopaganism of the humanistic movement, which is that the humanist was essentially Christian and remained so in spite of "the impact of the Revival of Learning upon the Christian scholar and his sense of calling." On this point Harbison is apparently in agreement with Walser and Kristeller. But his interpretation is quite different from either of theirs. His central thesis is that, while the Renaissance humanists remained Christian scholars as their predecessors had been, the Revival of Learning provided for them a new frame of reference of classical paganism which they were never quite able to square with that of traditional Christianity: and that ultimately the Christian scholar had to choose between his Christian and his scholarly calling.

The selection takes the form of a survey of selected humanists from Petrarch through Valla and Pico to the English scholar John Colet whose life and work reached to the eve of the Reformation. The author uses these figures to illustrate the various ways in which these men adjusted to the contradictions between classicism and Christianity; and he obviously prefers Colet as "the first to be able to absorb a good deal of the philological and historical interests and attitudes of the New Learning and to direct them to a purpose fully Christian." This preference awakens echoes of an earlier generation of scholars which made a clear distinction between the pagan humanists of the Italian Renaissance and the Christian scholars of the Northern Renaissance.

The student should attempt to "test" the thesis that Harbison presents against the case presented by Walser and Kristeller. How, for example, does Harbison's view square with the importance Kristeller attaches to "sacred philology"? He should consider the consistency between Harbison's underlying assumption and his main thesis. And he should ask whether Harbison has put himself closer to the revisionists or the traditionalists.

The implications of all this [i.e. the humanists' developing sense of historical time and distance] for the scholar who took his commitment to the Christian religion seriously were confused and unclear at first. It had not been easy to domesticate Greek philosophy in medieval Christianity, but Aquinas and others had done it. Abelard had found Christian uses for dialectic but was suspicious of grammar and rhetoric: "What has Horace to do with the Psalter, Virgil with the Gospel, Cicero with the Apostle?" he asked, echoing Jerome. The line of least resistance for the Christian Humanist was to castigate dialectic (and Scholasticism in general) as unchristian, to ask with Erasmus what has Aristotle to do with Christ, and to sing the praises of grammar and rhetoric as potential allies of Christian belief. This the Humanists did, from Petrarch on, but it was not so easy to persuade either themselves or others as it might have seemed. And it is this that gives the study of the Christian scholar and his calling during the Reformation its interest. For one thing, to reject Abelard and Aquinas was to be driven back to the equally fundamental questions raised by Jerome and Augustine as scholars and Christians. And to think more and more as historians and less and less as philosophers was to raise a disturbingly new question for Christian thinkers: What if there had been a breach of historical continuity within Christianity itself, a breach between a primitive apostolic Church close to its Founder's spirit and a corrupted institution of a later and darker age which had unwittingly broken the tie that bound it to Christ? What if the new history, archaeology, and philology should appear to shake to its foundations the structure of Christianity as a set of timeless beliefs? There was work enough for Christian scholars to do as a result of the Revival of Learning.

To suggest some of the facets of the problem we must select and concentrate as we did in the preceding chapter. The most important figures to understand if one would know something of the impact of the Revival of Learning upon the Christian scholar and his sense of calling are Petrarch, Lorenzo Valla, Pico della Mirandola, and John Colet. With these four we shall be concerned in this chapter.

Francesco Petrarca, or Petrarch (1304–1374), was the first to feel deeply the personal implications of the new scholarly interests and perspectives which we have discussed—or at least the first to be articulate about his doubts and worries. More clearly than anyone of his generation, Petrarch was able to conceive Roman antiquity historically, as it had been, a pagan society of infinite attractiveness. He knew this society was dead, but he found by experience that he could revive its greatest figures and their thoughts in his imagination and live in spiritual friendship with them. This gave peculiar poignancy to his sense of the gulf between the *Respublica Romana* and the *Respublica Christiana,* between civic and monastic ideals, between Cicero and Christ. He knew that the Voice might reproach him for being a Ciceronian rather than a Christian as it had reproached Jerome. But characteristically, it was an imaginative literary dialogue, not a vision, in which the conflict within him took place between his love for pagan antiquity and his devotion to Christianity. This was his *Secret,* the famous dialogue between St. Augustine and himself which he wrote in 1342 at the age of thirty-eight and always kept by his bedside to remind him of his soul-searchings at the height of his intellectual powers. The problem is Jerome's primarily, but the Father who Petrarch feels will best understand his own passions and problems is not Jerome but the author of the *Confessions.* The Augustine of the dialogue is a curious mixture, part Augustine as he was, part Petrarch's prudish medieval conscience. He is always right in his argument with Petrarch's more human half, but he is not always understanding enough of human failings. He wins the argument but loses Petrarch's soul.

Petrarch's *Secret* is an extraordinarily subtle piece of self-analysis. Augustine lays bare Petrarch's spiritual anatomy with the relentless touch of a skilled soul-surgeon: his infatuation for Laura, which Augustine insists was never so high-minded or ennobling an affair as Petrarch maintains it was; his ambition for literary fame, which the saint says

is more soaring and limitless than Petrarch is aware of; and his *accidia,* his inner melancholy and malaise, the result of a hopelessly divided mind and will. When Petrarch blames all these failings on external circumstances and agencies, Augustine brings him relentlessly back to their internal roots. The trouble is "your overcrowded mind," he says; you have "no considered plan"; you "can never put your whole strength to anything" because of the "worrying torment of a mind angry with itself [which] loathes its own defilements, yet cleanses them not away." Read Seneca or Cicero, he says, or for that matter read your own book on *Tranquillity of Soul;* you are "a past-master in the whole field," but like too many other writers of your generation, you do not practice what you preach.[1]

The root of the trouble, it develops, is a deep dichotomy between occupation and conscience. No man of his generation was ever more engrossed and seduced by the pleasures of scholarship and writing than Petrarch. All his life he sought some satisfying moral justification of the work he loved —in vain. He quoted Cicero's definition of glory to Augustine—"the illustrious and world-wide renown of good services rendered to one's fellow-citizens, to one's country, or to all mankind"—with the implication that this was what *he* was doing. But Augustine was not taken in: "Why and wherefore, I ask, this perpetual toil, these ceaseless vigils, and this intense application to study? You will answer, perhaps, that you seek to find out what is profitable for life. But you have long since learned what is needful for life and for death. What was now required of you was to try and put in practice what you know, instead of plunging deeper and deeper into laborious inquiries, where new problems are always meeting you, and insoluble mysteries, in which you never reach the end. . . . You write books on others, but yourself you quite forget."[2] Does this mean, asks Petrarch, that I must drop my work entirely? Yes, says Augustine, Rome has been celebrated before; think only on your approaching death. Petrarch says he wishes Augustine had told him all this earlier. "I will pull myself together and collect my scattered wits, and make a great endeavor to possess my soul in patience," he concludes,

[1] *Petrarch's Secret.* . . . trans. Wm. H. Draper, London, Chatto and Windus, 1911, pp. 45–46, 99, 138. The quotations that follow are used by permission.

[2] *Ibid.,* pp. 166–170.

The Eve of the Modern World

"but I have not strength to resist that old bent for study altogether." The "true order" is "that mortal men should first care for mortal things, and that to things transitory, things eternal should succeed." Meanwhile he prays that God will lead him "safe and whole out of so many crooked ways."[3]

In the course of the dialogue, Petrarch raised anew the question which had haunted both Augustine and Abelard, the question of the relation between learning and goodness, or more precisely, the problem of scholarship and sex: can a sinner be a good scholar? "Remember," says Augustine to Petrarch on the subject of Laura, "remember how ill your profession accords with a life like this; think how this woman has injured your soul, your body, your fortune."[4]

The whole question of learning and goodness came up again twenty-five years later in an amusing way. In 1366 four Venetian noblemen amused themselves after a good dinner by debating and declaring a formal legal sentence to the effect that Petrarch was certainly a good man but a poor scholar, "a good man without learning." This cut Petrarch to the quick. He waited a year, then wrote an elaborate answer in the classical form of an invective entitled *On my own ignorance and that of many others*. His line of defence — ignoring for the moment the various layers of irony — is that he may not know much but neither does anybody, and he is at least a devoted Christian, which is more than his enemies can say. At the same time he is careful to display his erudition by saturating the essay with classical quotations. Furthermore, he sketches the reply he would make if he were to be accused of Ciceronianism as Jerome was: "My incorruptible treasure and the superior part of my soul is with Christ; but because of the frailties and burdens of mortal life, which are not only difficult to bear but difficult merely to enumerate, I cannot, I confess, lift up, however ardently I should wish, the inferior parts of my soul, in which the irascible and concupiscible appetites are located." Cicero has done him no harm and much good, he insists. Augustine and Jerome both had the same experience. "I even feel sure that Cicero himself would have been a Christian if he had been able to see Christ and to comprehend his doctrine," he adds, as Augustine had thought of Plato.[5] Yet in all this there is no real justification of the scholarly or literary calling. In fact there is a deep undercurrent

of anti-intellectualism which seems more than merely ironical: "It is safer to strive for a good and pious will than for a capable and clear intellect. . . . It is better to will the good than to know the truth. . . . In this life it is impossible to know God in his fulness; piously and ardently to love Him is possible. . . ."[6] "It will be enough if I succeed in being wise within the limits of sobriety; and this can be achieved without much learning, even without any, as is clearly shown by the long line of illiterate saints of both sexes."[7] And yet Petrarch spent years of his life working over a scholarly book *On Illustrious Men* of classical antiquity and had really very little love for "illiterate saints."

It is too easy to make fun of Petrarch. A badly integrated personality, we would say today — and send him to the psychoanalyst's couch. But Petrarch's emotional tensions were the warning of a new era in the history of Christian scholarship. The particular kind of reconciliation between classicism and Christianity which was represented by Aquinas in philosophy, Dante in poetry, and the Gothic Cathedral in art could not last forever because it was based on hazy and inaccurate notions of the past, both classical and Christian. The rise of history, archaeology, and philology as scholarly disciplines was bound to sharpen the differences between Athens and Jerusalem and reveal the shaky historical foundations of the so-called medieval synthesis of Greek reason and Christian faith. As the philological and historical attitudes spread, they would reveal that the gulf between the classical point of view and the Christian was far wider than either Aquinas or Dante suspected. What Petrarch did was to dramatize and popularize these new scholarly attitudes. Elaboration of the disciplines themselves he left to others, but he did demonstrate vividly the psychological tensions that might result if the disciplines were taken seriously. Try as he might, Petrarch could never quite bring his scholarly activity and his Christian faith into any organic relationship with each other. He could never gain a sense of calling as a Christian and a scholar. His failure was an omen of how difficult the task was to be in the next

[3] *Ibid.*, pp. 176, 184–192.

[4] *Ibid.*, p. 163.

[5] *The Renaissance Philosophy of Man*, ed. Ernst Cassirer, P. O. Kristeller, and J. H. Randall, Chicago, University of Chicago Press, 1948, pp. 113–115. Copyright 1948 by the University of Chicago. The quotations that follow from Petrarch and Pico are used by permission.

[6] *Ibid.*, p. 105.

[7] *Ibid.*, p. 127.

two centuries of growing secularism and deepening religious strife.

The destructive possibilities, both for good and ill, of the new attitudes which accompanied the Revival of Learning became abundantly evident a century after Petrarch in the career of Lorenzo Valla (1405 – 1457), Valla exemplified better than anyone else of his generation and the triumph of grammar and rhetoric over dialectic, of the historical over the philosophical attitude. He had probably the keenest critical intelligence of any of the Italian Humanists. Like Jerome he was primarily a philologist—and like Jerome he was always getting into violent literary quarrels. Like Abelard he seems to have been primarily concerned to make his generation think, question, ponder its unexamined beliefs and assumptions.

His book *On the Elegancies of the Latin Language* (published 1444) was for its day a model of the best critical method in linguistic study and served as the foundation of good Latin style and sound method for later Humanists, notably Erasmus. Unlike Jerome, Valla's restless intellect applied the methods learned in philology to the criticism of doctrines and institutions. At twenty-six years of age he wrote a dialogue *On Pleasure* which attacked Petrarch's naive reconciliation of Stoicism with Christian ethics, questioned the validity of good works as a conscious moral goal and suggested ironically that a life lived according to Epicurean principles was a better introduction than Stoicism to the eternal bliss reserved for Christians. Soon he was applying his criticism to Scholasticism and monasticism. The Schoolmen, he said, really did not know their Aristotle, and they wrote very bad and obscure Latin; they should have paid more attention to rhetoric than to dialectic, which was after all a barren method. The monks, he said, had falsely usurped the name of "religious" and were trying to dodge the secular duties demanded of all Christians; there was only one moral perfection, he insisted, open to layman and cleric alike; the monks were rather a sect than a religion. His most famous work was his conclusive proof, on historical and philological grounds, that the *Donation of Constantine*, upon which so much of the papal claim to temporal power was based, was an arrant forgery. Typical of his method were his remarks about the "satraps" which the author of the document incautiously mentioned. "What have satraps got to do with the case?" asks the outraged historian and philologist. "Numskull, blockhead! Do Caesars speak thus? Are Roman decrees usually drafted thus? Whoever heard of satraps being mentioned in the councils of the Romans?"[8]

If the new criticism could be applied to the *Donation of Constantine*, why could it not be applied equally well to other documents of the Christian tradition? Valla's originality lay in his insight that if collation of manuscripts, analysis of language, and examination of historical context got one closer to the mind of Cicero or of Aristotle, the same techniques would presumably get one closer to the mind of the Fathers, or of St. Paul, or perhaps of Moses. No document was so sacred as to be exempt from philological analysis, providing that fundamental doctrines were not questioned. Valla demonstrated that a letter from King Abgar of Edessa to Jesus was apocryphal. He proved that the mystical writings attributed to Dionysius the Areopagite could not possibly have been written by a contemporary of St. Paul's, as generations of medieval students had believed. He argued that the Apostles' Creed was the work not of the Apostles but of the Council of Nicaea. But most important of all, he took in hand three Latin and three Greek codices of the New Testament and demonstrated that the Latin Vulgate was full of grammatical misunderstandings and unhappy translations. Paul had written extremely well in Greek, he pointed out; it was a shame that his meaning was so often twisted or obscured by the translator. He could not believe that the New Testament Vulgate was Jerome's work. Jerome was too good a scholar and stylist for that. The New Testament verses scattered through his works are always better translated than they are in the Vulgate. Either Jerome had nothing to do with it, or the copyists had ruined his work. . . .

He had the instincts of a true critic, writes his biographer: "to compare, to judge, to illuminate, to correct, to show literature the way to become a supremely effective force in ameliorating society."[9] But how much of this could be called Christian motivation we shall never know and it is useless to inquire. To assess the precise extent to which an individual mind or a whole society has become what we call "secularized" is the most difficult problem the historian of this period has to face. Valla never protested his Christian motives in the

[8] *The Treatise of Lorenzo Valla on the Donation of Constantine,* trans. C. B. Coleman, New Haven, Yale University Press, pp. 84 – 85.

[9] Girolamo Mancini, *Vita di Lorenzo Valla,* Florence, 1891, p. 331.

way Abelard and Petrarch felt called upon to do; nor did he ever proclaim his contempt for Christianity. His work exemplifies nicely how faint and fluctuating is the line that separates the religious from the secular in the motivation of critical scholarship at the close of the Middle Ages. What Valla did as a scholar was indispensable to Erasmus, Luther, and Calvin — and they all spoke well of him. He demonstrated what historical and philological criticism could accomplish. But we will never be able to fathom the combination of worldly motives, disinterested love of truth, and Christian aims, that inspired his work.

The ideal scholar, if there were one, would be composed of equal parts of critical ability and appreciative capacity. The two are not often united in the same man. Valla was long on critical acumen but short on appreciative insight (into Scholasticism, for instance). The most spectacular scholar of the next generation, Giovanni Pico della Mirandola (1463 – 1494), was long on the power of appreciation and short on critical penetration. Valla was a philologist who had little patience with philosophy; Pico, a philosopher who had no great interest in philology. If Valla illustrated the benefits and potential dangers of criticism, Pico demonstrated the strengths and weaknesses of a sort of indiscriminate appreciation as the foundation of scholarly work.

It is hard to describe Pico and make him believable. The attempt somehow reminds one of that remark of Montaigne's about stories of the same witch appearing one day in one place and the next a thousand miles away: "To tell the truth I would not believe my own eyes in such a case."[10] Apparently Pico had everything: brains, good looks, noble birth, money, ambition, and enormous energy. Above all, he had an insatiable thirst for learning, which he attempted to slake at Bologna, Padua, Florence, Rome, and Paris. In 1486 at the tender age of twenty-four — "full of pride and desirous of glory," his nephew-biographer tells us — he went to Rome and published nine hundred Theses or propositions drawn from the lore of all ages and places, Eastern and Western. To the startled scholarly world he proposed to defend these propositions before all comers and offered to pay the traveling expenses of any debaters who should come from a distance. The Pope was unimpressed. "This young man wants someone to burn him some day," he remarked. A

[10] *Essays*, III, II.

papal commission censured thirteen of the propositions — such as that Christ did not really and truly descend into Hell but only *quoad effectum,* and that no one's beliefs are simply the product of his will alone. Pico wrote a hasty *Apology* but this got him into more trouble. He fled to Paris where he was imprisoned for a short time, then escaped to Florence where he remained under the protection of Lorenzo de' Medici during most of his few remaining years. This conflict with ecclesiastical authority shook him deeply. Looking back on it, he told his nephew he thought it was by God's special providence that he had thus been falsely accused of heresy so that he would come to his senses, give up "the voluptuous use of women," to which he had been addicted, and correct his evil ways. Just what the character of his "conversion" was, it is hard to say. He sold his hereditary lands, burned some youthful love poetry, and talked of going out barefoot to preach Christ — after he finished writing "certain books" he had in hand. He came increasingly under the influence of Savonarola, who insisted in a sermon preached after his death that Pico had determined to become a Dominican friar. But he remained a layman, and except that he concentrated somewhat more on purely religious problems, the change in his life apparently did not affect his whole conception of learning, as it had Augustine's. In 1494 at the early age of thirty-one he died of a fever in three days of illness. . . .

One thing is evident. Pico was no more able than Petrarch or Valla to attain any clear sense of calling as a Christian scholar. Petrarch never found any final reconciliation between the Ciceronian and Christian halves of his split personality. Valla never made explicit the Christian roots (if there were any) of his philological crusade. Pico's personal devotion to Christ, the only-begotten Son, never found any adequate place in his vast and indiscriminate syncretism. All three considered themselves scholars and Christians, but none of the three had any consciousness, so far as I have been able to discover, of organic relationship between personal piety and scholarly endeavor.

Here, it would seem, is the importance of John Colet (1467? – 1519). Colet was the first to be able to absorb a good deal of the philological and historical interests and attitudes of the New Learning and to direct them to a purpose fully Christian. In him personal piety and professional purpose interpenetrated each other so thoroughly that when his friends wrote about him, the scholar always recalled the Christian and the Christian the scholar. "In London there is John Colet, Dean of St. Paul's, who has combined great learning with a marvellous piety," Erasmus wrote to a friend. Later he said that he had never seen "a more highly-gifted intellect," adding immediately that Colet liked to bend this intellect to what would fit him for immortality. At table, Erasmus reported, his conversation was "all either about literature or about Christ." "A book was ever his companion on the road, and his talk was always of Christ." Thomas More said of him after his death: "None more learned or more holy has lived among us for many ages past."[11]

The thing that strikes the historian most about Colet at this distance is the extraordinary balance and harmony in him between conflicting impulses and aims which tore other men of his generation to pieces — or made hypocrites of them. In a little devotional tract that he wrote, an admonition to the reader is repeated like a refrain: order your life "by reason and grace." And its last words are: "Use well temporal things. Desire eternal things. Finis."[12] The balance between this world and the next in his mind gave him an inner assurance that made those who knew him best rely on him for judgment and courage. He had the power, as Lupton notes, "of uniting and attaching others to himself, or rather of drawing them through himself to a higher object."[13] He did not come by this emotional stability easily. "It was but a very small portion of this religious spirit that he owed to nature," Erasmus thought. By nature he was irascible, covetous, and inclined to sensuous pleasures. He had to discipline these three weaknesses all his life, "by philosophy and sacred studies, watching, fasting, and prayer" — that is, by both mind and will. His anger sometimes blazed out in righteous indignation. He founded St. Paul's School with the money he inherited from his wealthy merchant father, partly because he knew his tendency to covetousness. He never married (he was ordained priest in 1498) and his dinners were notoriously frugal, "yet," says Erasmus, "if an occasion ever presented itself, either of conversing with ladies, or being a

guest at sumptuous repasts, you might have seen some traces of the old nature in him." Erasmus concluded the warm pen-portrait which is the chief source of our knowledge of Colet's life by remarking that although he never noted any sign of human weakness in his saintly friend Vitrier, "In Colet were some traits which showed him to be but man." . . .

Colet was no Humanist in the ordinary sense of the word. He seems never to have felt any guilty love for pagan literature like Jerome or Petrarch. He saw no value in reading the ancient poets and philosophers. In his Oxford lectures he specifically condemned the idea that a man had to study the classics in order to understand Scripture. Truth is understood by grace, grace is procured by prayers, and prayers are heard through devotion and self-denial.[14] Man's natural reason has no autonomous power of arriving at the truth without God's aid. Theology is not a "science" to be attained by reason — this was Aquinas' error, he thought — it is a "wisdom" revealed to faith by the divine illumination.[15] Colet steeped himself in Paul's radical pessimism about the natural man and emerged an Augustinian — almost a "Lutheran," in fact — on the helplessness of the unaided intellect. In his lectures on the Dionysian writings, he showed how much he had absorbed of the Neo-Platonic doctrine that mere learning will never save a man. "Not knowledge, but love, leads to eternal life. . . . Ignorant love has a thousand times more power than cold wisdom." He condemned "indiscriminate erudition," saying that it dulled Christian innocence and simplicity.[16] Probably he was referring to the Schoolmen, but it is not impossible that he was thinking of Pico.

Yet when all is said on the side of Colet's narrow intellectual interests and almost puritanical Christianity (he had absorbed Paul's view of marriage as a mere concession to human infirmity), the fact remains that he was able to direct a penetrating mind and a devout heart into a brief scholarly career of considerable significance. Within the Christian tradition itself, his tastes were not narrow or dogmatic. He read heretical books with attention, says Erasmus, and got more out of them than he did out of

[11] Erasmus to Servatius Roger, 8 July 1514, Allen, *Opus Epistolarum,* I, Ep. 296; Erasmus, *Vitrier and Colet,* pp. 31–32, 26; Thomas More to a Monk, 1519–20, *The Correspondence of Sir Thomas More,* ed. Elizabeth F. Rogers, Princeton, 1947, p. 192.

[12] "A ryght fruitfull monicion concernynge the order of a good christen mannes lyfe," in Lupton, *Life,* pp. 305–310.

[13] Lupton, *Life,* p. 265.

[14] Colet, *I Corinthians,* p. 110.

[15] Rice, "John Colet and the Annihilation of the Natural," *loc. cit.,* pp. 152–161.

[16] Colet, *Two Treatises on the Hierarchies of Dionysius,* ed. J. H. Lupton, London, 1869, p. 219; Erasmus, *Vitrier and Colet,* p. 37.

orthodox scholastic hair-splitters.[17] His scholarly ideal, even when he failed to live up to it in his own writing, was directness and simplicity. He once read a copy of Reuchlin's *Cabalistica* and wrote Erasmus that he was not really qualified to discuss it, but that as he read, it seemed to him at times that "the wonders were more verbal than real."[18] What came to his mind in commenting on Romans 1:17 was quite characteristic. He chose to remark on how simple was the Apostles' method of citation when quoting from the Old Testament (in this case, Paul was quoting "The just shall live by faith" from Habakkuk). In contrast, he said, modern theologians and lawyers are so afraid no one will believe them that they pile citation upon citation to show off their erudition.[19]

Christian scholarship to Colet begins in prayer and divine illumination; it concerns itself with the whole of a scriptural writer's thought and his historical surroundings; it moves on from historical analysis to ethical and religious understanding; and it ends in social reform and the deepening of personal piety. Unlike any of the moving spirits of the Revival of Learning in Italy whom we have considered, Colet was able to adapt the historical and philological approach to the reverent study of Scripture and to bring his own Christian piety into fruitful relationship with humanistic scholarship. His example was to have important effects upon the greatest scholar of the age, Erasmus of Rotterdam.

[17] Erasmus, *Vitrier and Colet*, p. 38.

[18] Lupton, *Colet*, pp. 225–226.

[19] Colet, *Romans*, p. 209.

3

THE REFORMATION: THE PROBLEM OF CAUSE

There was in the medieval church a long prior history of religious dissent stretching back for centuries before the Protestant Reformation. Time after time dissent had taken the shape of monastic reform movements — the Cluniac reform of the tenth and eleventh centuries, the Cistertian Order of the twelfth century, and the mendicant orders of the thirteenth. And these movements had succeded, in their times, in reforming and reinvigorating the church. There had been individual critics who had railed against the church; others who quietly lamented its perennial corruption; and mystics who had turned from it to look for God within themselves. Dissent had expressed itself in the form of violent heretical movements which increased in frequency and virulence through the High Middle Ages in spite of the best efforts of the Church, first to ignore them, then to correct them, and finally to destroy them.

In a hundred ways the church had somehow dealt with its dissenters and contained them. But with the increasing internal troubles of the church in the fourteenth and fifteenth centuries and the increasing pressure of conflicts with the emerging national monarchies, the vigor which in earlier ages had been summoned to deal with religious dissent had begun to fail. At the same time the abuses which had long lent credence to the charges of critics of the church were on the increase. The church of the High Middle Ages had committed itself to continued concern for temporalities: the church of the later Middle Ages now bore the onus of that commitment. The need for reform was so patent that it became the major program of the whole string of church councils that stretched across the fifteenth century. The cry for reform of the church in head and members was raised again and again. Many highly placed churchmen were concerned for church reform, even most of the fifteenth century popes were for it. But they refused to accept even a program of reform with which they were in fundamental agreement from the hands of the hated councils, and the energies which might have been effectively employed in reform were dissipated in constitutional strife. The Conciliar Movement was a massive failure and with it faded the hope for either systematic constitutional change or reform of the church. Heretical critics multiplied and men of good will turned in despair to lay religious movements, to fanatic revivalists, and to their own dark thoughts. There seemed no alternative but the violence of religious revolution: and this came at last with the Protestant Reformation. In this context the Reformation becomes part of the pattern of dissent running back through the history of the church. But is this pattern a fundamental cause of the Reformation or is it merely its historical setting and background? Two of the selections that follow take opposing views on this question.

Much of the modern speculation about the causes of the Reformation focuses on the square and stalwart figure of Martin Luther, who seems to embody so much of its strength and purpose in himself. His importance is certainly fundamental in any discussion of the Reformation. But many scholars see the basic cause of the Reformation—either to praise or to condemn it—in the troubled soul of Luther and in the truculence and success with which he maintained his convictions. They reject the notion that the background to the Reformation was its cause. They point out that the condition of the church was no worse in the early sixteenth century than it had been for centuries: indeed, there were some signs of recovery. They point out that there was astonishingly little that was either original or new in Luther's position, that much of what he said had been said before by Hus, Occam, Wyclif and others. Thus, they say, why should Luther have succeeded in making a religious revolution when earlier reformers had failed, except for some special magic in the man himself? The scholars who take this position subscribe to some variety of what has been called the "hero thesis" in history, which sees the moving force of things in great men rather than in the ebb and flow of large, impersonal forces. Three of the following selections set forth the view that Luther was the cause of the Reformation—but they see Luther in very different ways.

The student should be aware that the two points of view represented in the selections of this problem, while important, are not the only points of view. For example, if it is true that much of what Luther said Hus had said before, why was it that the spark of Luther's words caught fire in so many other men of his time? Was it only the man Luther himself? If the abuses of the church were on their way to being cured, why were so many men ready to follow Luther to the destruction of the church? Is it not possible to see the cause of the Reformation in the coincidence of the man and his time? Is there not a middle ground on which the critic may stand?

HENRY CHARLES LEA

THE EXTERNAL VIEW

One of the oldest and most durable explanations for the Reformation is that it was a reaction against the abuses of the medieval church and a movement to correct those abuses. The very term Reformation reflects this contention. Among the most passionate advocates of this view was Henry Charles Lea (1825–1909) from whose chapter-essay, "The Eve of the Reformation" in the *Renaissance* volume of the old *Cambridge Modern History,* the following selection is taken.

Lea argues that it is an error to regard the Reformation as primarily a religious movement; that "the motives, both remote and proximate, which led to the Lutheran revolt were largely secular rather than spiritual"; and that "the existing ecclesiastical system was the practical evolution of dogma, and the overthrow of dogma was the only way to obtain permanent relief from the intolerable abuses of that system." He goes on to detail the familiar story of church abuse—the corrupt and cynical financial practices of the papacy and its agents, the intrusion of the church into the proper affairs of the emerging secular states, the conflict of lay and ecclesiastical courts for jurisdiction. He concludes that, on the one hand, the church forfeited the respect and confidence of the secular world by its very secularism and, on the other, destroyed true spirituality by its dependence on the empty forms of religious observance.

The student should note, in light of our previous problem, Lea's gratuitous charge that Renaissance humanism was both paganistic and a contributing factor to the coming of the Reformation. He should weigh the reasons Lea gives for the Reformation's having occurred in Germany. But most of all the student should observe that Lea's concept of the cause of the Reformation is basically external. This view is predictable enough given the fact that the bulk of Lea's writings—including the massive *A History of the Inquisition of the Middle Ages* and *History of Sacerdotal Celibacy in the Christian Church*—was devoted to the examination of the institutions of the medieval church, and that his verdict on those institutions was fundamentally negative. In the final analysis, then, the student should ponder whether the external view of cause can really be entertained for so fundamental a religious revolution as the Reformation.

As the sixteenth century opened, Europe was standing unconscious on the brink of a crater destined to change profoundly by its eruption the course of modern civilisation. The Church had acquired so complete a control over the souls of men, its venerable antiquity and its majestic organisation so filled the imagination, the services it had rendered seemed to call for such reverential gratitude, and its ac-

From Henry Charles Lea, "The Eve of the Reformation," Chapter XIX of *The Cambridge Modern History*, Vol. I: *The Renaissance* (New York, 1907), pp. 653–57, 660, 665–68, 673–80, 686–87, 690–91. Reprinted by permission of the Cambridge University Press.

knowledged claim to interpret the will of God to man rendered obedience so plain a duty, that the continuance of its power appeared to be an unchanging law of the universe, destined to operate throughout the limitless future. To understand the combination of forces which rent the domination of the Church into fragments, we must investigate in detail its relations with society on the eve of the disruption, and consider how it was regarded by the men of that day, with their diverse grievances, more or less justifying revolt. We must here omit from consideration the benefits which the Church had conferred, and confine our attention to the antagonisms which it provoked and to the evils for which it was held responsible. The interests and the motives at work were numerous and complex, some of them dating back for centuries, others comparatively recent, but all of them growing in intensity with the development of political institutions and popular intelligence. There has been a natural tendency to regard the Reformation as solely a religious movement; but this is an error. In the curious theocracy which dominated the Middle Ages, secular and spiritual interests became so inextricably intermingled that it is impossible wholly to disentangle them; but the motives, both remote and proximate, which led to the Lutheran revolt were largely secular rather than spiritual. So far, indeed, as concerns our present purpose we may dismiss the religious changes incident to the Reformation with the remark that they were not the object sought but the means for attaining that object. The existing ecclesiastical system was the practical evolution of dogma, and the overthrow of dogma was the only way to obtain permanent relief from the intolerable abuses of that system. . . .

This sovereignty was temporal as well as spiritual. The power of the Pope, as the earthly representative of God, was illimitable. The official theory, as expressed in the *De Principum Regimine,* which passes under the name of St Thomas Aquinas, declared the temporal jurisdiction of kings to be simply derived from the authority intrusted by Christ to St Peter and his successors; whence it followed that the exercise of the royal authority was subject to papal control. . . .

While it is true that the extreme exercise of papal authority in making and unmaking Kings was exceptional, still the unlimited jurisdiction claimed by the Holy See was irksome in many ways to the sovereigns of Europe and, as time wore on and the sec-

ular authority became consolidated, it was endured with more and more impatience. There could be no hard and fast line of delimitation between the spiritual and the temporal, for the two were mutually interdependent, and the convenient phrase, *temporalia ad spiritualia ordinata,* was devised to define those temporal matters, over which, as requisite to the due enjoyment of the spiritual, the Church claimed exclusive control. Moreover it assumed the right to determine in doubtful matters the definition of this elastic term and the secular ruler constantly found himself inconveniently limited in the exercise of his authority. The tension thence arising was increased by the happy device of legates and nuncios, by which the Holy See established in every country a representative whose business it was to exercise supreme spiritual jurisdiction and to maintain the claims of the Church, resulting in a divided sovereignty, at times exceedingly galling and even incompatible with a well-ordered State. Rulers so orthodox as Ferdinand and Isabel asked the great national Council of Seville, in 1478, how they could best prevent the residence of legates and nuncios who not only carried much gold out of the kingdom but interfered seriously with the royal pre-eminence. In this they only expressed the desires of the people; for the Estates of Castile, in 1480, asked the sovereigns to make some provision with respect to the nuncios who were of no benefit and only a source of evil.

Another fruitful source of complaint, on the part not only of the rulers but of the national Churches, was the gradual extension of the claim of the Holy See to control all patronage. Innocent III has the credit of first systematically asserting this claim and exploiting it for the benefit of his Cardinals and other officials. The practice increased, and Villani tells us that, in 1319, John XXII assumed to himself the control of all prebends in every collegiate church, from the sale of which he gathered immense sums. Finally the assertion was made that the Holy See owned all benefices and in the rules of the papal Chanceries appear the prices to be charged for them, whether with or without cure of souls, showing that the traffic had become an established source of revenue. Even the rights of lay patrons and founders were disregarded and in the provisions granted by the popes there was a special clause derogating their claims. Partly this patronage was used for direct profit, partly it was employed for the benefit of the Cardinals and their retainers, on whom pluralities were heaped with unstinted hand,

and the further refinement was introduced of granting to them pensions imposed on benefices and monastic foundations. Abbeys, also, were bestowed *in commendam* on titular abbots who collected the revenues through stewards, with little heed to the maintenance of the inmates or the performance of the offices. In the eager desire to anticipate these profits of simony, vacancies were not awaited, and rights of succession, under the name of expectatives, were given or sold in advance. The deplorable results of this spiritual commerce were early apparent and formed the subject of bitter lamentation and complaint, but to no purpose. . . .

Another ecclesiastical abuse severely felt by all sovereigns who were jealous of their jurisdiction and earnest in enforcing justice was the exemption enjoyed by all ranks of the clergy from the authority of the secular tribunals. They were justiciable only by the spiritual Courts, which could pronounce no judgments of blood, and whose leniency towards clerical offenders virtually assured to them immunity from punishment—an immunity long maintained in English jurisprudence under the well-known name of Benefit of Clergy. So complete was the freedom of the priesthood from all responsibility to secular authority that the ingenuity of the doctors was taxed to find excuses for the banishment of Abiathar by Solomon. The evil of this consisted not only in the temptation to crime which it offered to those regularly bred to the Church and performing its functions, but it attracted to the lower orders of the clergy, which were not bound to celibacy or debarred from worldly pursuits, numberless criminals and vagabonds, who were thus enabled to set the officers of justice at defiance. The first defence of a thief or assassin when arrested was to claim that he belonged to the Church and to display his tonsure, and the episcopal officials were vigilant in the defence of these wretches, thus stimulating crime and grievously impeding the administration of justice. Frequent efforts were made by the secular authorities to remedy these evils; but the Church resolutely maintained its prerogatives, provoking quarrels which led to increased antagonism between the laity and the clergy. The *Gravamina* of the German Nation, adopted by the Diet of Nürnberg, in 1522, stated no more than the truth in asserting that this clerical immunity was responsible for countless cases of adultery, robbery, coining, arson, homicide, and false-witness committed by ecclesiastics; and there was peculiar significance in the declaration that, unless the clergy were subjected to the secular

Courts, there was reason to fear an uprising of the people, for no justice was to be had against a clerical offender in the spiritual tribunals. . . .

Under the circumstances the Holy See could inspire neither respect nor confidence. Universal distrust was the rule between the States, and the papacy was merely a State whose pretensions to care for the general welfare of Christendom were recognised as diplomatic hypocrisy. When, in 1462, Pius II took the desperate step of resolving to lead in person the proposed crusade, he explained that this was the only way to convince Europe of his sincerity. When he levied a tithe, he said, for the war with the infidel, appeal was made to a future Council; when he issued indulgences he was accused of greed; whatever was done was attributed to the desire to raise money, and no one trusted the papal word; like a bankrupt trader, he was without credit. This distrust of the papacy with regard to its financial devices for the prosecution of the war with the Turk was universally entertained, and it lent a sharper edge to the dissatisfaction of those called upon to contribute. . . .

In every way the revenues thus enjoyed and squandered by the Curia were scandalous and oppressive. To begin with, the cost of their collection was enormous. The accounts of the papal agent for first-fruits in Hungary, for the year 1320, show that of 1913 florins collected only 732 reached the papal treasury. With a more thorough organisation in later periods the returns were better; but when the device was adopted of employing bankers to collect the proceeds of annates and indulgences, the share allotted to those who conducted the business and made advances, was ruinously large. In the contract for the fateful St Peter's indulgence with the Fuggers of Augsburg, their portion of the receipts was to be fifty *per cent*. Even worse was it when these revenues were farmed out, for the banker who depended for his profits on the extent of his sales or collections was not likely to be overnice in his methods, nor to exercise much restraint over his agents. Europe was overrun with pardon-sellers who had purchased letters empowering them to sell indulgences, whether of a general character or for some church or hospital; and for centuries their lies, their frauds, their exactions, and their filthy living were the cause of the bitterest and most indignant complaints.

Even more demoralising were the revenues derived

from the sale of countless dispensations for marriage within the prohibited degrees, for the holding of pluralities, for the numerous kinds of "irregularities" and other breaches of the canon law; so that its prescriptions might almost seem to have been framed for the purpose of enabling the Holy See to profit by their violation. Not less destructive to morals were the absolutions, which amounted to a sale of pardons for sin of every description, as though the Decalogue had been enacted for this very purpose. There was also a thriving business done in the composition for unjust gains, whereby fraudulent traders, usurers, robbers, and other malefactors, on paying to the Church a portion of their illegal acquisitions, were released from the obligation of making restitution. In every way the power of the keys and the treasure of the merits of Christ were exploited, without any regard for moral consequences. . . .

In fact, one of the most urgent symptoms of the necessity of a new order of things was the complete divorce between religion and morality. There was abundant zeal in debating minute points of faith, but little in evoking from it an exemplary standard of life—as Pius II said of the Conventual Franciscans: they were generally excellent theologians but gave themselves little trouble about virtue. The sacerdotal system, developed by the dialectics of the Schoolmen, had constructed a routine of external observances through which salvation was to be gained not so much by abstinence from sin as by its pardon through the intervention of the priest, whose supernatural powers were in no way impaired by the scandals of his daily life. Except within the pale of the pagan Renaissance, never was there a livelier dread of future punishment, but this punishment was to be escaped, not by amendment but by confession, absolution, and indulgences. This frame of mind is exemplified by the condottiere Vitelozzo Vitelli who, when after a life steeped in crime, he was suddenly strangled by Cesare Borgia, in 1502, felt no more poignant regret than that he could not obtain absolution from the Pope—and that Pope was Alexander VI. Society was thoroughly corrupt—perhaps less so in the lower than in the higher classes—but no one can read the Lenten sermons of the preachers of the time, even with full allowance for rhetorical exaggeration, without recognising that the world has rarely seen a more debased standard of morality than that which prevailed in Italy in the closing years of the Middle Ages. Yet at the same time never were there greater outward manifesta-

tions of devotional zeal. A man like San Giovanni Capistrano could scarce walk the streets of a city without an armed guard to preserve his life from the surging crowds eager to secure a rag of his garments as a relic or to carry away some odour of his holiness by touching him with a stick. Venice, which cared little for an interdict, offered in vain ten thousand ducats, in 1455, for a seamless coat of Christ. Siena and Perugia went to war over the wedding-ring of the Virgin. At no period was there greater faith in the thaumaturgic virtue of images and saintly relics; never were religious solemnities so gorgeously celebrated; never were processions so magnificent or so numerously attended; never were fashionable shrines so largely thronged by pilgrims. In his *Encheiridion Militis Christiani*, written in 1502 and approved by Adrian VI, then head of the University of Louvain, Erasmus had the boldness to protest against this new kind of Judaism which placed its reliance on observances, like magic rites, which drew men away from Christ; and again, in 1519, in a letter to Cardinal Albrecht of Mainz, he declared that religion was degenerating into a more than Judaic formalism of ceremonies, and that there must be a change.

A priesthood trained in this formalism, which had practically replaced the ethical values of Christianity, secure that its supernatural attributes were unaffected by the most flagitious life, and selected by such methods as were practised by the Curia and imitated by the prelates, could not be expected to rise above the standards of the community. Rather, indeed, were the influences, to which the clergy were exposed, adapted to depress them below the average. They were clothed with virtually irresponsible power over their subjects, they were free from the restraints of secular law, and they were condemned to celibacy in times when no man was expected to be continent. For three hundred years it had been the constant complaint that the people were contaminated by their pastors and the complaint continued. . . .

The popular literature of the period similarly reflects this mingled contempt and hatred for the priesthood. The Franciscan Thomas Murner, who subsequently was one of the most savage opponents of Luther, in the curious rhymed sermons which, in 1512, he preached in Frankfort-on-the-Main, and which, under the names of the *Schelmenzunft* and the *Narrenbeschweerung*, had a wide popularity, is never tired of dwelling on the scandals of all classes of the clergy, from bishops to monks and nuns. All are worldly, rapacious, and sensual. When the lay lord has shorn the sheep, the priest comes and fairly disembowels it, the begging friar follows and gets what he can and then the pardoner. If a bishop is in want of money he sends around his fiscal among the parish priests to extort payment for the privilege of keeping their concubines. In the nunneries the sister who has the most children is made the abbess. If Christ were on earth to-day He would be betrayed, and Judas would be reckoned an honest man. The devil is really the ruler of the Church, whose prelates perform his works; they are too ignorant to discharge their duties and require coadjutors — it would be well for them could they likewise have substitutes in hell. The wolf preached and sang mass so as to gather the geese around him, and then seized and ate them; so it is with prelate and priest who promise all things and pretend to care for souls until they get their benefices, when they devour their flocks. The immense applause with which these attacks on the abuses of the Church were everywhere received, and others of a similar character in Eulenspiegel, Sebastian Brant's *Narrenschiff*, Johann Faber's *Tractatus de Ruine Ecclesie Planctu*, and the *Encomium Moriae* of Erasmus, their translation into many languages and wide circulation throughout Europe, show how thoroughly they responded to the popular feeling, how dangerously the Church had forfeited the respect of the masses, and how deeply rooted was the aversion which it had inspired. The priests hated Rome for her ceaseless exactions and the people hated the priests with perhaps even better reason. So bitter was this dislike that, in 1502, Erasmus tells us that among laymen to call a man a cleric or a priest or a monk was an unpardonable insult. . . .

While thus the primary cause of the Reformation is to be sought in the all-pervading corruption of the Church and its oppressive exercise of its supernatural prerogatives, there were other factors conducing to the explosion. Sufficient provocation had long existed, and since the failure at Basel no reasonable man could continue to anticipate relief from conciliar action. The shackles which for centuries had bound the human intellect had to be loosened, before there could be a popular movement of volume sufficient to break with the traditions of the past and boldly tempt the dangers of a new and untried career for humanity. The old reverence for authority had to be weakened, the sense of intellectual independence had to be awakened and the spirit of en-

quiry and of more or less scientific investigation had to be created, before pious and devout men could reach the root of the abuses which caused so much indignation, and could deny the authenticity of the apostolical deposit on which had been erected the venerable and imposing structure of scholastic theology and papal autocracy.

It was the New Learning and the humanistic movement which supplied the impulse necessary for this, and they found conditions singularly favourable for their work. The Church had triumphed so completely over her enemies that the engines of repression had been neglected and had grown rusty, while the Popes were so engrossed in their secular schemes and ambition that they had little thought to waste on the possible tendencies of the fashionable learning which they patronised. Thus there came an atmosphere of free thought, strangely at variance with the rigid dogmatism of the theologians, and even in theology there was a certain latitude of discussion permissible, for the Tridentine decrees had not yet formulated into articles of faith the results of the debates of the Schoolmen since the twelfth century. It is a remarkable proof of the prevailing laxity that Nicholas V commissioned Gianozzo Manetti to make a new translation of the Bible from the original Hebrew and Greek, thus showing that the Vulgate was regarded as insufficient and that it enjoyed no such authority as that attributed to it at Trent. In view of this laxity it is not surprising that in Italy the New Learning assumed various fantastic shapes of belief — the cult of the Genius of Rome by Pomponio Leto and his Academy, the Platonism of Marsiglio Ficino, the practical denial of immortality by Pomponazzi, and the modified Averrhoism of Agostino Nifo. So long as the profits of the Curia or the authority of the Pope remained undisputed there was little disposition to trouble the dreamers and speculators. Savonarola declares, with some rhetorical exaggeration, that culture had supplanted religion in the minds of those to whom the destinies of Christianity were confided, until they lost belief in God, celebrated feasts of the devil, and made a jest of the sacred mysteries. In the polite Court circles of Leo X, we are told, a man was scarce accounted as cultured and well-bred unless he cherished a certain amount of heretical opinion; and after Luther's doctrines had become rigidly defined Melanchthon is said to have looked back with a sigh to the days before the Reformation as to a time when there was freedom of thought. It is true that there was occasional spasmodic repression. Pico della Mirandola, because of thirteen heretical propositions among the nine hundred which he offered to defend in 1487, was obliged to fly to Spain and to make his peace by submission; but, as a rule, the humanists were allowed to air their fancies in peace. When the disputations of the schools on the question of the future life became overbold and created scandal, the Lateran Council, in 1513, forbade the teaching of Averrhoism and of the mortality of the soul; but it did so in terms which placed little restraint on philosophers who shielded themselves behind a perfunctory declaration of submission to the judgment of the Church. . . .

The combination of all these factors rendered an explosion inevitable, and Germany was predestined to be its scene. The ground was better prepared for it there then elsewhere, by the deeper moral and religious earnestness of the people and by the tendencies of the academies and associations with which society was honeycombed. In obedience to these influences the humanistic movement had not been pagan and aesthetic as in Italy, but had addressed itself to the higher emotions and had sought to train the conscience of the individual to recognise his direct responsibility to God and to his fellows. But more potent than all this were the forces arising from the political system of Germany and its relations with the Holy See. The Teutonic spirit of independence had early found expression in the *Sachsenspiegel* and *Sächsische Weichbild*—the laws and customs of Northern Germany—which were resolutely maintained in spite of repeated papal condemnation. Thus not only did the Church inspire there less awe than elsewhere in Europe, but throughout the Middle Ages there had been special causes of antagonism actively at work.

If Italy had suffered bitterly from the *Tedeschi,* Germany had no less reason to hate the papacy. The fatal curse of the so-called Holy Roman Empire hung over both lands. It gave the Emperor a valid right to the suzerainty of the peninsula; it gave the papacy a traditional claim to confirm at its discretion the election of an Emperor. Conflicting and incompatible pretensions rendered impossible a permanent truce between the representatives of Charlemagne and St Peter. Since the age of Gregory VII the consistent policy of Rome had been to cripple the Empire by fomenting internal dissension and rendering impossible the evolution of a strong and centralised government, such as elsewhere in Europe was gradually overcoming the centrifugal forces of feudalism. This policy had been successful and Germany had become a mere geographical expression—a congeries of sovereign princes, petty and great, owning allegiance to an Emperor whose dignity was scarce more than a primacy of honour and whose actual power was to be measured by that of his ancestral territories. The result of this was that Germany lay exposed defenceless to the rapacity and oppression of the Roman Curia. Its multitudinous sovereigns had vindicated their independence at the cost of depriving themselves of the strength to be derived from centralised union. Germany was the ordinary resource of a Pope in financial straits, through the exaction of a tithe, the raising of the annates, or the issue in unstinted volume of the treasure of the merits of Christ in the form of an unremitting stream of indulgences which sucked up as with a sponge the savings of the people. Nor could any steady opposition be offered to the absorption of the ecclesiastical patronage by the Curia, through which benefices were sold or bestowed on the cardinals or their creatures, and no limits could be set on appeals to the Holy See which enlarged its jurisdiction and impoverished pleaders by involving them in interminable and ruinous litigation in the venal Roman Courts. . . .

If Germany was thus the predestined scene of the outbreak, it was also the land in which the chances of success were the greatest. The very political condition which baffled all attempts at self-protection likewise barred the way to the suppression of the movement. A single prince, like the Elector Frederick of Saxony, could protect it in its infancy. As the revolt made progress other princes could join it, whether moved by religious considerations, or by way of maintaining the allegiance of their subjects, or in order to seize the temporalities and pious foundations, or, like Albrecht of Brandenburg, to found a principality and a dynasty. We need not here enquire too closely into the motives of which the League of Schmalkalden was the outcome, and may content ourselves with pointing to the fact that even Charles V was, in spite of the victory of Mühlberg, powerless to restore the imperial supremacy or to impose his will on the Protestant States.

The progress of the Reformation, and still more so that of the Counter-Reformation, lie outside the limits of the present chapter; but it may be concluded by a few words suggesting why the abuses which, in the sixteenth century, could only be cured by rending the Church in twain, have to so large an extent disappeared since the Reformation, leading many enthusiasts to feel regret that the venerable ecclesiastical structure was not purified from within—that reform was not adopted in place of schism. The abuses under which Christendom groaned were too inveterate, too firmly entrenched, and too profitable to be removed by any but the sternest and sharpest remedies.

PRESERVED SMITH

ANOTHER VIEW FROM THE OUTSIDE

The following passage is from the introductory chapter of *The Age of the Reformation* by Preserved Smith (1880–1941), who may be taken as a fair representative of the reaction of his generation of Reformation scholars against the generation of Henry Charles Lea. Like Lea, Smith deals in this selection with the financial abuses of the old church, with its secularism, with the immorality of the clergy, and the consequent evil reputation of the clergy in the eyes of laymen on the eve of the Reformation. He even cites the same passage from Pius II which Lea had used. He points out, like Lea, the barrenness of the religious formalism that the sixteenth century had inherited from the medieval church and the inability of that formalism to cope with the vigorous new spirit beginning to stir in the generation of Martin Luther.

But there are fundamental differences between Lea and Smith, beginning with their basic assumptions. Smith denies that the "principal cause" of the Reformation "was the corruption of the church," an assumption diametrically opposed to that of Lea. Thus, Smith's recitation of many of the same charges and arguments that Lea had used stemmed from a very different motive: "though the corruptions of the church were not a main cause of the Protestant secession, they furnished good excuses for attack." What Lea presented as basic causes, Smith regards as pretexts.

Another difference the student should note is the difference in tone between the two selections. Where Lea exhibits outraged moral conscience, Smith adopts a tone almost of mocking superiority. For he belonged to a generation of rationalistic historians who thought they were beginning at last to understand the past in terms of larger social and economic patterns which had not been understood either by their predecessors or by their subjects, the blind wretches who had struggled vainly against those patterns in ages past. Thus, while Smith disagrees with the external view taken by Lea, his own view of the causes of the Reformation is itself external. As he says in the concluding chapter of this same book, "The Reformation, like the Renaissance and the sixteenth-century Social Revolution, was but the consequence of the operation of antecedent changes in environment and habit, intellectual and economic."

In the eyes of the early Protestants the Reformation was a return to primitive Christianity and its principal cause was the corruption of the church. That there was great depravity in the church as elsewhere cannot be doubted, but there are several reasons for thinking that it could not have been an important cause for the loss of so many of her sons. In the first place there is no good ground for believing that the moral condition of the priesthood was worse in 1500 than it had been for a long time; indeed, there is good evidence to the contrary, that things were tending to improve, if not at Rome yet in many parts of Christendom. If objectionable practices of the priests had been a sufficient cause for the secession of whole nations, the Reformation would have come long before it actually did. Again, there is good reason to doubt that the mere abuse of an institution has ever led to its complete otherthrow; as long as the institution is regarded as necessary, it is rather mended than ended. Thirdly, many of the acts that seem corrupt to us, gave little offence to contemporaries, for they were universal. If the church sold offices and justice, so did the civil governments. If the clergy lived impure lives, so did the laity. Probably the standard of the church (save in special circumstances) was no worse than that of civil life, and in some respects it was rather more decent. Finally, there is some reason to suspect of exaggeration the charges preferred by the innovators. Like all reformers they made the most of their enemy's faults. Invective like theirs is common to every generation and to all spheres of life. It is true that the denunciation of the priesthood comes not only from Protestants and satirists, but from popes and councils and canonized saints, and that it bulks large in medieval literature. Nevertheless, it is both a *priori* probable and to some extent historically verifiable that the evil was more noisy, not more potent, than the good. But though the corruptions of the church were not a main cause of the Protestant secession, they furnished good excuses for attack; the Reformers were scandalized by the divergence of the practice and the pretensions of the official representatives of Christianity, and their attack was envenomed and the break made easier thereby. It is therefore necessary to say a few words about those abuses at which public opinion then took most offence.

Many of these were connected with money. The common man's conscience was wounded by the smart in his purse. The wealth of the church was enormous, though exaggerated by those contemporaries who estimated it at one-third of the total real estate of Western Europe. In addition to revenues from her own land the church collected tithes and taxes, including "Peter's pence" in England, Scandinavia and Poland. The clergy paid dues to the curia, among them the *servitia* charged on the bishops and the annates levied on the income of the first year for each appointee to high ecclesiastical office, and the price for the archbishop's pall. The priests recouped themselves by charging high fees for their ministrations. At a time when the Christian ideal was one of "apostolic poverty" the riches of the clergy were often felt as a scandal to the pious.

Though the normal method of appointment to civil office was sale, it was felt as a special abuse in the church and was branded by the name of simony. Leo X made no less than 500,000 ducats annually from the sale of more than 2000 offices, most of which, being sinecures, eventually came to be regarded as annuities, with a salary amounting to about 10 per cent. of the purchase price.

Justice was also venal, in the church no less than in the state. Pardon was obtainable for all crimes for, as a papal vice-chamberlain phrased it, "The Lord wishes not the death of a sinner but that he should pay and live." Dispensations from the laws against marriage within the prohibited degrees were sold. Thus an ordinary man had to pay 16 grossi for dispensation to marry a woman who stood in "spiritual relationship" to him; a noble had to pay 20 grossi for the same privilege, and a prince or duke 30 grossi. First cousins might marry for the payment of 27 grossi; an uncle and niece for from three to four ducats, though this was later raised to as much as sixty ducats, at least for nobles. Marriage within the first degree of affinity (a deceased wife's mother or daughter by another husband) was at one time sold for about ten ducats; marriage within the second degree was permitted for from 300 to 600 grossi. Hardly necessary to add, as was done: "Note well, that dispensations or graces of this sort are not given to poor people." Dispensations from vows and from the requirements of ecclesiastical law, as for example those relating to fasting, were also to be obtained at a price.

One of the richest sources of ecclesiastical revenue was the sale of indulgences, or the remission by the pope of the temporal penalties of sin, both penance in this life and the pains of purgatory. The practice of giving these pardons first arose as a means of assuring heaven to those warriors who fell fighting the infidel. In 1300 Boniface VIII granted a plenary indulgence to all who made the pilgrimage to the jubilee at Rome, and the golden harvest reaped on this occasion induced his successors to take the same means of imparting spiritual graces to the faithful at frequent intervals. In the fourteenth century the pardons were extended to all who contributed a sum of money to a pious purpose, whether they came to Rome or not, and, as the agents who were sent out to distribute these pardons were also given power to confess and absolve, the papal letters were naturally regarded as no less than tickets of admission to heaven. In the thirteenth century the theologians had discovered that there was at the disposal of the church and her head an abundant "treasury of the merits of Christ and the saints," which might be applied vicariously to anyone by the pope. In the fifteenth century the claimed power to free living men from purgatory was extended to the dead, and this soon became one of the most profitable branches of the "holy trade."

The means of obtaining indulgences varied. Sometimes they were granted to those who made a pilgrimage or who would read a pious book. Sometimes they were used to raise money for some public work, a hospital or a bridge. But more and more they became an ordinary means for raising revenue for the curia. How thoroughly commercialized the business of selling grace and remission of the penalties of sin had become is shown by the fact that the agents of the pope were often bankers who organized the sales on purely business lines in return for a percentage of the net receipts plus the indirect profits accruing to those who handle large sums. Of the net receipts the financiers usually got about ten per cent.; an equal amount was given to the emperor or other civil ruler for permitting the pardoners to enter his territory; commissions were also paid to the local bishop and clergy, and of course the pedlars of the pardons received a proportion of the profits in order to stimulate their zeal. On the average from thirty to forty-five per cent. of the gross receipts were turned into the Roman treasury.

It is natural that public opinion should have come to regard indulgences with aversion. Their bad moral effect was too obvious to be disregarded, the compounding with sin for a payment destined to satisfy the greed of unscrupulous prelates. Their economic effects were also noticed, the draining of the country of money with which further to enrich a corrupt Italian city. Many rulers forbade their sale in their territories, because, as Duke George of Saxony, a good Catholic, expressed it, before Luther was heard of, "they cheated the simple layman of his soul." Hutten mocked at Pope Julius II for selling to others the heaven he could not win himself. Pius II was obliged to confess: "If we send ambassadors to ask aid of the princes, they are mocked; if we impose a tithe on the clergy, appeal is made to a future council; if we publish an indulgence and invite contributions in return for spiritual favors, we are charged with greed. People think all is done merely for the sake of extorting money. No one trusts us. We have no more credit than a bankrupt merchant."

Much is said in the literature of the latter Middle Ages about the immorality of the clergy. This class has always been severely judged because of its high pretensions. Moreover the vow of celibacy was too hard to keep for most men and for some women; that many priests, monks and nuns broke it cannot be doubted. And yet there was a sprinkling of saintly parsons like him of whom Chaucer said

Who Christes lore and his apostles twelve
He taught, but first he folwed it himselve,

and there were many others who kept up at least the appearance of decency. But here, as always, the bad attracted more attention than the good.

The most reliable data on the subject are found in the records of church visitations, both those undertaken by the Reformers and those occasionally attempted by the Catholic prelates of the earlier period. Everywhere it was proved that a large proportion of the clergy were both wofully ignorant and morally unworthy. Besides the priests who had concubines, there were many given to drink and some who kept taverns, gaming rooms and worse places. Plunged in gross ignorance and superstition, those blind leaders of the blind, who won great reputations as exorcists or as wizards, were unable to understand the Latin service, and sometimes to repeat even the Lord's prayer or creed in any language.

The Reformation, like most other revolutions, came

not at the lowest ebb of abuse, but at a time when the tide had already begun to run, and to run strongly, in the direction of improvement. One can hardly find a sweeter, more spiritual religion anywhere than that set forth in Erasmus's *Enchiridion,* or in More's *Utopia,* or than that lived by Vitrier and Colet. Many men, who had not attained to this conception of the true beauty of the gospel, were yet thoroughly disgusted with things as they were and quite ready to substitute a new and purer conception and practice for the old, mechanical one.

Evidence for this is the popularity of the Bible and other devotional books. Before 1500 there were nearly a hundred editions of the Latin Vulgate, and a number of translations into German and French. There were also nearly a hundred editions, in Latin and various vernaculars, of *The Imitation of Christ.* There was so flourishing a crop of devotional handbooks that no others could compete with them in popularity. For those who could not read there were the *Biblia Pauperum,* picture-books with a minimum of text, and there were sermons by popular preachers. If some of these tracts and homilies were crude and superstitious, others were filled with a spirit of love and honesty. Whereas the passion for pilgrimages and relics seemed to increase, there were men of clear vision to denounce the attendant evils. A new feature was the foundation of lay brotherhoods, like that of the Common Life, with the purpose of cultivating a good character in the world, and of rendering social service. The number of these brotherhoods was great and their popularity general.

Had the forces already at work within the church been allowed to operate, probably much of the moral reform desired by the best Catholics would have been accomplished quietly without the violent rending of Christian unity that actually took place. But the fact is, that such reforms never would or could have satisfied the spirit of the age. Men were not only shocked by the abuses in the church, but they had outgrown some of her ideals. Not all of her teaching, nor most of it, had become repugnant to them, for it has often been pointed out that the Reformers kept more of the doctrines of Catholicism than they threw away, but in certain respects they repudiated, not the abuse but the very principle on which the church acted. In four respects, particularly, the ideals of the new age were incompatible with those of the Roman communion.

The first of these was the sacramental theory of salvation and its corollary, the sacerdotal power. According to Catholic doctrine grace is imparted to the believer by means of certain rites: baptism, confirmation, the eucharist, penance, extreme unction, holy orders, and matrimony. Baptism is the necessary prerequisite to the enjoyment of the others, for without it the unwashed soul, whether heathen or child of Christian parents, would go to eternal fire; but the "most excellent of the sacraments" is the eucharist, in which Christ is mysteriously sacrificed by the priest to the Father and his body and blood eaten and drunk by the worshippers. Without these rites there was no salvation, and they acted automatically *(ex opere operato)* on the soul of the faithful who put no active hindrance in their way. Save baptism, they could be administered only by priests, a special caste with "an indelible character" marking them off from the laity. Needless to remark the immense power that this doctrine gave the clergy in a believing age. They were made the arbiters of each man's eternal destiny, and their moral character had no more to do with their binding and loosing sentence than does the moral character of a secular officer affect his official acts. Add to this that the priests were unbound by ties of family, that by confession they entered into everyone's private life, that they were not amenable to civil justice—and their position as a privileged order was secure. The growing self-assurance and enlightenment of a nascent individualism found this distinction intolerable.

Another element of medieval Catholicism to clash with the developing powers of the new age was its pessimistic and ascetic other-worldliness. The ideal of the church was monastic; all the pleasures of this world, all its pomps and learning and art were but snares to seduce men from salvation. Reason was called a barren tree but faith was held to blossom like the rose. Wealth was shunned as dangerous, marriage deprecated as a necessary evil. Fasting, scourging, celibacy, solitude, were cultivated as the surest roads to heaven. If a good layman might barely shoulder his way through the strait and narrow gate, the highest graces and heavenly rewards were vouchsafed to the faithful monk. All this grated harshly on the minds of the generations that began to find life glorious and happy, not evil but good.

Third, the worship of the saints, which had once been a stepping-stone to higher things, was now widely regarded as a stumbling-block. Though far from a scientific conception of natural law, many men had become sufficiently monistic in their philosophy to see in the current hagiolatry a sort of polytheism. Erasmus freely drew the parallel between the saints and the heathen deities, and he and others scourged the grossly materialistic form which this worship often took. If we may believe him, fugitive nuns prayed for help in hiding their sin; merchants for a rich haul; gamblers for luck; and prostitutes for generous patrons. Margaret of Navarre tells as an actual fact of a man who prayed for help in seducing his neighbor's wife, and similar instances of perverted piety are not wanting. The passion for the relics of the saints led to an enormous traffic in spurious articles. There appeared to be enough of the wood of the true cross, said Erasmus, to make a ship; there were exhibited five shin-bones of the ass on which Christ rode, whole bottles of the Virgin's milk, and several complete bits of skin saved from the circumcision of Jesus.

Finally, patriots were no longer inclined to tolerate the claims of the popes to temporal power. The church had become, in fact, an international state, with its monarch, its representative legislative assemblies, its laws and its code. It was not a voluntary society, for if citizens were not born into it they were baptized into it before they could exercise any choice. It kept prisons and passed sentence (virtually if not nominally) of death; it treated with other governments as one power with another; it took principalities and kingdoms in fief. It was supported by involuntary contributions.

The expanding world had burst the bands of the old church. It needed a new spiritual frame, and this frame was largely supplied by the Reformation. Prior to that revolution there had been several distinct efforts to transcend or to revolt from the limitations imposed by the Catholic faith; this was done by the mystics, by the pre-reformers, by the patriots and by the humanists.

ROLAND H. BAINTON

A SYMPATHETIC VIEW FROM THE INSIDE

The following passage from the best-selling biography, *Here I Stand: A Life of Martin Luther,* by Roland H. Bainton represents the nearly complete departure of contemporary scholars from the "environmental" or "external" analysis of the causes of the Reformation such as we have seen in the excerpt from Henry Charles Lea and, to a degree, in that from Preserved Smith. Bainton's view may in contrast be called an essentially interior view. The Reformation was to him neither primarily a social revolution nor the result of the movement of massive, impersonal economic forces. It was primarily a religious revolt and it was generated in the religious disquiet of a single man—Martin Luther. As Bainton says, ". . . Luther was above all else a man of religion. The great outward crises of his life which bedazzle the eyes of dramatic biographers were to Luther himself trivial in comparison with the inner upheavals of his questing after God." By the same token, such things as the corruption of the church, the peculiar socio-political configuration of the Holy Roman Empire, the emergence of capitalism, and the intellectual revolution of Renaissance humanism, while perhaps not trivial, must be relegated by such a view to the status of contributing background factors rather than primary causes of the Reformation.

In this selection Bainton deals in some detail with the series of inner crises in

Luther's young manhood which led him to that "revelation" which may be called the starting point of the Reformation. The first of these crises was the terror-stricken vow to become a monk, made in the midst of a thunderstorm. The second was the "terror of the holy" that overtook him at the celebration of his first mass. The third was his realization of a "way out" for him from the hopelessness of man's sin and the awfulness of God's majesty through a new understanding of scripture, in particular of the famous passage from Romans which "became to me a gate to heaven" and the origin of the cardinal Lutheran doctrine of justification by faith.

On a sultry day in July of the year 1505 a lonely traveler was trudging over a parched road on the outskirts of the Saxon village of Stotternheim. He was a young man, short but sturdy, and wore the dress of a university student. As he approached the village, the sky became overcast. Suddenly there was a shower, then a crashing storm. A bolt of lightning rived the gloom and knocked the man to the ground. Struggling to rise, he cried in terror, "St. Anne help me! I will become a monk."

The man who thus called upon a saint was later to repudiate the cult of the saints. He who vowed to become a monk was later to renounce monasticism. A loyal son of the Catholic Church, he was later to shatter the structure of medieval Catholicism. A devoted servant of the pope, he was later to identify the popes with Antichrist. For this young man was Martin Luther.

His demolition was the more devastating because it reinforced disintegrations already in progress. Nationalism was in process of breaking the political unities when the Reformation destroyed the religious. Yet this paradoxical figure revived the Christian consciousness of Europe. In his day, as Catholic historians all agree, the popes of the Renaissance were secularized, flippant, frivolous, sensual, magnificent, and unscrupulous. The intelligentsia did not revolt against the Church because the Church was so much of their mind and mood as scarcely to warrant a revolt. Politics were emancipated from any concern for the faith to such a degree that the Most Christian King of France and His Holiness the Pope did not disdain a military alliance with the Sultan against the Holy Roman Empire. Luther changed all this. Religion became again a dominant factor even in politics for another century and a half. Men cared enough for the faith to die for it and to kill for it. If there is any sense remaining of Christian

civilization in the West, this man Luther in no small measure deserves the credit.

Very naturally he is a controversial figure. The multitudinous portrayals fall into certain broad types already delineated in his own generation. His followers hailed him as the prophet of the Lord and the deliverer of Germany. His opponents on the Catholic side called him the son of perdition and the demolisher of Christendom. The agrarian agitators branded him as the sycophant of the princes, and the radical sectaries compared him to Moses, who led the children of Israel out of Egypt and left them to perish in the wilderness. But such judgments belong to an epilogue rather than a prologue. The first endeavor must be to understand the man.

One will not move far in this direction unless one recognizes at the outset that Luther was above all else a man of religion. The great outward crises of his life which bedazzle the eyes of dramatic biographers were to Luther himself trivial in comparison with the inner upheavals of his questing after God. For that reason this study may appropriately begin with his first acute religious crisis in 1505 rather than with his birth in 1483. . . .

The Church taught that no sensible person would wait until his deathbed to make an act of contrition and plead for grace. From beginning to end the only secure course was to lay hold of every help the Church had to offer: sacraments, pilgrimages, indulgences, the intercession of the saints. Yet foolish was the man who relied solely on the good offices of the heavenly intercessors if he had done nothing to insure their favor!

And what better could he do than take the cowl? . . .

From *Here I Stand* by Roland H. Bainton, pp. 21–22, 30–34, 37, 39, 41–42, 44, 60–66. Copyright 1950 by Pierce & Smith (Abingdon Press). Reprinted by permission of Abingdon Press.

These were the ideas on which Luther had been nurtured. There was nothing peculiar in his beliefs or his responses save their intensity. His depression over the prospect of death was acute but by no means singular. The man who was later to revolt against monasticism became a monk for exactly the same reason as thousands of others, namely, in order to save his soul. The immediate occasion of his resolve to enter the cloister was the unexpected encounter with death on that sultry July day in 1505. He was then twenty-one and a student at the University of Erfurt. As he returned to school after a visit with his parents, sudden lightning struck him to earth. In that single flash he saw the denouement of the drama of existence. There was God the all-terrible, Christ the inexorable, and all the leering fiends springing from their lurking places in pond and wood that with sardonic cachinnations they might seize his shock of curly hair and bolt him into hell. It was no wonder that he cried out to his father's saint, patroness of miners, "St. Anne help me! I will become a monk." . . .

Luther in later life remarked that during the first year in the monastery the Devil is very quiet. We have every reason to believe that his own inner tempest subsided and that during his novitiate he was relatively placid. This may be inferred from the mere fact that at the end of the year he was permitted to make his profession. The probationary period was intended to give the candidate an opportunity to test himself and to be tested. He was instructed to search his heart and declare any misgivings as to his fitness for the monastic calling. If his companions and superiors believed him to have no vocation, they would reject him. Since Luther was accepted, we may safely assume that neither he nor his brethren saw any reason to suppose that he was not adapted to the monastic life. . . .

Thus he might have continued had he not been overtaken by another thunderstorm, this time of the spirit. The occasion was the saying of his first mass. He had been selected for the priesthood by his superior and commenced his functions with this initial celebration.

The occasion was always an ordeal because the mass is the focal point of the Church's means of grace. Here on the altar bread and wine become the flesh and blood of God, and the sacrifice of Calvary is re-enacted. The priest who performs the miracle of transforming the elements enjoys a power and

privilege denied even to angels. The whole difference between the clergy and the laity rests on this. The superiority of the Church over the state likewise is rooted here, for what king or emperor ever conferred upon mankind a boon comparable to that bestowed by the humblest minister at the altar?

Well might the young priest tremble to perform a rite by which God would appear in human form. But many had done it, and the experience of the centuries enabled the manuals to foresee all possible tremors and prescribe the safeguards. The celebrant must be concerned, though not unduly, about the forms. . . .

The day began with the chiming of the cloister bells and the chanting of the psalm, "O sing unto the Lord a new song." Luther took his place before the altar and began to recite the introductory portion of the mass until he came to the words, "We offer unto thee, the living, the true, the eternal God." He related afterward:

At these words I was utterly stupefied and terror-stricken. I thought to myself, "With what tongue shall I address such Majesty, seeing that all men ought to tremble in the presence of even an earthly prince? Who am I, that I should lift up mine eyes or raise my hands to the divine Majesty? The angels surround him. At his nod the earth trembles. And shall I, a miserable little pygmy, say 'I want this, I ask for that'? For I am dust and ashes and full of sin and I am speaking to the living, eternal and the true God."

The terror of the Holy, the horrors of Infinitude, smote him like a new lightning bolt, and only through a fearful restraint could he hold himself at the altar to the end.

The man of our secularized generation may have difficulty in understanding the tremors of his medieval forebear. There are indeed elements in the religion of Luther of a very primitive character, which hark back to the childhood of the race. He suffered from the savage's fear of a malevolent deity, the enemy of men, capricious, easily and unwittingly offended if sacred places be violated or magical formulas mispronounced. His was the fear of ancient Israel before the ark of the Lord's presence. Luther felt similarly toward the sacred host of the Savior's body; and when it was carried in procession, panic took hold of him. His God was the God who inhabited the storm clouds brooding on the brow of Sinai, into whose presence Moses could not enter with unveiled face and live. Luther's experience, however, far exceeds the primitive and should not be so unintelligible to the modern man who, gazing upon the uncharted nebulae through instruments of his own devising, recoils with a sense of abject littleness.

Luther's tremor was augmented by the recognition of unworthiness. "I am dust and ashes and full of sin." Creatureliness and imperfection alike oppressed him. Toward God he was at once attracted and repelled. Only in harmony with the Ultimate could he find peace. But how could a pigmy stand before divine Majesty; how could a transgressor confront divine Holiness? Before God the high and God the holy Luther was stupefied. For such an experience he had a word which has as much right to be carried over into English as *Blitzkrieg*. The word he used was *Anfechtung*, for which there is no English equivalent. It may be a trial sent by God to test man, or an assault by the Devil to destroy man. It is all the doubt, turmoil, pang, tremor, panic, despair, desolation, and desperation which invade the spirit of man.

Utterly limp, he came from the altar to the table where his father and the guests would make merry with the brothers. After shuddering at the unapproachableness of the heavenly Father he now craved some word of assurance from the earthly father. How his heart would be warmed to hear from the lips of old Hans that his resentment had entirely passed, and that he was now cordially in accord with his son's decision! They sat down to meat together, and Martin, as if he were still a little child, turned and said, "Dear father, why were you so contrary to my becoming a monk? And perhaps you are not quite satisfied even now. The life is so quiet and godly."

This was too much for old Hans, who had been doing his best to smother his rebellion. He flared up before all the doctors and the masters and the guests, "You learned scholar, have you never read in the Bible that you should honor your father and your mother? And here you have left me and your dear mother to look after ourselves in our old age." . . .

This second upheaval of the spirit set up in Luther an inner turmoil which was to end in the abandonment of the cowl, but not until after a long interval. In fact he continued to wear the monastic habit for three years after his excommunication. Altogether

he was garbed as a monk for nineteen years. His development was gradual, and we are not to imagine him in perpetual torment and never able to say mass without terror. He pulled himself together and went on with the appointed round and with whatever new duties were assigned. The prior, for example, informed him that he should resume his university studies in order to qualify for the post of lector in the Augustinian order. He took all such assignments in stride.

But the problem of the alienation of man from God had been renewed in altered form.

Luther set himself to learn and expound the Scriptures. On August 1, 1513, he commenced his lectures on the book of Psalms. In the fall of 1515 he was lecturing on St. Paul's Epistle to the Romans. The Epistle to the Galatians was treated throughout 1516–17. These studies proved to be for Luther the Damascus road. The third great religious crisis which resolved his turmoil was as the still small voice compared to the earthquake of the first upheaval in the thunderstorm at Stotternheim and the fire of the second tremor which consumed him at the saying of his first mass. No *coup de foudre*, no heavenly apparition, no religious ceremony, precipitated the third crisis. The place was no lonely road in a blinding storm, nor even the holy altar, but simply the study in the tower of the Augustinian monastery. The solution to Luther's problems came in the midst of the performance of the daily task.

His first lectures were on the book of Psalms. We must bear in mind his method of reading the Psalms and the Old Testament as a whole. For him, as for his time, it was a Christian book foreshadowing the death of the Redeemer.

The reference to Christ was unmistakable when he came to the twenty-second psalm, the first verse of which was recited by Christ as he expired upon the cross. "My God, my God, why hast thou forsaken me?" What could be the meaning of this? Christ evidently felt himself to be forsaken, abandoned by God, deserted. Christ too had *Anfechtungen*. The utter desolation which Luther said he could not endure for more than a tenth of an hour and live had been experienced by Christ himself as he died. Rejected of men, he was rejected also of God. How much worse this must have been than the scourging, the thorns, the nails! In the garden he sweat blood as he did not upon the cross. Christ's descent into hell was nothing other than this sense of alienation from God. Christ had suffered what Luther suffered, or rather Luther was finding himself in what Christ had suffered, even as Albrecht Dürer painted himself as the Man of Sorrows.

Why should Christ have known such desperation? Luther knew perfectly well why he himself had had them: he was weak in the presence of the Mighty; he was impure in the presence of the Holy; he had blasphemed the Divine Majesty. But Christ was not weak; Christ was not impure; Christ was not impious. Why then should he have been so overwhelmed with desolation? The only answer must be that Christ took to himself the iniquity of us all. He who was without sin for our sakes became sin and so identified himself with us as to participate in our alienation. He who was truly man so sensed his solidarity with humanity as to feel himself along with mankind estranged from the All Holy. What a new picture this is of Christ! Where, then, is the judge, sitting upon the rainbow to condemn sinners? He is still the judge. He must judge, as truth judges error and light darkness; but in judging he suffers with those whom he must condemn and feels himself with them subject to condemnation. The judge upon the rainbow has become the derelict upon the cross.

A new view also of God is here. The All Terrible is the All Merciful too. Wrath and love fuse upon the cross. The hideousness of sin cannot be denied or forgotten; but God, who desires not that a sinner should die but that he should turn and live, has found the reconciliation in the pangs of bitter death. It is not that the Son by his sacrifice has placated the irate Father; it is not primarily that the Master by his self-abandoning goodness has made up for our deficiency. It is that in some inexplicable way, in the utter desolation of the forsaken Christ, God was able to reconcile the world to himself. This does not mean that all the mystery is clear. God is still shrouded at times in thick darkness. There are almost two Gods, the inscrutable God whose ways are past finding out and the God made known to us in Christ. He is still a consuming fire, but he burns that he may purge and chasten and heal. He is not a God of idle whim, because the cross is not the last word. He who gave his Son unto death also raised him up and will raise us with him, if with him we die to sin that we may rise to newness of life.

Who can understand this? Philosophy is unequal to it. Only faith can grasp so high a mystery. This is the foolishness of the cross which is hid from the wise and prudent. Reason must retire. She cannot understand that "God hides his power in weakness, his wisdom in folly, his goodness in severity, his justice in sins, his mercy in anger."

How amazing that God in Christ should do all this; that the Most High, the Most Holy should be the All Loving too; that the ineffable Majesty should stoop to take upon himself our flesh, subject to hunger and cold, death and desperation. We see him lying in the feedbox of a donkey, laboring in a carpenter's shop, dying a derelict under the sins of the world. The gospel is not so much a miracle as a marvel, and every line is suffused with wonder.

What God first worked in Christ, that he must work also in us. If he who had done no wrong was forsaken on the cross, we who are truly alienated from God must suffer a deep hurt. We are not for that reason to upbraid, since the hurt is for our healing.

Repentance which is occupied with thoughts of peace is hypocrisy. There must be a great earnestness about it and a deep hurt if the old man is to be put off. When lightning strikes a tree or a man, it does two things at once — it rends the tree and swiftly slays the man. But it also turns the face of the dead man and the broken branches of the tree itself toward heaven. . . . We seek to be saved, and God in order that he may save rather damns. . . . They are damned who flee damnation, for Christ was of all the saints the most damned and forsaken.

The contemplation of the cross had convinced Luther that God is neither malicious nor capricious. If, like the Samaritan, God must first pour into our wounds the wine that smarts, it is that he may thereafter use the oil that soothes. But there still remains the problem of the justice of God. Wrath can melt into mercy, and God will be all the more the Christian God; but if justice be dissolved in leniency, how can he be the just God whom Scripture describes? The study of the apostle Paul proved at this point of inestimable value to Luther and at the same time confronted him with the final stumbling block because Paul unequivocally speaks of the justice of God. At the very expression Luther trembled. Yet he persisted in grappling with Paul, who plainly had agonized over precisely his problem and had found a solution. Light broke at last through the examination of exact shades of meaning in the Greek language. One understands why Luther could never join those who discarded the humanist tools of scholarship. In the

Greek of the Pauline epistle the word "justice" has a double sense, rendered in English by "justice" and "justification." The former is a strict enforcement of the law, as when a judge pronounces the appropriate sentence. Justification is a process of the sort which sometimes takes place if the judge suspends the sentence, places the prisoner on parole, expresses confidence and personal interest in him, and thereby instills such resolve that the man is reclaimed and justice itself ultimately better conserved than by the exaction of a pound of flesh. Similarly the moral improvement issuing from the Christian experience of regeneration, even though it falls far short of perfection, yet can be regarded as a vindication of the justice of God.

But from here on any human analogy breaks down. God does not condition his forgiveness upon the expectation of future fulfillment. And man is not put right with God by any achievement, whether present or foreseen. On man's side the one requisite is faith, which means belief that God was in Christ seeking to save; trust that God will keep his promises; and commitment to his will and way. Faith is not an achievement. It is a gift. Yet it comes only through the hearing and study of the Word. In this respect Luther's own experience was made normative. For the whole process of being made new Luther took over from Paul the terminology of "justification by faith."

These are Luther's own words:

I greatly longed to understand Paul's Epistle to the Romans and nothing stood in the way but that one expression, "the justice of God," because I took it to mean that justice whereby God is just and deals justly in punishing the unjust. My situation was that, although an impeccable monk, I stood before God as a sinner troubled in conscience, and I had no confidence that my merit would assuage him. Therefore I did not love a just and angry God, but rather hated and murmured against him. Yet I clung to the dear Paul and had a great yearning to know what he meant.

Night and day I pondered until I saw the connection between the justice of God and the statement that "the just shall live by his faith." Then I grasped that the justice of God is that righteousness by which through grace and sheer mercy God justifies us through faith. Thereupon I felt myself to be reborn and to have gone through open doors into paradise. The whole of Scripture took on a new meaning, and whereas before the "justice of God" had filled me with hate, now it became to me inexpressibly sweet in greater love. This passage of Paul became to me a gate to heaven. . . .

If you have a true faith that Christ is your Saviour, then at once you have a gracious God, for faith leads you in and opens up God's heart and will, that you should see pure grace and overflowing love. This it is to behold God in faith that you should look upon his fatherly, friendly heart, in which there is no anger nor ungraciousness. He who sees God as angry does not see him rightly but looks only on a curtain, as if a dark cloud had been drawn across his face.

Luther had come into a new view of Christ and a new view of God. He had come to love the suffering Redeemer and the God unveiled on Calvary. But were they after all powerful enough to deliver him from all the hosts of hell? The cross had resolved the conflict between the wrath and the mercy of God, and Paul had reconciled for him the inconsistency of the justice and the forgiveness of God, but what of the conflict between God and the Devil? Is God lord of all, or is he himself impeded by demonic hordes? Such questions a few years ago would have seemed to modern man but relics of medievalism, and fear of demons was dispelled simply by denying their existence. Today so much of the sinister has engulfed us that we are prone to wonder whether perhaps there may not be malignant forces in the heavenly places. All those who have known the torments of mental disorder well understand the imagery of satanic hands clutching to pull them to their doom. Luther's answer was not scientific but religious. He did not dissipate the demons by turning on an electric light, because for him they had long ago been routed when the veil of the temple was rent and the earth quaked and darkness descended upon the face of the land. Christ in his utter anguish had fused the wrath and the mercy of God, and put to flight all the legions of Satan.

HARTMANN GRISAR

A HOSTILE VIEW FROM THE INSIDE

In the following passage another scholar, the Jesuit Hartmann Grisar (1845 – 1932) sees the basic cause or, in this case, the basic blame for the Reformation in the same critical period of Luther's life and in much the same series of events as does Bainton. The passage is taken from his *Martin Luther, His Life and Work,* a somewhat abbreviated and sharpened work based upon Grisar's larger and more famous *Luther,* Eng. tr. E. M. Lamond, 6 vols. (London: Herder, 1913 – 17). Grisar is probably the most important modern Catholic scholar of Lutheranism but he is still very much in the mainstream of a hostile tradition going back to the age of the Reformation itself. While some of the partisan reactions of the traditional Catholic biography no longer enjoy a place in Grisar's pages, his "home base" in interpreting Luther and the Reformation is always Catholic orthodoxy, understandably enough, and from this base his view of Luther is often hostile. This is true in spite of his considerable and perceptive insight into the psychology of religion, in spite of his candid admission that "the existing discontent" with the condition of the church "accelerated the revolution," and in spite even of his formidable knowledge of his subject. Largely then as a result of Grisar's point of view there emerges from his account of the same events quite a different picture of Martin Luther. Instead of the frightened and solitary religious striving against "the terror of the holy" and finally finding illumination in his understanding of St. Paul, we find a rebel, wilfully distorting the rules of his own order and arrogantly preferring his own interpretation of scripture and Christian tradition to that of the church. Grisar finds Luther selfish, overbearing, and neglectful of his proper religious duties. He finds him misled by his attraction to mysticism and excessive in his ascetic exercise. In short, what Grisar builds is a case of Luther's suffering from "a serious aberration." What other interpretation is open to him?

LUTHER'S FIRST BIBLICAL LECTURES— HIS MYSTICISM

The first lectures of the new professor of Biblical science were delivered in the years 1513 to 1515 and dealt with the Psalms. Those of his pupils who were monks and had to recite the Divine Office in choir, were particularly interested in the Psalms. The interpretation offered them by Luther has been preserved in his works. It is, however, not an explanation made in accordance with our modern ideas, but rather a collection of allegorical and moral sentences based upon the text, as was the custom in those days. Luther justly abandoned this allegorical manner of interpretation in later life. Non-Catholics have endeavored, without justification, to discover in these lectures the germs of his later teaching. His manner of expression is often indefinite and elastic and generally more rhetorical than theologically correct. His teaching on justification, grace, and free will, is, like his other doctrines, still fundamentally Catholic, or at least can be so interpreted if the dog-

From Hartmann Grisar, S. J., *Martin Luther, His Life and Work,* adapted from the 2nd German edition by F. J. Eble, ed. A. Preuss (Westminster, Md., 1950), pp. 58–70. Reprinted by permission of The Newman Press.

matic teaching of the Church is properly understood. Still there are a few indications of the coming change. Take, for instance, his emphatic assertion that Christ died for all men and his exaggerated opposition to the doctrine of justification by means of good works. In general these lectures reveal talent, religious zeal, and fertile imagination — qualities which must have charmed his auditors to an unusual degree.

Luther was very amiable and communicative towards his pupils. His entire personality, the very gleam of his eye, exerted a certain fascination over those who associated with him.

The young professor of Sacred Scripture displayed a pronounced inclination towards mysticism. Mysticism had always been cultivated to a certain extent in the religious orders of the Catholic Church. The reading of Bonaventure had pointed Luther, even as a young monk, to the pious union with God at which Mysticism aims. Toward the close of his lectures on the Psalms, he became acquainted with certain works on Mysticism which he imbibed with great avidity. They were the sermons of Tauler and the tract "Theologia deutsch." They dominate his thoughts in 1515. Although these works were not designed to do so, they helped to develop his unecclesiastical ideas. His lively experience of the weakness of the human will induced him to hearken readily to the mystical voices which spoke of the complete relinquishment of man to God, even though he did not understand them perfectly. His opposition to good works opened his mind to a fallacious conception of the doctrines of those books of the mystical life. It appeared to him that, by following such leaders, his internal fears could be dispelled by a calm immersion in the Godhead.

John Tauler, an ornament of the Dominican Order (died in 1361), was a famous preacher in the pulpits of Strasburg. His writings and sermons are filled with profound thoughts and have a strong popular appeal. They abound in attractive imagery and are replete with devotion. Tauler stands four-square on the basis of Catholic teaching and the best scholastic theology. Two points in his mystical admonitions found a special echo in Luther's soul, namely, the interior calmness with which God's operations are to be received, and the darkness which fills the souls of pious persons, of whom he speaks consolingly. Luther, however, introduced his own erroneous ideas into the teaching of Tauler. His demand that

the soul be calmly absorbed in God, Luther interpreted as complete passivity, yea, self-annihilation. And what Tauler says concerning trials arising from the withdrawal of all religious joy, of all emotions of grace in the dark night of the soul, he referred directly to his own morbid attacks of fear, to which he endeavored to oppose a misconceived quietism, a certain repose generated by despair. In brief, he tried to transform all theology into what he called a theology of the Cross. Misconstruing Tauler's doctrine of perfection he would recognize only the highest motives, namely, reasons of the greatest perfection for himself as well as for others. Fear of divine punishment and hope of divine reward were to be excluded.

These were extravagances which could not aid him, but, on the contrary, involved great danger to his orthodoxy; in fact, constituted a serious aberration. But he trusted his new lights with the utmost self-confidence. Writing of Tauler to his friend Lang at Erfurt, who was also fascinated by the works of that mystic, Luther compares him with contemporary and older theologians and says that while Tauler was unknown to the Schoolmen, he offered more real theology than the combined theological professors of all the universities.

The other mystical writer who interested him, was discovered by Luther in a manuscript. He lived in the fourteenth century and was the author of the "Theologia deutsch." His name is unknown to us. He was a priest at Frankfort on the Main. His work, which is a didactic treatise on perfection, is Catholic, although not exempt from obscurities. Luther esteemed it as a book of gold, particularly in view of its praise of the sole domination of God in the soul that suffers for Him. He edited this book, at first incompletely, in 1516, then in its entirety, in 1518. It is remarkable that a book on Mysticism was his first publication. Soon he occupied himself with the mystical writings of the so-called Dionysius the Areopagite, the father of Mysticism, and with those of Gerard Groote, a more modern author.

His style in those days, as also later on, reveals how profoundly he was animated by the devout tone of these mystics. Thus, in writing to George Leiffer, a fellow-monk at Erfurt, who was afflicted by persecutions and interior sufferings, he says (1516): "Do not cast away thy little fragment of the Cross of Christ, but deposit it as a sacrosanct relic in a golden shrine, namely, in a heart filled with gentle charity.

For even the hateful things which we experience, are priceless relics. True, they are not, like the wood of the Cross, hallowed by contact with the body of the Lord, yet, in as far as we embrace them out of love for His most loving heart and His divine will, they are kissed and blessed beyond measure." In discussing the idea of self-annihilation under the guidance of God, which was his favorite thought in these days, he shows that he has gone astray. He says that man should not choose among good works, but abandon himself to God's inspiration, as the steed is governed by the reins. In an address delivered in 1516 he declares: "The man of God goeth, whithersoever God directs him as a rider. He never knows whither he is headed; he is passive rather than active. He journeys ever onward, no matter what the condition of the road, through water, mud, rain, snow, wind, etc. Thus are the men of God who are led by the divine spirit." Such are the doctrines which he opposed to those who became distasteful to him on account of their insistence on good works and what he called their Pharisaical observance of external practices.

On May 1, 1515, a chapter of the Augustinian congregation was held at Gotha under the presidency of Staupitz. Luther preached the sermon at the opening assembly. The theme which he selected treated of the contrasts which must have developed in the monasteries of the congregation, namely, the "little saints" and their calumnies against the monastic brethren who disagreed with them in matters of discipline. With extreme acerbity, and employing the crudest and most repulsive figures of speech, he scourged their criticism of others as inspired by love of scandal and malevolent detraction. Apparently the majority of the brethren of his Order sided with him, for they elected him to the office of rural vicar, *i.e.*, special superior of a number of monasteries as the representative of Staupitz.

At stated times he visited the monasteries thus entrusted to him. There were eleven of them, including Erfurt and Wittenberg. After the middle of April, 1516, he made a visitation of the congregations of the Order at Dresden, Neustadt on the Orla, Erfurt, Gotha, Langensalza, and Nordhausen. The letters written by him during his term of office as rural vicar, which normally lasted three years, contain practical directions and admonitions concerning monastic discipline and are, in part, quite edifying. Some of his visitations, however, were conducted with such astonishing rapidity that no fruitful results

could be expected of them. Thus the visitation of the monastery at Gotha occupied but one hour, that at Langensalza two hours. "In these places," he wrote to Lang, "the Lord will work without us and direct the spiritual and temporal affairs in spite of the devil." At Neustadt he deposed the prior, Michael Dressel, without a hearing, because the brethren could not get along with him. "I did this," he informed Lang in confidence, "because I hoped to rule there myself for the half-year."

In a letter to the same friend he writes as follows about the engagements with which he was overwhelmed at that time: "I really ought to have two secretaries or chancellors. I do hardly anything all day but write letters. . . . I am at the same time preacher to the monastery, have to preach in the refectory, and am even expected to preach daily in the parish church. I am regent of the *studium* [*i.e.*, of the younger monks] and vicar, that is to say prior eleven times over; I have to provide for the delivery of the fish from the Leitzkau pond and to manage the litigation of the Herzberg fellows [monks] at Torgau; I am lecturing on Paul, compiling an exposition of the Psalter, and, as I said before, writing letters most of the time. . . . It is seldom that I have time for the recitation of the Divine Office or to celebrate Mass, and then, too, I have my peculiar temptations from the flesh, the world, and the devil."

INTERIOR STATE

The last sentence quoted above contains a remarkable declaration about his spiritual condition and his compliance with his monastic duties at that time. He seldom found time to recite the Divine Office and to say Mass. It was his duty so to arrange his affairs as to be able to comply with these obligations. The canonical hours were strictly prescribed. Saying Mass is the central obligation of every priest, especially if he is a member of a religious order. If Luther did not know how to observe due moderation in his labors; if he was derelict in the principal duties of the spiritual life; it was to be feared that he would gradually drift away from the religious state, particularly in view of the fact that he had adopted a false Mysticism which favored the relaxation of the rule. As rural vicar, it is probable that he did not sustain among the brethren the good old spirit which the zealous Proles had introduced into the society. Of the "temptations of the flesh" which he mentions we learn nothing definite. He was not yet in conflict with his vows. His wrestlings with the devil may signify the fears and terrors to which he was subject.

He continued to be on good terms with his friend Staupitz, who was interested in the young monk's manifold activities. Staupitz also posed as a mystic, and favored the spiritual tendency which Luther followed. This talented and sociable man was very popular as a useful adviser in the homes of the rich and as an entertainer at table. Whilst Luther could not accompany him on such errands, he enjoyed his company on monastic visitations. In July, 1515, he accompanied Staupitz to Eisleben, when the latter opened the new Augustinian monastery at that place. As he walked in his sacerdotal vestments in the procession through the city of his birth at the side of his vicar, who carried the Blessed Sacrament, Luther was suddenly seized with unspeakable fright at the thought of the proximity of Christ. On mentioning the incident to his superior afterwards, the latter comforted him by saying: "Your thought is not Christ," and assuring him that Christ did not desire this fear. At times, in consequence either of a disordered affection of the heart or of overwork, he was so distressed that he could not eat or drink for a long time. One day he was found seemingly dead in his cell, so completely was he exhausted as a result of agitation and lack of food. His friend Ratzeberger, a physician, mentions this incident, without, however, indicating the exact time of its occurrence. Luther was relieved of this pitiable condition by recourse to music, which always stimulated him. After he had regained his strength, he was able once more to prosecute his labors. As a result of his suffering and worry he became very much emaciated.

Did Luther subject himself to extraordinary deeds of penance at any period of his monastic life, as he frequently affirmed in his subsequent conflict with the papacy and monasticism, when he was impelled by polemical reasons to describe himself as the type of a holy and mortified monk, one who could not find peace of mind during his whole monastic career? Holding then that peace of mind was simply impossible in the Catholic Church, he arbitrarily misrepresents monasticism, in order to exhibit in a most glaring manner the alleged inherent impossibility of "papistic" ethics to produce the assurance of God's mercy. "I tormented my body by fasting, vigils, and cold. . . . In the observance of these matters I was so precise and superstitious, that I imposed more burdens upon my body than it could bear without danger to health." "If ever a monk got to heaven by monkery, then I should have got there." "I almost died a-fasting, for often I took neither a drop of water nor a morsel of food for three days."

Such exaggerated penitential exercises were prohibited by the statutes of the congregation, which were distinguished for great discretion, and insisted upon proper moderation as a matter of strict duty.

The above picture of singular holiness is produced not by early witnesses, but by assertions which Luther made little by little at a later period of life. The established facts contradict the legend. Perhaps his description is based partly on reminiscences of his distracted days in the monastery, or on eccentric efforts to overcome his sombre moods by means of a false piety. His greatest error, and the one which most betrays him, is that he ascribes his fictitious asceticism to all serious-minded members of his monastery, yea, of all monasteries. He would have it that all monks consumed themselves in wailing and grief, wrestling for the peace of God, until he supplied the remedy. It is a rule of the most elementary criticism finally to cut loose from the distorted presentation of the matter which has maintained itself so tenaciously in Protestant biographies of Luther.

It may be admitted that, on the whole, Luther was a dutiful monk for the greatest part of his monastic life. "When I was in the monastery," he stated on one occasion, in 1535, "I was not like the rest of men, the robbers, the unjust, the adulterous; but I observed chastity, obedience, and poverty."

Yet, after his transfer to Wittenberg, and in consequence of the applause which was accorded to him there, the unpleasant traits of his character, especially his positive insistence on always being in the right, began to manifest themselves more and more disagreeably. In his opinion, the Scholastic theologians, even the greatest among them, were sophists. They were a herd of "swine theologians," while he was the enlightened pupil of St. Paul and St. Augustine. The finer achievements of Scholasticism, especially those of its intellectual giant, Thomas of Aquin, were scarcely known to him. Could his confused mysticism perhaps supplement his deficient knowledge of Scholasticism? No, it only made him more self-conscious and arbitrary in the sphere of theology. He gave free vent to his criticism of highly respected ascetical writers. An example of his egotistical excess in this respect is furnished by his glosses for the year 1515, which he indited on the Psalter of Mary, a work of Mark of Weida. In addition to these characteristics, there was his peculiar irritability, which is strikingly exhibited in his correspondence during 1514. The theologians of Erfurt, led by Nathin, had reproved him for taking the doctorate at Erfurt instead of at Wittenberg, since the Erfurt school had claims on him as one of its own pupils. It is possible that some harsh words were exchanged in regard to this matter. The young professor in a letter addressed to the monastery at Erfurt says that he had well nigh resolved to "pour out the entire vial of his wrath and indignation upon Nathin and the whole monastery" on account of their lies and mockery. They had received two shocking letters (litterae stupidae) from him, for which he now wants to excuse himself, though his indignation "was only too well founded," especially since he now heard even worse things about Nathin and his complaints against his (Luther's) person. In the meantime, God had willed his separation from the Erfurt monastery, etc.

The ill-feeling between Nathin and his Erfurt colleagues, on the one hand, and Luther and his monastic partisans on the other, arose from the controversy concerning the stricter observance of the rule within the Order.

OPPOSITION TO SELF-RIGHTEOUSNESS AND RELIGIOUS OBSERVANCE

Contradictory conceptions of monastic life continued to be harbored in the Augustinian congregation even after the settlement of the contention with regard to Staupitz's plans of union.

Those brethren who treasured the ancient monastic discipline, protected by papal privileges and exemptions, were accused of self-righteous Pharisaism and of disobedience towards the General of the order by Luther and his party. They were the "Little Saints" against whom he had inveighed in his impetuous address at Gotha. In his lectures and sermons he reproached, though often only in allusions, their "observantine" practices, their adherence to the doctrine of good works, and their want of charity. His invectives, however, were

launched with a bitterness which those concerned assuredly did not merit, even though there might have been reasons for complaint. It may be said that the ancient and the modern wings opposed each other in the Wittenberg monastery. Probably there was friction also in the monastery at Erfurt, where Luther's friend Lang was prior, as well as in other monasteries of the congregation. Luther's monastery, however, was the center of the contention. The young students of the Order brought with them their divergent views out of the cloisters whence they came and they carried the new atmosphere of Wittenberg along with them when they left. Luther's partisans at Wittenberg boasted that they were more closely attached to the General of the Order at Rome than their opponents. The General, they contended, was not in favor of the singularities of the Observantines.

At the commencement of his first series of lectures on the Psalms, Luther delivered a sarcastic address on the obedience due to religious superiors. "How many do we not find," he says, "who believe they are very religious, and yet they are, if I may so express it, only men of an extremely sanguine temperament (sanguinicissimi) and true Idumaeans [i.e., paganminded]. There are people who so revere and praise their monastic state, their order, their Saints, and their institutions, that they cast a shadow upon all others, not wishing to grant them their proper place. In a very unspiritual manner they are humble followers (observantes) of their fathers and boast of them. Oh, the frenzy that prevails in this day! It has almost come to this that every monastery repudiates the customs of all others and is imbued with such pride as to preclude taking over or learning anything at all from another. That is the pride of Jews and heretics, with which we, unfortunate ones, are also encompassed," etc. In the addresses which he delivered in the monastery church he frequently alludes to the obstinate pride of the Jews and heretics, in condemnation of those members of his order or of other orders who adhered to the strict observance. These "Observantines, exempted and privileged characters"—thus he fulminates in another lecture, are devoid of obedience, which is the very soul of good works. It will be seen—he continues—how detrimental to the Church they are; in the interests of the rule, they were determined to insist upon exceptions; "but that is a light that comes from the devil."

This was the contest which led the fiery monk to enter upon doubtful ways. His opposition to the so-called doctrine of self-righteousness caused him to form a false conception of righteousness; instead of attacking an heretical error, he combated the true worth of good works and the perfections of the monastic life.

Voluntary poverty, as practiced by the mendicants, was one of the foundations of his Order. The inmates of monastic houses were to live on alms according to the practice introduced by the great Saint Francis of Assisi and for the benefactions received were to devote themselves gratis to the spiritual needs of their fellowmen. Many abuses, it is true, had attached themselves to the mendicant system; self-interest, avarice, and worldly-mindedness infected the itinerant mendicants. But in his explanation of the Psalms Luther attacks the life of poverty *per se:* "O mendicants! O mendicants! O mendicants!" he pathetically exclaims, "who can excuse you? . . . Look to it yourselves," etc. He places the practice of poverty in an unfavorable light. In his criticism of the "self-righteousness of his irksome enemies, he confronts them with the righteousness of the spirit that cometh from Christ. These people, whom he believed it his duty to expose, were guilty, in his opinion, of a Pharisaical denial of the true righteousness of Christ. His righteousness, and not our good works, effect our salvation; works generate a fleshly sense and boastfulness. These thought-processes evince how false mysticism, unclear theological notions, a darkening of the monastic spirit, and passionate obstinacy conspired in Luther's mind.

In the years 1515 and 1516, the phalanx of the self-righteous, the *justitiarii*, as he styles them, again constitute the object of his attacks. There is Christ, the hen with its protecting wings, which he must defend against the vultures that pounce upon us in their self-righteousness. These enemies of the sweet righteousness imputed to us by God are "a pestilence in the Church; intractable, nay, rebellious against their superiors, they decry others and clothe themselves with the lamb-skins of their good works."

An Augustinian friend of his, George Spenlein, having become weary of certain persecutions, had had himself transferred from Wittenberg to the monastery at Memmingen. Luther sent him a peculiar letter of condolence on April 8, 1516. According to this missive, it would seem that the self-righteous Spenlein had been for a long time "in opposition to the self-righteousness of God, which had been bestowed most lavishly and gratuitously upon him by Christ"; whereas he (Spenlein) desired to stand before God with his own works and merits, which, of course, is impossible. He (Luther), too, had harbored this notion, and says he still wrestles with this error. "Learn, therefore, my sweet brother," thus he addresses Spenlein in the vocabulary of mysticism, "learn to sing to the Lord Jesus and, distrusting yourself, say to Him: Thou, O Lord Jesus, art my righteousness, but I am Thy sin. Thou hast accepted what was mine and hast given to me what was Thine. Oh, that thou wouldst boldly appear thyself as a sinner, yea, be a sinner in reality; for Christ abides only in sinners." "But, if you are a lily and a rose of Christ, then learn to bear persecution with patience, lest your secret pride convert you into a thorn."

The germ of Luther's reformatory doctrine is plainly contained in this species of Mysticism. Step by step he had arrived at his new dogma in the above described manner. The system which attacked the basic truths of the Catholic Church, was complete in outline. Before giving a fuller exposition of it, we must consider the individual factors which cooperated in its development in Luther's mind.

Confession and penance were a source of torturing offense to the young monk. Can one obtain peace with God by the performance of penitential works? He discussed this question with Staupitz on an occasion when he sought consolation. Staupitz pointed out to him that all penance must begin and end with love; that all treasures are hidden in Christ, in whom we must trust and whom we must love. These words contain nothing new; but the exhortation to combine love with penance entered the inflammable soul of Luther as a voice from heaven. According to his own expression, it "clung to his soul as the sharp arrows of the mighty" (Ps. CXIX, 4); henceforward, he says, he would execrate the hypocrisy by means of which he had formerly sought to express a "fabricated and forced" penitential spirit during the tortures of confession. Now that the merits of Christ covered everything, penance appeared easy and sweet to him. He expresses himself on this point in a grateful letter to Staupitz, written in 1518.

On the occasion referred to, it is probable that Staupitz, as was his custom, expressed himself in a vague and sentimental manner, rather than in clear theological terms. His writings are susceptible of improvement in many respects. The influence which he exerted on Luther was not a wholesome one. He was too fond of him to penetrate his character. He perceived in him a rising star of his congregation, a very promising ornament of his Order. Even in the most critical period anterior to Luther's apostasy, he eulogized his courage and said: Christ speaks out of your mouth,—so well it pleased him that Luther, in the matter of righteousness and good works, ascribed everything to Christ, to whom alone glory should be given. Certain of a favorable response on the part of his superior, Luther wrote thus in the above letter to him: "My sweet Saviour and Pardoner, to whom I shall sing as long as I live (Ps. CIII, 33), is sufficient for me. If there be anyone who will not sing with me, what is that to me? Let him howl if it please him." The short-sighted Staupitz sided with Luther even after he had been condemned by the Church.

Nor was Staupitz the man who could thoroughly free Luther from his doubts about predestination, although Luther says he helped him. His general references to the wounds of Christ could not permanently set the troubled monk aright. He should have placed definitely before him the Catholic dogma, based on Sacred Scripture, that God sincerely desires the salvation of all men, and should have made clear to the doubter that voluntary sin is the sole cause of damnation. But he himself seems not to have grasped these truths, for in certain critical passages of his writings he allows them to retreat before a certain mysterious predestination. Luther's fear of predestination constituted the obscure substratum of his evolving new religious system. Recalling Staupitz's exhortations, he says, in 1532: We must stop at the wounds of Christ, and may not ponder over the awful mystery. The only remedy consists in dismissing from our minds the possibility of a verdict of damnation. "When I attend to these ideas, I forget what Christ and God are, and sometimes arrive at the conclusion that God is a scoundrel. . . . The idea of predestination causes us to forget God, and the *Laudate* ceases and the *Blasphemate* begins." The part which these struggles had in the origin of his new doctrine, is to be sought in Luther's violent efforts to attain to a certain repose in the face of his presumptive predestination.

It is also remarkable that the last-quoted utterance is followed by one concerning his "great spiritual temptations." In contrast with the struggles of despair which he underwent, he is not deeply impressed by ordinary temptations. "No one," he writes, "can really write or say anything about grace, unless he has been disciplined by spiritual temptations." His opponents, he says elsewhere, not having had such experiences, it behooved them to observe silence. When his doctrine encountered opposition in Rome, he wrote to Staupitz that Roman citations and other matters made no impression on him. "My sufferings, as you know, are incomparably greater, and these force me to regard such temporal flashes as extremely trivial." He meant "doubtlessly, personal, inward sufferings and attacks which were connected with bodily ailments . . . , whereby, as formerly, he was always seized with fear for his personal salvation when he pondered on the hidden depths of the divine will."

In his interpretation of the Epistle of St. Paul to the Romans, given during the years 1515 and 1516, Luther completely unfolded his new doctrine.

NORMAN O. BROWN

A VISCERAL VIEW FROM THE INSIDE

We have identified in the last two selections what Protestant scholarship has come to call Luther's "Thurmerlebnis" or "experience in the tower," that is, the sudden understanding of the famous passage from St. Paul, that "gate to heaven" which eventually led Luther to the fundamental premise of his theology and made a religious revolution. Bainton noted with some delicacy that "the solution to Luther's problem came in the midst of the performance of the daily task." Grisar (in a passage not included in the previous selection) was considerably more direct. In the present selection Norman O. Brown is more direct still and, with the same candor as Luther himself exhibited, states that this central experience of divine illumination came to Luther "on the privy in the tower." What is more to the point, he asserts that this is not simply an unfortunate or embarrassing incident that history and Luther might well have left unrecorded. On the contrary, he insists that what, in another frame of reference, is an uncomfortable triviality, in his view reveals "a hidden connection between higher spiritual activity and lower organs of the body."

We have already observed that contemporary scholarship has tended to abandon the "external" concept of the causes of the Reformation and to seek its more basic cause in the history of the man Luther. Brown's thesis is an example of another approach to this search, the psychoanalytic approach. Without exception, the books and articles which have attempted to demonstrate this approach have been attacked—and in many instances they have deserved attack. Psychoanalytic interpreters have been faulted for their historical inaccuracy, their ignorance of theology, and the presuppositions of their methodology. It has been charged, for example, that even in the case of Luther about whom we have more day-to-day, ordinary information than about any other man of his time, we still cannot know enough that is pertinent to psychoanalysis to make a trustworthy judgment. It has even been charged that the basic assumption of psychoanalysis—that man is always and in every age motivated by self-interest—fails as an assumption when dealing with an essentially religious man.

This selection from Brown's *Life Against Death, The Psychoanalytical Meaning of History,* while certainly still controversial, is one of the most solid representatives of its type and the student must attempt to assess not only the work but the method.

Luther describes the circumstances under which he received the illumination which became the fundamental axiom of the Protestant Reformation— the doctrine of justification by faith—in the following words:

These words "just" and "justice of God" were a thunderbolt in my conscience. They soon struck terror in me who heard them. He is just, therefore He punishes. But once when in this tower I was meditating on those words, "the just lives by faith," "justice of God," I soon had the thought whether we ought to live justified by faith, and God's justice ought to be the salvation of every believer, and soon my soul was revived. Therefore it is God's justice which justifies us and saves us. And these words became a sweeter message for me. This knowledge the Holy Spirit gave me on the privy in the tower.

Luther with his freedom from hypocrisy, his all-embracing vitality, and his all-embracing faith, records the scene of his crucial religious experience with untroubled candor. It was in a tower of the Wittenberg monastery, where the privy was located. Grisar explains, "In olden times it was very usual to establish this adjunct on the city wall and its towers, the sewage having egress outside the town boundaries."

Luther's candor has been too much for the Lutherans. Recognizing the crucial importance of the "experience in the tower," the *Thurmerlebnis,* as it is called in Lutheran hagiography, Lutheran scholars have either monkeyed with the texts in an attempt to separate the tower from the privy, or else interpreted the tower not as a geographical location but as an allegory of spiritual captivity. It was thus left to the Jesuit Father Grisar (1911) to recover the facts, only to be received by outcries, from Harnack and a pack of lesser Lutherans, that he was hitting below the belt, indulging in "vulgar Catholic polemics."

When the smoke of controversy died away, the location of the *Thurmerlebnis* was established, but both the Jesuit and his Lutheran critics were agreed that the location was of no significance. Grisar agreed with Harnack that "the locality in which Luther first glimpsed this thought is of small importance"; he agreed with the Lutheran Scheel that Roman Catholics, like all Christians, believe that God is present everywhere.

Psychoanalysis, alas! cannot agree that it is of no significance that the religious experience which in-

From Norman O. Brown, *Life Against Death, The Psychoanalytical Meaning of History* (Middletown, Conn., 1959), pp. 202–3, 206–210, 211–17. Reprinted by permission of Wesleyan University Press and Routledge & Kegan Paul Ltd.

augurated Protestant theology took place in the privy. The psychoanalytical theory of infantile sexuality and its sublimation insists that there is a hidden connection between higher spiritual activity and lower organs of the body. Ever since Freud's essay on "Character and Anal Erotism" (1908), psychoanalysis has accepted as a demonstrated theorem that a definite type of ethical character, exhibiting a combination of three traits—orderliness, parsimony, and obstinacy—is constructed by the sublimation of a special concentration of libido in the anal zone, and it is therefore labeled the anal character. . . .

At the abstract theoretical level, psychoanalytical paradox and historical common sense are so far apart that one can only despair of ever unifying them. It therefore seems inevitable that progress will be made, if at all, by concrete empirical investigation. And since in general psychoanalytical considerations grope so far beneath the surface that they can easily be dismissed as arbitrary constructions not based on facts, such concrete empirical investigations must take as their point of departure, not psychoanalytical imputations as to what may (or may not) be going on in the Unconscious, but historical fact.

Such a solid point of departure is provided by the historical fact that the Protestant illumination came to Luther while seated on the privy. Such historical facts are hard to come by (few of the world's great men had Luther's honesty), and historical science should make the most of them. The hypothesis to be investigated is that there is some mysterious intrinsic connection between the Protestant illumination and the privy. The issue is: What exactly does the privy mean to Luther? But since the theory of sublimation is at stake in such an investigation, we cannot use the theory of sublimation to impute to Luther's unconscious meanings for the privy. Rather we must rely on the historical evidence of his writings for documented fact as to what the privy meant to Luther (in psychoanalytical terms, his "associations" to the idea of the privy). Such an empirical investigation of Luther's writings reveals the existence of a middle term, unexplored by both the psychoanalysts and the historians, connecting the privy with Protestantism on the one hand and capitalism on the other. This middle term is the Devil.

Psychoanalytical studies of the Devil, following Freud himself, have emphasized the Oedipal aspect of the Devil, his status as a father-substitute, the ambivalent combination of emulation of and hostility against the father in the Devil, and the identity of God and the Devil (as father-substitutes) underlying their opposition. The persistently anal character of the Devil has not been emphasized enough. The color pre-eminently associated with the Devil and the Black Mass is black—not because of his place of abode (a circular explanation) but because of the association of black and filth. "The painters paint the Devil black and filthy," says Luther. Equally persistent is the association of the Devil with a sulphurous or other evil smell, the origin of which is plainly revealed in the article "De crepitu Diaboli" in an eighteenth-century compendium of folklore. The climax of the ritual of the Witches' Sabbath was to kiss the Devil's posteriors or a facial mask attached to the Devil's posteriors. In the central ceremony of the Black Mass, as the Queen of the Sabbath lay prone, "The sacred host was prepared by kneading on her buttocks a mixture of the most repulsive material, faeces, menstrual blood, urine, and offal of various kinds." Hence Dante makes the still point of the turning world, round which he passes upward to Purgatory, Satan's anus; hence Bosch, in the panel depicting this world as Hell, enthrones Satan on a privy, from which the souls that have passed out of his anus drop into the black pit.

Luther's idea of the Devil is a compound of current folklore, personal experience, and theological speculation; but of these ingredients the element of personal experience is decisive. It is an error to think of Luther's diabolism, or the general diabolism of the period, as a reverberation of a medieval theme. The age which gave birth to Protestantism experienced the Devil with a peculiar immediacy, power, and pervasiveness, and Luther, who personally experienced the Devil with more immediacy, power, and pervasiveness than any other leader of the age, is in this respect only the most representative man of the age. Personal experience was the touchstone by which Luther tested current folklore of the Devil; and personal experience was, of course, the touchstone for his theological speculations.

In Luther's personal encounters with the Devil—remember we are dealing with materialized apparitions—the anal character of the Devil is sensuously perceived and sensuously recorded by Luther (in his Table-Talk) with a gross concreteness that latter-day Protestantism cannot imagine and would not tolerate. An encounter with the Devil is for Luther an encounter with something black and "filthy." Latter-day Lutheranism has encouraged the circulation of the stories of how the Devil threw ink at Luther, and Luther threw ink at the Devil; here the anality has a thin but sufficient disguise. But there is no disguise in Melancthon's additional details: "Having been worsted by this saying the Demon departed indignant and murmuring to himself, after having emitted a crepitation of no small size, which left a train of foul odour in the chamber for several days afterwards." Personal experience therefore authorized Luther to give credibility to the story of a Lutheran pastor to whom the Devil appeared in the confessional, blasphemed Christ, and "departed leaving a horrible stench." The materialized anality which is the Devil consists not only of anal smells but also anal sights; twice at least Luther was assaulted by an apparition of the Devil "showing him his posterior." And, as passages too numerous to cite show, Luther's most general word for the assaults of the Devil is the homely German verb *bescheissen.*

As striking as the anality of the Devil's attacks is the anality of Luther's counterattacks. When Luther pours verbal abuse at the Devil or throws the ink at him, the anality of his weapons is perhaps disguised. But there is no disguise when Luther records that in one encounter, when Lutheran doctrines had not sufficed to rout the Devil, he had routed him *"mit einem Furz"*—the same weapon the Devil used against Luther in Melancthon's story. Personal experience therefore authorized Luther to tell with approval the story of the lady who had routed the Devil with the same device. Other anal weapons employed by Luther in his fight with the Devil—my language is here more refined than Luther's—are injunctions to "lick (or kiss) my posteriors" or to "defecate in his pants and hang them round his neck," and threats to "defecate in his face" or to "throw him into my anus, where he belongs."

The last quotation exhibits the psychic logic and psychoanalytical understanding underlying Luther's warfare with the Devil. The Devil is virtually recognized as a displaced materialization of Luther's own anality, which is to be conquered by being replaced where it came from. The same pattern of anal attack and counterattack is exhibited in Luther's notions of witchcraft. Luther says that "people who eat butter that has been bewitched, eat nothing but mud"; and as a counterattack on the witchcraft that is spoiling the butter-churning, he recommends "Dr. Pommer's plan" as the best—"Dr. Pommer came to the res-

cue, scoffed at the Devil, and emptied his bowels into the churn."

Given the importance of the Devil in Lutheran theology—a subject to which we shall come in a moment—it is Luther's grossly concrete image of the anal character of the Devil that made the privy the appropriate scene for his critical religious experience. And the appropriate comment is not that milk-and-water piety, proposed by nineteenth-century Lutherans and assented to by the Jesuit Grisar, that "God is everywhere." We are reminded of Luther's acid test of a Christian teacher: "Does he know of death and the Devil? Or is all sweetness and light?" Protestantism was born in the temple of the Devil, and it found God again in extremest alienation from God. The dark ambivalence of the situation is expressed in Luther's story of the proper answer to the Devil given by a monk sitting on the privy:

Monachus super latrinam
Non debet orare primam?
Deo quod supra,
Tibi quod cadit infra.

The situation is apparently proverbial. Sir John Harrington wrote the same answer to the Devil on an emblem hung in the privy of his house: "To God my pray'r I ment, to thee the durt." Whether or not there was a materialized apparition of the Devil in Luther's experience in the tower, the Devil was present in some sense of psychic reality. Again we must remember the intimate and everyday familiarity of Luther's experience with the Devil. The Wartburg castle was full of devils, who never left him at peace but "behave in such a way that he is never alone even when he seems to be so." In his old age Luther's steps were dogged by two particular devils, who walked with him whenever he went in the dormitory (*auf dem Schlafhause*). And the Wittenberg cloister, where the *Thurmerlebnis* took place, was no less full of devils.

We have established the relation between the Devil and anality. We have now to establish the relation between the Devil and Protestantism. Everybody knows that Luther and Luther's Protestantism are haunted by a sense of the Devil; every time we sing *"Ein feste Burg"* and celebrate the victory over our "ancient foe" it stares us in the face. But rationalists nursed on eighteenth-century Enlightenment, and optimists nursed on nineteenth-century Liberalism, who themselves cannot take the Devil seriously, could not take Luther's Devil seriously. We are reminded of Baudelaire's epigram—"The neatest trick of the Devil is to persuade you he does not exist." Luther's diabolism was regarded as either an individual psychological aberration or as a hang-over from medieval superstition. In this spirit Troeltsch, Weber, Tawney and their countless followers (including Fromm) have defined Protestantism simply as a new relation to God. Thus Troeltsch: "The whole change of view in Protestantism is summed up and expressed in its Idea of God"; the essence of Protestantism is "the reduction of the whole of religion . . . to that idea of God."

But Protestantism and its social and psychological implications must be understood as a new relation to the Devil, a relation which explains the new relation to God. If we want to understand Luther, we may, if we like, take neither his God nor his Devil seriously, and substitute psychological explanations for both. What we may not do is to take one seriously and explain away the other. . . .

"Far from decreasing the power of the Devil in the world, the Reformation brought him strong reinforcements"; so speaks the Devil's most authoritative historian. The psychological premise of Protestantism is conviction of sin. Protestantism, as a new relation to God, is a response to a new experience of evil. The novelty consists first in the scope and intensity of the evil experienced, and second in the sense of absolute powerlessness in the face of it. This new experience of evil reaches back into the waning period of the Middle Ages; Protestantism and Protestant diabolism are the offspring of a long gestation. Huizinga writes of the fifteenth century:

Is it surprising that the people could see their fate and that of the world only as an endless succession of evils? Bad governments, exactions, the cupidity and violence of the great, wars and brigandage, scarcity, misery and pestilence—to this is contemporary history nearly reduced in the eyes of the people. The feeling of general insecurity which was caused by the chronic form wars were apt to take, by the constant menace of the dangerous classes, by the mistrust of justice, was further aggravated by the obsession of the coming end of the world, and by the fear of hell, of sorcerers and of devils. The background of all life in the world seems black. Satan covers a gloomy earth with his sombre wings.

In Luther this experience of omnipresent and uncontrollable evil generates the theological novelty that this world, in all its outward manifestations, is ruled not by God but by the Devil. "It is an article of faith," says Luther, "that the Devil is *Princeps mundi, Deus huius seculi.*" It is an article of faith, based on experience: "The Devil is the lord of the world. Let him who does not know this, try it. I have had some experience of it: but no one will believe me until he experiences it too." "The world and all that belongs to it must have the Devil as its master." "We are servants in a hostelry, where Satan is the householder, the world his wife, and our affections his children." "The whole world is possessed by Satan." "The whole world is enslaved to his machinations." "The world is the Devil and the Devil is the world." "Everything is full of devils, in the courts of princes, in houses, in fields, in streets, in water, in wood, in fire."

Luther finds the autonomous demonic power of evil not only in the macrocosm of society but also in the microcosm of the individual. It is his experience of the dominion of Satan over the individual that generates another theological innovation, the denial of free will; Melancthon (in 1559) and other critics correctly apprehend the trend of Luther's thought when they call his predestinarianism Manichaean. Luther's predestinarianism is partly based on a sense of the power of temptation—"No man could face the devil with his free will"—but at a deeper level it is based on the sense that temptation and sin are the work of an autonomous force outside of the individual. The result is to eliminate the traditional notion of vices, faults for which the individual is responsible, and substitute the Devil. "The German reformer and his disciples thus filled Germany with devils by diabolizing all vices." A Lutheran compilation, the *Theatrum Diabolorum* (1569), lists the new discoveries, the devil of blasphemy, the dance-devil, the laziness-devil, the pride-devil, etc.

Not content with diabolizing the vices, Luther diabolizes the virtues also. Man is justified not by works but by faith alone; and faith is not a virtue in our power but a gift of God. The whole domain of traditional virtue, pejoratively re-evaluated as mere "works," is handed over to the Devil. "For seeing that, outside of Christ, death and sin are our masters and the devil our God and sovereign, there can be no power or might, no wit or understanding whereby we could make ourselves fit for, or could even strive after, righteousness and life, but on the contrary we must remain blind and captive, slaves of sin and the devil." Therefore, "in the man who does not believe in Christ not only are all sins mortal, but even his good works are sins." Hence piety in the Romish style is the devil's work: "The Devil lets his own do many good works, pray, fast, build churches, establish Masses and holy days, and behave as if he were quite holy and pious." "Men of holy works (*die Werkheiligen*) are Satan's captive servants, no matter how much they appear outwardly to surpass others in good works and in strictness and holiness of life." Thus the Devil as "lord of the world," so that "men must think, speak and do what the Devil wills," is the guiding spirit behind the traditional religious virtue of pious works. . . .

True, Luther cannot permit his experience of dualism to submerge Christianity's traditional faith in the monarchy of God; to reconcile the two he has such formulations as that God *permits* the Devil to rage or that God *withdraws* to leave space for the Devil. But the net effect is still to recognize the Devil's power as a positive antidivine structure in its own right. Hence when Luther is arguing for man's lack of free will, he does not simply argue from the omnipotence of God, but also from the power and rights of the Devil and from original sin, which established and perpetuates Satan's domination over mankind. "In the Protestant Church, the Devil must have his pay, and the Devil's pay is the soul of the sinner. Thus ever since the days of the Reformation, Satan's power in this world has considerably increased." According to the more merciful Catholic tradition, even those who had made pacts with the Devil might, even in the eleventh hour, be saved by some outward act of penitence (the "works" that Luther despised) or by the intercession of the saints (another concept that fell victim to Protestant fundamentalism). The new Lutheran notion of inescapable damnation takes over the Faust legend and makes it a profound symbol of modern man.

Nor does Christian faith withdraw the Christian from the domination of Satan. Here the central doctrine is the impossibility of overcoming sin, a Lutheran innovation which, as Troeltsch says, is all the more remarkable for being a divergence from Pauline Christianity. The doctrine of the impossibility of overcoming sin can be deduced from the doctrine of the vanity of good works, and it results in the Lutheran dualism between the inner world of grace and the outer world of works, the world of the spirit and the world of the flesh. Following Troeltsch's explication of the Lutheran position, we may say

that an active fulfillment of the Christian ideal is impossible upon earth and realizable only in the future life. Hence the Lutheran conception of grace and of the impossibility of overcoming sin leaves no outwardly visible distinction between Christian and non-Christian. Christianity consists in the inner possession of grace, not in any outward achievement. Although to some extent faith should issue in good works, such good works affect neither the quality of Christian piety nor the fact of personal salvation. This is tantamount to saying—and Luther says it—that the Christian remains under the dominion of the Devil, and nevertheless is lord over the Devil and the Devil has no power over him. This paradox means that the Christian is split into two dimensions, spirit that belongs to Christ and flesh that belongs to the Devil. Again we see the tremendous extension of the Devil's empire in Protestantism. The whole realm of visible reality, the world and the flesh, belong to the Devil; God has retired into invisibility—*Deus absconditus.* . . .

It would be hard to find a clearer illustration of the actuality and effective power of that death instinct which Freud postulated and which the non-Freudian world has ridiculed. For hell, Luther said, is not a place, but is the experience of death, and Luther's devil is ultimately personified death. Luther's new *theologia crucis* rejects the traditional Aristotelian-Thomistic goal of actualizing the potentialities of life as *amor concupiscentiae,* and calls us to experience hell on earth, to experience life on earth as ruled by the death instinct, and to die to such a death-in-life, in the hope of a more joyful resurrection. . . .

It is the hope of a more joyful resurrection that alone saves Luther from the dominion of death. Satan is the lord of this life, but there is another life where Christ is King, and to have faith in the existence of that other life is to conquer this death-in-life while in it. To make psychological sense of Luther's central paradox we had to invoke Freud's two immortal antagonists, the life instinct and the death instinct. Under Luther's symbols, we perceive that Luther sees this life as being under the domination of the death instinct. Those who take Freud's *Civilization and Its Discontents* seriously can only agree, and must recognize Luther's insight as a decisive advance in the task, as old as human history, of reclaiming id territory for the human ego. This recognition of life as death-in-life reflects and crystallizes an immense withdrawal of libido from life. In other words, whereas in previous ages life had been a

The Eve of the Modern World

mixture of Eros and Thanatos, in the Protestant era life becomes a pure culture of the death instinct. Luther's faith and grace—the hope of a more joyful resurrection—form an enclave in the dominion of death which will not bow the knee and call death life, but on the other hand they form no real exception to the fact that death has dominion over life. Luther cannot affirm life, but can only die to this death-in-life. Therefore for him, too, holy living is holy dying. "God . . . makes alive by slaying."

Thus the insight of Protestantism is its insight into the dominion of death in life, and its service to life and to love is its hope in another life which would be true life. The positive features in Luther are his diabolism and his eschatology. Actually the diab-olism and the eschatology are two sides of the same coin. It would be psychically impossible for Luther to recognize the Devil's dominion over this world (Luther is not yet de Sade) without the faith that the Devil's dominion is doomed, and that the history of man on earth will end in the kingdom of God, when grace will be made visible. Hence it is an integral part of Luther's position to believe, as the earliest Christians had, that he is living in the last age of time. In fact, in Luther's eyes the new power of the Devil points to the end of time: our devils are far worse than those known in previous ages; compared to ours, medieval devils are child's play; the whole age is Satanic; the world cannot last much longer, and "from so Satanic a world" Luther would fain be "quickly snatched."

4

CALVINISM AND REVOLUTION

Important as Luther was as the first major reformer—whether or not the "cause" of the Reformation—his younger contemporary, the French reformer Jean Calvin was probably more important. For Lutheranism and, for that matter, most of the Protestant groups and sects which developed prior to the Calvinist movement were closely related to ethnic, national, regional, or class interests. It was only with Calvinism that the Reformation gained an internationalism and universality to set against the ancient, ecumenical claims of Catholicism.

The center of the Calvinist universe was Geneva, the "Protestant Rome." It was to this Swiss city that the young Calvin fled from persecution in his native France in 1536. It was at this very time that his religious ideas were beginning to crystalize. With the exception of one brief exile, Calvin spent the rest of his life in Geneva, intent upon making that city the Protestant "City of God." To an astonishing extent he succeeded.

Calvinism, like most of the evangelical sects, was a militant and concerned faith and from Calvin's Geneva a steady stream of preachers and missionaries and agents went out to preach the reformed doctrine, to enter into the religious and political strife of the time, and to seize upon local movements and protests and convert their disparate energies to Calvinism. All across Europe the division between Catholic and reformed had hardened into implacable hostility and this religious hostility had embittered older economic or political or sectional differences. The wars of religion had already begun and Calvinism was rapidly becoming a dominant factor in them. As the fortunes of religious war and persecution swayed back and forth, religious refugees came to Geneva—from the England of Mary Tudor, from the Huguenot south of France, from the Low Countries, and the Rhine valley. And in time they returned to their countries strengthened in faith and determination by the iron doctrines of Calvinism. By the later sixteenth century Calvinism had, in one way or another, set its stamp upon the Huguenot movement in France, the Reformed Church of the Low Countries and Germany, English Puritanism, and Scots Presbyterianism. Wherever Calvinism went, and in whatever form, it was followed by political upheaval and revolution. The formation of the Huguenot church in France was followed by the formation of the Huguenot party and the outbreak of the Wars of Religion. With the appearance of organized Calvinism in the Low Countries the long smouldering hostility to Spain became a war for independence from which eventually emerged the Protestant-Calvinist Dutch Republic. The civil war which broke out at last in England in the 1640's is customarily called the Puritan—that is to say, Calvinist—Revolution.

This seductive sequence of religious and political events, repeated time and again, has naturally enough suggested that Calvinism *caused* the religious wars and revolutions. Indeed, the suggestion has become a thesis. And it is that thesis which is the subject of the selections which follow in this problem. The selections represent widely divergent views with reference to this traditional framework of interpretation but, in one sense or another, they all test the thesis. And the student, as he ponders the readings, should do the same. He might ask himself, is what seems the logical conclusion really a logical conclusion at all or a form of the logical fallacy expressed in the dictum *post hoc ergo propter hoc?* Do the facts, as marshalled by the authorities quoted here, bear out the thesis? Is it generally supportable enough to be a thesis or do we impose upon very different and very complex sets of events the dangerous oversimplification of "the single cause"?

RUPERT E. DAVIES

THE THEOLOGICAL BASIS

The central problem of this section is posed by the question, to what extent was Calvinism a principal cause for the rash of social and political revolutions that broke out among the European states of the later sixteenth and seventeenth centuries? In the last three selections we shall look at specific cases in France, the Low Countries, and England. But in this first selection we must be concerned with a necessary item of background. Calvinism was primarily a theological system and, no matter how important its socio-political implications may have been, they were nonetheless implications. Thus we must see if there is a "Doctrine of Revolution" inherent in Calvin's theology. For this purpose we turn to an important critical book by Rupert E. Davies, *The Problem of Authority in the Continental Reformers,* and specifically to that portion of the book devoted to Calvin who, in this frame of reference, Davies regards as the most important of the major reformers.

The basis of Calvin's concept of authority is starkly simple: "Religious truth is to be found in the Word of God, and elsewhere only in so far as it is derived from the Word of God; there is no appeal from the Word of God, and no man, nor any body of men, is competent to set aside, add to, or disagree with, the Word of God." Thus the Bible becomes the source of supreme authority for individual men. It is also the source of authority for the church because the "visible Church" is composed of those who model their lives upon the Word of God and model the form of their ecclesiastical organization upon the principles and precedents to be found in the Word of God.

If the Word of God is the supreme authority in man's private life and in his religious life, is it not also the supreme authority in his relations with the exterior world—the state? And if the state fails to conform to the Word of God, what is the Christian citizen to do? This is the burden of the following selection. The student should note carefully the arguments that are developed with a view to applying them to the "cases" he will encounter later in this section.

What, on Calvin's view, is the relation of the Word of God to the State, in the sense of the legally constituted government? Does the Bible exercise authority over it? We must first discover the nature of the State in Calvin's idea of it. All power and authority belong ultimately and essentially to God. In view of the corruption of mankind God has delegated some of His power to men by directly setting up governments and magistrates, which will be necessary as long as man remains in his imperfect state—that is, as long as he remains on earth; they are "the vicars of God," "the ministers of the divine justice," their tribunals are "the throne of the living God," their mouths "the organ of the divine truth." Their God-given functions are "to cherish and protect the outward worship of God, to defend the sound doctrine of piety and the position of the Church, to adjust our lives to the society of men, to conform our characters to civil justice, to reconcile us to one another, to nourish common peace and tranquillity." This divine institution and these divine functions give magistrates a divine vocation, one that is not only "holy and legitimate in the sight of God, but also most sacred, and one that is by far the most honourable of all vocations in the whole life of mortals." In the performance of its functions the State has the right and duty to shed the blood of its citizens in punishment, since it is carrying out the judgements of God, and it also has the right and duty to declare and prosecute war against other States for

the protection of its citizens, although it will do everything in its power to preserve peace.

It is very clear that Calvin thus ascribes complete independence to the State in virtue of its direct divine institution. And this independence includes independence of the Church; or rather, it implies complete distinctness of province. The Church is concerned with the "soul, or the inner man," the State "with the setting up of civil and external justice of morals." Thus a man lives under two "regiments." The State may not interfere with the Church, though it is charged with the task of facilitating and protecting its operations, but the Church must not interfere with the State either.

Here, perhaps, it is necessary to pause. It is well known that in Calvin's Geneva the Church took a much greater part in politics than it has been allowed to do in any ancient or modern State, and as large a part as it took in any medieval State. It appears difficult to reconcile this fact with Calvin's conception of the functions of Church and State. No respectable reconciliation is in fact possible. Calvin's theory was what we have stated it to be. In conformity with it, Calvin himself never sought or obtained any magistracy at Geneva (although he sat on the constitutional commission of 1543); he was not even a citizen until 1559; and he exerted no influence in politics, as far as he knew, except as a

From Rupert E. Davies, *The Problem of Authority in the Continental Reformers, A Study in Luther, Zwingli, and Calvin* (London, 1946), pp. 130–38. Reprinted by permission of the Epworth Press.

private man and not as representative of the Church. He was probably unaware that any breach of his theory had occurred during his lifetime in Geneva. But here he did not see things as they really were. There were factors in the actual situation with which his theory had not reckoned. In the first place, he was himself constantly consulted on all matters which affected the city's welfare and always gave his advice on religious grounds; it was frequently taken, and his influence on politics came more and more to be virtually the interference of the Church through its leading minister. Secondly, his great love for the city of Geneva made him extremely zealous that it should be the model of a Christian city, and so he was the more urgent in his advice when it was asked for, and this intensified the impression of ecclesiastical interference. But the third factor was by far the most important: in Calvin's view, private morals were part of man's inner life and therefore within the scope of the Church; to deal with them and punish breaches of the moral law, he set up the Consistory, which was a Church court imposing spiritual penalties, including excommunication. But everyone in Geneva was a Church member, and the city was virtually identical with the congregation, so that excommunication was tantamount to banishment; and it is impossible to seclude the sphere of morals in such a way that the civil law is not related to them, so that the Consistory necessarily invaded the province of the State on numerous occasions. Thus the Church did not in practice allow the State the independence which Calvin's theory ascribed to it. A struggle naturally ensued, from which the Church emerged victorious over the State, although Calvin thought that it had merely vindicated its own rights, whereas in fact it had virtually disfranchised the State. Thus Reformed Geneva out-medievalized the Middle Ages, and the Church securely held the two swords. But Calvin's theory is not in the least affected, and to it we now return.

It is clear that it is a Biblical theory, based on the thirteenth chapter of the Epistle to the Romans, and supported by various passages in the Old and New Testaments. And Calvin quotes Scripture to prove his case at every point, according to his usual custom. Especially does he use the Biblical arguments to confute the anarchists and pacifists, who both denied in effect that government was necessary for Christians. But he nowhere says of the State what he has emphasized in respect of the Church, that it is created and formed by the Word of God, but only that it is set up by God. It seems, then, that Calvin thought of the State as having a function and authority, within its proper limits, which was derivative not from the Word, but only from God Himself. This function and authority are described and confirmed by the Word, but not created by it.

Calvin does not shift from this position when he treats of two other major aspects of politics—the right form of constitution and the nature and authority of law. On the former question, he says that it is useless for private men to speak and argue. For a great deal depends on circumstances, and even if one looks at the matter abstractly it is by no means easy to determine the best constitution. For himself, Calvin says, he has a preference for aristocracy—an interesting preference, in view of the democratic strain in his ideas of Church government, but one which he indulged when sitting on the Constitutional Commission of 1543 in Geneva, if the result of that commission's work may be used as evidence—and gives several reasons for this. But it has been "brought about by the divine providence that different regions" of the earth's surface "should be administered under different constitutions."

It is evident from this that Calvin regarded each constitution as having been determined and established by the will and direct act of God—he says in so many words in the course of the passage just quoted that God "set up an aristocracy among the Jews . . . until such time as He produced in David the archetype of Christ." Moreover, he nowhere says that we are to learn the true form of polity from the Bible, for although he uses the aristocracy, which he imagined the pre-Davidic Jews as having, as an argument in favour of his personal preference for that form of government, he does not regard the argument as in any way decisive; in fact, the implication of the passage is that we are not to go to the Bible for instructions in the matter, but rather to accept the already existing divine arrangements. It might be thought that he came to this conclusion because the Bible in various places approves of various types of polity and therefore consultation of it on this point would not be particularly fruitful, but in view of his general position in this regard it is legitimate to treat the conclusion as genuinely arrived at from Calvin's true premises.

In his treatment of law, Calvin first of all denies at some length the contention that the Mosaic law should be taken as the model of all subsequent legislation; having divided it into the moral law, the ceremonial law, and the judicial law, he says that only the first is universally applicable and that the third gives a juridical system suited to the Jews and intended for them only. Each State has to make its own laws according to the circumstances of its time and place and characters of its people, and it is entitled to make special laws, often of particular severity, in times of emergency; these laws are to be founded on one principle of the moral law—which is written, not only in the books of Moses, but on the consciences of all humanity and is rightly called Natural Law—and that principle is equity ((aequitas); but otherwise they are to be as different as circumstances demand. He goes on from this point to show that it is quite legitimate for Christians to go to law, so long as they are free from the spirit of litigiousness, despite the apparent prohibition of St. Paul in I Corinthians vi. I ("Dare any of you, having a matter against his neighbour, go to law before the unrighteous?").

We see that the position here is much the same as it is with forms of constitution; in fact, Calvin himself explicitly equates the two matters, and adds to what he has previously said about constitutions the remark that they must aim at equity. Law must differ from place to place and age to age and country to country as circumstances demand. The Bible does not prescribe the character and content of such laws; in fact, the actual legislation which it does contain is to be disregarded as being of a purely temporary nature. But there is one difference which is worthy of note. Constitutions are of direct divine appointment; laws are made by the government which results from the constitution, and their authority, like that of the taxes which a government may impose, is divine only at the first remove. But this fact does not affect the relation of the law to the Word of God, which is not invoked in the matter at all.

It may be objected that as laws (and, according to Calvin's afterthought, constitutions) are to be expressions of the principle of equity, and as the principle of equity is derived from the Word of God, they are after all subordinate to the Bible. But this objection takes no account of the sharp distinction between morals and law in the mind of Calvin, morals being within the province of the Bible and the Church, law within the province of the State. It is quite true that this distinction cannot really be maintained and that the attempt to maintain it had unpleasant results in practice in Geneva; it is also true that Calvin's de-

mand that laws should be based on the moral principle of equity is a virtual, though unconscious, admission that the distinction is untenable. But Calvin did make and maintain the distinction, and we must therefore deny that Calvin subordinated law to the Word of God.

The last aspect of politics with which Calvin deals in the *Institutes* is the question of the subject's obedience to his rulers. This was, of course, a matter of supreme importance to those of the Reformed faith, in view of widespread persecution, actual or imminent, at the time at which Calvin was writing. He discussed it therefore with care and at length. What he has to say follows logically from what he has said about the nature and functions of governments, constitutions, and laws. The authority of rulers is from God; therefore they are to be obeyed; to resist one's ruler is to resist God. It is quite true, he points out, that it is difficult to see in many rulers the representatives of God, but God is using them for His purposes none the less. The ruler has, of course, duties towards us, but they are not our business. We must do our duty, and, if need be, suffer as a consequence. If we feel disposed to rebel because of the sin or incapacity of our rulers, we must resist the temptation; their punishment will be carried out in due course by God Himself, and it is no concern of ours.

So far Calvin seems almost to have overstated the conclusion which follows from the delegation of divine power to human rulers—no doubt in his eagerness to prevent civil strife in as many countries as possible and to clear the Protestants of the charge of stirring up rebellion and internal dissension. But he has two modifications to make. Firstly, he says: "I am speaking all the time about private persons. For if there are now any magistrates of the people set up to restrain the licence of kings (as, for instance, the ephors who were opposed to the Spartan kings, or the tribunes of the people who were opposed to the Roman consuls, or the officers of the *demos* who were opposed to the Athenian Senate; and whatever power in present circumstances the three orders have in individual kingdoms when they hold their primary assemblies), so far am I from forbidding their opposition in accordance with their office to the mad licence of kings that, if they connive at the unrestrained aggressions of kings and their outrages against the humble common people, I assert that their deceit amounts to criminal treachery; for they are fraudulently betraying the liberty of the people which God has ordained them to protect." We are entitled to suppose that the "opposition" here virtually enjoined on "magistrates of the people" may take violent forms, and we have therefore here a concession to those who assert the right to rebel which is capable of having important practical consequences. Yet it must be observed that the right of the "magistrates of the people" to oppose the ruler is derived from their own position as rulers, and therefore set up by God; there is nothing here to limit the duty of subjects to obey.

In the last section of all he makes the second, and larger, modification. "But in the obedience which we have decided to be due to the commands of our rulers, we must always make this exception—or rather, this must be our primary consideration—that it may not lead us away from our obedience to Him, to whose will the wishes of all kings must be subject, to whose decrees their commands must give way, to whose majesty the emblems of their majesty must submit." We are to disobey the commands of our rulers when they are against God; and this he interprets by saying that we must "endure anything rather than turn away from piety." In other words, as his examples from the Old Testament show, we are to disobey when we are commanded to follow a false religion—and only then. There is no sign, however, that we, as private citizens, are to go farther than passive disobedience; violent action is not open to us.

This whole account of the duties of subjects is, of course, amply established and confirmed throughout by the evidence of Holy Writ, and in a certain sense it is true to say that the subject is to obey his rulers and rebel against his rulers because he is commanded to do so by the Bible. He is thus subject in his political relations to the authority of Scripture. But the principal reason why he is so to obey is the fact that the rulers' power comes to them straight from God, whom it is his prime duty in the whole of life to obey, and the principal reason why he is on certain occasions to rebel is the fact that the rulers on these occasions have ceased to be the instruments of God and have set themselves against Him, and consequently obedience to God involves disobedience to the rulers. And there is certainly nothing in the whole account to suggest that the rulers have their power from any source but God, or that they are subordinate to the Word of God. Thus Calvin here, it appears, is strictly consistent with his general view of government.

A charge of inconsistency might, however, be brought against him on one count. A subject is to disobey his rulers when they command anything against God; now only the Bible reveals what is against God. Therefore it seems that the subject disobeys his rulers whenever they issue a command which is contrary to the Bible; and this means that the rulers, despite Calvin's professions to the contrary, are to legislate after all in accordance with the Bible. But the inconsistency dissolves if we remember once again Calvin's distinction between the provinces of Church and State. The State, if it truly conceives its function, cannot possibly issue commands which are against God; if it does issue such commands, it must be that the State has gone beyond its province and intruded on that of the Church and Bible. And the permission on certain occasions to disobey means in fact permission to disobey when the State has exceeded its functions.

Here, perhaps, it is worth while comparing Calvin's view of politics with that of Luther. Both Reformers held that God set up the State directly, and that the State therefore derives its authority from God, and not from the Word. But whereas Luther asserts that the State once set up must govern and make its laws according to the prescriptions of the Word, Calvin says that it does so in its own derived right. Thus Calvin takes a step, wholly alien to the thought of Luther, in the direction of autonomizing the State. He is, of course, nowhere near to saying that the State is autonomous in the sense of being independent of divine law altogether; but he does free it from any subordination to Church or Bible. It is ironical, therefore, that while Luther's Church became subservient to the State, Calvin's Church aimed at and often achieved domination of the State.

We may now sum up as follows the scope and nature of the Bible's authority according to Calvin: for the individual in religious matters, the Bible is completely authoritative; in political matters he is under its authority to the extent of being commanded authoritatively by it to obey his rulers, but much more he is under the authority of God as mediated to him by his rulers. The Church derives all its authority from the Bible, and the Bible is for it completely authoritative. The State derives its authority immediately from God, and the Bible has no authority over it.

It is clear that we cannot ascribe to Calvin the Biblical totalitarianism which we found in the case of

The Eve of the Modern World

Luther; and the former's partial recognition of the autonomy of the State and of the individual in his political relations puts him beyond the Middle Ages. We have, too, in Calvin the beginnings of the distinction between religious and other kinds of truth, implied by the right of the State to publish its own valid ordinances. Of course, the distinction in Calvin is merely inchoate, since the State's edicts are to him derived from God, but the door has been pushed slightly ajar for the State to enter later with a claim of absolute right to speak in its own sphere, and then for science, art, and the rest to do the same.

J. E. NEALE

THE WARS OF RELIGION: A SPECIAL CASE?

The clearest and most often cited example of Calvinist revolution are the so-called Wars of Religion in France. Even this conventional label betrays the thesis. And it is thoroughly understandable: Calvin was French himself; he felt most deeply the religious disabilities under which "true religion" suffered in France; he directed his most passionate efforts to the conversion of his fellow Frenchmen; and he was successful to the extent that the earliest major organization of Calvinism outside the city of Geneva itself was the Huguenot organization in France. It is to that organization that we turn in the following selection excerpted from Sir John Neale's *The Age of Catherine de Medici*. There are several chapter-essays in the book dealing with various aspects of the Wars of Religion, but we are concerned with his chapter on the religious background and the formation of the Huguenot church organization which Neale regards as "the most striking feature in the history of the French Calvinist . . . movement." In this assessment he is in basic agreement with Davies, the author of the preceding selection, who said in an earlier passage of his book, "It is in the matter of church government that [Calvin's] influence has been, and remains, most profound and far reaching." The shape of the Huguenot church became the shape of the Huguenot rebel state that supported the Wars of Religion.

While Neale's account is not cluttered with special pleading or religious partisanship he, nonetheless, is in substantial agreement with the conventional thesis that the religious wars were caused by the special character of Calvinism. He contends, for example, that the French reform movement "was bound to assume the shape of rebellion." The student should keep this idea in mind as he deals with the last two selections in this section for he must decide if the thesis which explains so well the Wars of Religion in France can be equally well applied to the Dutch Revolt or the English Civil War; or whether the case of the Wars of Religion is a special case.

Our story begins in March 1559 with the Peace of Cateau-Cambrésis. It was primarily a peace between Spain and France, though England too was a party, for Mary Tudor had entered the war in the train of

From J. E. Neale, *The Age of Catherine de Medici* (New York, 1959), pp. 9–11, 13–22, 24–32. Reprinted by permission of Barnes & Noble, Inc., and Jonathan Cape Ltd.

her husband, Philip II, and had lost Calais. This peace marks the close of an epoch in European as well as French history.

The most obvious change in the European scene was its new rulers. Only three to four years before, Philip II had taken over Spain and the Spanish Netherlands from his father, the Emperor Charles V; in England Elizabeth had become Queen the previous November; and in France celebrations connected with the Peace were to result in the death of Henry II and thus lead to the gradual emergence of the Queen-Mother, Catherine de Medici, as the director of French policy. By a striking coincidence all three of these rulers were long-lived. Catherine de Medici died at the turn of the year 1588-89: she was sixty-nine. Philip II died in 1598: he was seventy-one. Elizabeth died in 1603: she was sixty-nine. The second half of the sixteenth century was dominated by these three personalities, and, according to one's national standpoint, is the Age of Philip II, of Elizabeth, or of Catherine de Medici.

The Peace of Cateau-Cambrésis closed the period of the Italian Wars, which had gone on intermittently for over sixty years and ended, from the French point of view, in complete humiliation. France finally gave up the challenge to Spanish hegemony in Italy, and Italy was left to itself and Spain. The Italian states could no longer disturb the peace by playing off one great power against another; they passed out of the main current of international affairs.

The Italian Wars were ended. So also was the second great theme of that period of history—the German Reformation. After years of disorder and civil war, in which the Emperor had tried and failed to accomplish the miracle of uniting rival theologies in a compromise, exhaustion and realism had propounded their own solution—the solution which is described by the Latin tag, *cuius regio eius religio*: the prince determines the faith of his kingdom. The sixteenth century was totalitarian in its political creed: its motto was "One King, One Faith." Germany preserved this creed in its Reformation settlement, but paid a heavy price. It shattered itself. The Prince, not the Emperor, was the beneficiary of the German Reformation; and a country which in law was a federal state became in consequence a confederation of states. German unity had to wait until the nineteenth century—or perhaps one should say, until the twentieth. The Reformation settlement was

embodied in the Peace of Augsburg in 1555; and thereafter Germany, like Italy, receded from the main current of European affairs and did not re-emerge until the eve of the Thirty Years War, half a century or so later. In that half-century it is western Europe that occupies the stage of history.

Modern research, with its emphasis on economic factors, has a very up-to-date reason for the making of the Peace of Cateau-Cambrésis: money, or rather, the lack of it. Of that I must say a word in a later chapter. But in the mind of the King of France, Henry II, who wanted peace so desperately that he was prepared to surrender almost anything, money was not the only reason. He had an overwhelming desire to tackle a domestic problem, the urgency of which had been growing in recent years. That problem was heresy; and it is the theme of this chapter.

We have all heard, maybe to the point of staleness, about the causes of the Reformation; about the state of the Catholic Church in the early sixteenth century, about worldly and non-resident bishops, ignorant and unspiritual clergy, and the monasteries. The story is the same in France, only perhaps more so, for there, in addition to the general slackness of the age, there was a peculiar reason for the deplorable condition of the Church. It was the Concordat of 1516; an agreement made between the French monarchy and the Papacy, which can only be described as a deal in the spoils of the Gallican Church. It gave the King the nomination to bishoprics, abbeys, and conventual priories in France; and its effect can be put quite briefly. Not a single French bishop obtained his post because of religious zeal or spiritual worthiness. Fifty per cent of benefices were given for Court services, the rest to please influential local magnates; and benefices were actually given to two Italian princes to further French diplomacy in Italy. These appointments were regarded, not as ecclesiastical preferment, but as grants of revenue, a conception that was blatant enough when the grants consisted of all future vacant benefices until their combined revenue should reach a certain sum. . . .

In its early phases the French Reform movement was moderate and respectable. It was the spiritual facet of Humanism, a blending of Erasmian and Lutheran impulses, and had the King's sister for patron. Though admirable in many ways, it lacked the qualities to shape a great rebel cause. Indeed, neither Lutheranism nor Humanism possessed the

The Eve of the Modern World

practical genius required for sustained and successful rebellion. This may seem a strange remark when one thinks of the explosive force of the Lutheran Reformation in Germany: it had been dynamic enough to rouse a whole nation and had accomplished a revolution. But the practical success of the movement had been due to the support of the secular princes. It was they and not Luther who had supplied the Lutheran Church with its organization. Luther was a mystic, not an administrator. To him the Church was not an organized, earthly society, but an invisible body, the mystic communion of saints; and it needed the mundane mind of the Prince to fetch the Church down from the heavens, where Luther had left it suspended, and clothe it in the necessary garments to move about the earth. There were no essential Lutheran doctrines about the form of church organization, and everywhere the Prince supplied that form. Consequently we find the Lutheran Church episcopal in one state and non-episcopal in another. . . .

If French Protestantism had remained Lutheran it would indeed have been a weak plant.

It would have been weak because in the nature of things the Reformation in France could not count on the support of the King. However much on occasions the French monarchy might seem to wobble, there can be little doubt that it was fated to remain Catholic. What had it to gain from going Reformist? In the all-important business of appointing to bishoprics and wealthy abbeys, the King of France, under the Concordat of 1516, was as much the Head of the Church as Henry VIII of England. A government that was desperately and permanently bankrupt, as France was for the next half-century, that relied on its ecclesiastical patronage to pay officials and courtiers, and that in dire need was able to tax the Church without mercy, could not afford to discard a system which served it so well.

True, the French King might have broken with Rome and, like Henry VIII, become the titular as well as the practical Head of the Church. There was an old and strong tradition of Gallicanism in the French Church, a tradition of national independence which might seem to have suggested a move of this sort; and in the first year or two of our period there actually was an occasional hint to the Papacy that if it did not mind its p's and q's France might follow the example of England. But even if such a change had been practical policy, it would not have satisfied the Reformers. On doctrinal questions a breach with Rome would no doubt have brought some concessions to Protestants, but the last thing the Reformers wanted was the perpetuation of that scandalous laxity and irreligion associated with royal control of the Church. No. The French monarchy was fated to remain Catholic. Its vested interests in the *ancien régime* were too great, and so also were those of powerful elements in the country. Moreover, though Protestant communities developed in Paris and were troublesome, this city was always staunchly, nay fanatically Catholic. It was not an accident that England ultimately took the religious complexion of its capital: London was worth a sermon. Nor was it an accident that France ultimately took the religious complexion of its capital: Paris was worth a Mass.

Thus the French Reform movement, being opposed to the interests of the monarchy, was bound to assume the shape of rebellion. Now, there are certain essentials for prolonged and successful rebellion; and the chief is organization. Here lies the significance of Calvinism. If I am inclined to stress organization over against doctrine or anything else, the reason is my profound conviction of its vital importance. Much of English history, Scottish history, and Dutch history in the second half of the sixteenth century might be written round the organization of Calvinism; and I am often tempted to speak of this period as the Age of Calvin, although in fact Calvin died in 1564. . . .

The theological or doctrinal aspect of Calvinism need not detain us. On this subject it is sufficient to note that at a moment when the inherent individualism of the German Reformation was producing confusion in Protestant theology, Calvin, with his legal training and the clarity and rigour of the French genius, rethought Protestant theology into an ordered and logical system. The Gallic qualities of his mind naturally fitted his teaching to become the Protestant gospel of the French people. There was one doctrine of Calvinism—that of predestination, to which Calvin was driven by the relentless logic of his thought—which deserves mention because of its value to a fighting faith. In time of hazard and persecution it was no small fortification to the spirit to know that one was among the elect, predestined by God to salvation.

But it is not the theology, it is the organization of this Church that is the most striking feature in the history of the French Calvinist, or, as it was called,

Huguenot movement. Unlike Luther, Calvin did not regard the organization of the Church as a negligible consideration and let the State have its own way. It was an integral part of his teaching. After all, the secret of the power wielded throughout the centuries by the Catholic Church lay in its organization and discipline as well as its dogma. And, as one eminent French historian has put it, Calvin's unique achievement, the sign of his originality, was to construct a new Catholicism outside the old and opposed to it.

This organization, which is better known to most of us by the name Presbyterian, must be examined in some detail. The officers of Calvin's Church were divided into three categories: ministers, elders, and deacons. The elders joined with the ministers in the government and discipline of the Church, while the deacons had charge of the sick and poor. In appearance the scheme had a democratic basis since each minister—and the same was true of elders and deacons—had ultimately to be elected by the particular congregation that he was to serve. But in fact Calvin's Church was oligarchic and conservative. The real choice of candidates for the ministry was in the hands of the body of ministers, who put them through a preliminary and searching examination of their doctrinal views and knowledge of scripture, their preaching ability, and their moral fitness. In Geneva Calvin gave the title of the Venerable Company to his ministers, and he meant them to live up to the title. Discipline was the very essence of his Church, among both officers and rank and file.

Each individual church, in the scheme of ecclesiastical government for countries like France, was governed by its minister and elders, the laity in the persons of the elders joining with the ministry here as throughout the whole organization. Minister and elders together formed a disciplinary committee known as the Consistory, which, by domiciliary visits or otherwise, maintained a constant supervision over the mode of life of every member of the church; an activity which Queen Elizabeth, to whom the Genevan system was anathema, described as an intolerable inquisition to pry into people's lives. This committee might even, and in France did, exercise a minor police power.

Above the Consistory, or ruling body of the single church, was another committee known in France as the Colloquy. It consisted of the ministers and elders of a number of neighbouring churches, grouped into a district, over which they exercised a general supervision, dealing with business brought to them by the individual churches. Above the Colloquy was the Synod, also a governing body of ministers and elders. In a large country like France there would be Provincial Synods, and, capping the whole ecclesiastical organization, a National Synod.

Think what this organization meant; think, especially, how well it was adapted to the cause of rebellion. Isolation, which breeds fear, doubt, and surrender in all but the most courageous, was impossible. No sooner was a community formed than it was organized; no sooner were there several communities than they were linked together by the Colloquy; and on top of this came the Provincial Synod and finally the National Synod to weld all the churches into a single unit.

Throughout every grade of this organization ran the remarkable Calvinist discipline, which maintained unity of belief and a high code of personal conduct. . . .

So much for the organization and discipline of the Calvinist Church. We must next see how Calvin meant his Church to fit into the State. Once more he was precise and logical. State and Church were separate powers, but they were fused, first by the assumption that every citizen would be a member of the Church, and secondly by the unique position accorded to the Bible. Calvin regarded the Bible as the word of God, in the full and literal sense. Consequently, in a godly society it should be the fundamental law both of the State and the Church. Now the Bible is full of moral injunctions, and the Old Testament in particular, with its Mosaic laws, embodies a whole penal code. These injunctions and this code, being the word of God, should therefore be part of the law of the State: for example, death is the punishment for adultery in the Old Testament, and it should be the same in the Calvinist State. From our point of view the conception reveals a monstrous confusion of morality and law; the sort of confusion which, in a minor degree perhaps, the contemporary totalitarian State has made. But it is not my object to condemn or praise; and I hasten to make a final point about Calvin's State. It is this: since the Bible was to be the fundamental law of the State, and since the professional expositors of the Bible were the ministers, it followed that the ministers would in fact dominate State as well as Church. In other words, Calvin's State would be a theocracy; a

The Eve of the Modern World

natural conclusion, for he drew his inspiration from the Old Testament and the Israelitish theocracy.

This in brief was Calvin's theory of Church and State — his vision of Utopia. In the course of the centuries many authors have written Utopias; few indeed have had the opportunity and the ideal conditions for putting them to the actual experiment. This perfect and rarest of Fortune's gifts was Calvin's. Geneva became his theocracy. . . .

It was from Geneva that the French Huguenot movement was organized. From here and neighbouring Protestant cities, Protestant literature was carried secretly through France by colporteurs and distributed surreptitiously by booksellers. It is significant that between 1549 and 1557 no less than fifty-six printers and booksellers sought refuge in Geneva. From here also missionaries went forth. As Huguenot congregations were formed it was to Geneva that they applied for ministers, and it was there that they sent their young men to be trained for the ministry. On questions of government and policy they were continually writing to Calvin. Once more I think that a contemporary parallel may be helpful. Calvin's Geneva was in many ways like Moscow during those years after the war of 1914–1918 when the Soviet State dreamed of a world communist revolution: it was as much a thorn in the side of the French government as Moscow in the side of capitalist Germany before 1933.

Though this account of Calvin and Geneva has not, I hope, exceeded the length that their place in French history warrants, it is time that we examined the growth of the Calvinist movement in France itself.

First, let us look at the classes of people who responded to Reformist propaganda. We can best begin with the one class that it scarcely touched — the peasantry. With certain exceptions they were hostile. They were completely illiterate and thus could not be affected by the clandestine literature that played so large a part in Huguenot propaganda; and as was inevitable with people rooted to the soil, they were profoundly conservative. They were attached to the worship of saints and the cult of the dead; and it was only when Reformist ideas began to grip the nobility and gentry that any of them were won over to the cause, and then by tenant-loyalty rather than religious conversion.

As might be expected, it was among the educated,

at the universities, that the new doctrine spread first. Many university teachers and also tutors in noble households were converted, and in due course influenced the minds of their pupils. Medical men, lawyers, and notaries, and other professional men figured prominently in Huguenot ranks. The lawyer class in France was very large and, in comparison with the less bureaucratic government of England, was used in great numbers in the administration of the country. They formed almost an estate in themselves, and their traditions were anti-clerical. It was generally from the rank and file of the profession that Huguenot converts were obtained. They played an important part in the movement, for they were able secretly to shelter heretics from the operation of the laws against them.

These professional men were mostly the sons of merchants, whose trade connections with other countries brought them into touch with new-fangled ideas, and who, by their independent spirit and quality of mind, as a class were everywhere inclined to anticlericalism and heresy. In France they had additional cause for discontent in the grave financial drain caused by the Italian Wars. Their professional sons had no small part in converting them to Calvinism; and the organization of the Huguenot Church, by providing through the offices of elders and deacons for bourgeois laity in church government, appealed to their *amour-propre*. The spirit of Calvinism was, as I have said, essentially oligarchic and bourgeois.

Among the clergy, the bishops kept more or less clear of the infection. Only four went over to Geneva; five more were restless. Otherwise, in contrast with the English Reformation, the episcopacy was the great obstacle to heresy. It was the lower clergy and especially the Friars who became Huguenots. For three centuries the Friars had been the militia of the Church. They thronged the universities, and by their preaching, their mysticism, and their contacts with the people, were the true leaders of the crowd. They were a great asset and a great nuisance: speculators in doctrine and rebels against discipline, their tradition was one of independence and turbulence. They proved readily accessible to Genevan ideas, and were invaluable in the early stages of the Reform movement as peripatetic preachers of heresy, profiting by the non-residence of bishops and the immunities of their orders to overrun the country. They provided the new Church in France with its first ministers. But their indiscipline and their democratic spirit, both of which Calvin loathed, detracted from their service. One of Calvin's correspondents described them as "these horrible beasts"; and Calvin himself was far from enamoured of such turbulent pioneers.

The nobility—a class which included what we in England would term the country gentry—was the last class to be won over in large numbers. Very few were Calvinists in 1547, but twelve years later the situation had changed remarkably. Education and the influence of their women-folk were important factors in their conversion. With the women it was religious feeling—a revulsion against the moral and religious laxity of Francis I's reign; but with their men-folk the motive was often revolt against a social and political regime of which they were the victims. Moreover, they had lost a good deal by the Concordat of 1516, before which they had been able to secure high ecclesiastical positions for their sons. They tended to be anticlerical and anticipated spoils for themselves in the form of Church lands if the Reform movement triumphed.

The recruiting of the lesser nobility—the country gentry—was of great practical service. They might be described as the Storm-Troopers of the Huguenot movement. As a class they were entitled and accustomed to carry swords, and they therefore constituted a natural protection for meetings of heretic congregations. There was need for this. At first Huguenot congregations met in secret and often at night, in cellars or in the countryside outside the towns. Their meetings were illegal and liable to be broken up by the authorities. A more frequent danger was attack by hostile bands of Catholics, for, as the movement spread, it inflamed passions, as the growth of the Nazi movement did in Germany; and just as there were incessant clashes and fights between Communists and Nazis in the days before Hitler succeeded to power, so there were clashes and fights between Catholics and Huguenots. The gentry were needed to protect the Huguenot ministers and their flocks from assault, and congregations often met with a body of armed protectors forming a circle of defence round them. The churches came to place themselves, each under some nobleman as their protector.

As the number of converts increased, the situation deteriorated, breeding further aggression on both sides, for there were few ministers available in the earlier stages of the movement and congregations were therefore apt to grow so large that they were

forced to meet in public. Secrecy was no longer possible. An extract from the minutes of the Consistory of Mans, dated August 6th, 1561, illustrates this transition to public meetings: "It has been decided that M. Merlin shall commence to preach publicly under the town hall of this town on Sunday next at 7.0 a.m. Superintendents will make haste to warn faithful noblemen (gentilshommes) so that all the faithful of this town shall be at the meeting." After this beginning, the minister at Mans preached in public four times a week.

Naturally, when secret meetings gave place to public, ministers were no longer able to exercise adequate control over the recruiting of their audiences, and rowdy elements appeared, only too ready to start image-breaking. Moreover, there was an impulse, which the ministers could not well restrain, to seize buildings, especially churches, for Huguenot services. This was often done in a hot-headed and riotous way. In Languedoc and Guienne bands of fanatics drove priests and worshippers out of churches and attacked convents. Similar happenings took place in other parts of the country, though occasionally, where Catholics were lukewarm, amicable arrangements were made with them and churches were shared between the new and the old faiths.

The change from secret to open worship—a significant stage in the Huguenot story—took place during the years 1560 and 1561. Disorder spread through France. Where Catholics were in a majority they turned on the Huguenots and engaged in bloody strife; where the Huguenots were strong, extremists often got out of hand and terrorized the Catholics.

Speaking in general terms—for it would be wearisome, and not very illuminating, to discuss the question in detail, province by province—the Huguenot movement tended to be strong in centres of international trade; for example, at Lyons, the great entrepôt near to the Genevan and German centres of Protestantism, and in the east in Brittany where trade connections with England and the Netherlands encouraged its growth. Normandy too was badly infected with heresy, though here the chief inducement was social and political discontent among the gentry of a province where the evils of French government were exceptionally rife. The movement also flourished in the south, from the Rhône and Provence through Languedoc to the King of Navarre's territory in the south-west. Paris had heretics, but

The Eve of the Modern World

remained predominantly and fervently Catholic: the Huguenot stronghold over against Catholic Paris was Orleans, where some idea of the numbers may be gathered from the fact that in May 1561 five to six thousand persons attended Communion and more than ten thousand followed Protestant funerals. In May 1561 there were said to be two thousand one hundred and fifty separate Huguenot churches in France.

The important years for the organization of the Church were 1555 to 1559. Since 1555 the separate churches had been organizing themselves, largely under the influence and direction of Calvin, who wanted to put a stop to disorder and establish a responsible ministry and proper discipline. Then in May 1559 the first National Synod was held in Paris. The meeting was in a lodging house, so that the coming and going would not attract attention; and the number present may have reached fifty. They were obscure men, for as yet the nobility had not imposed itself upon the leadership of the Church; and all of them risked death by their presence. They drew up a confession of faith and articles of discipline, including a constitution or organization for the whole Church. . . .

Such an organization—the organization of a rebel movement within the State—would be remarkable at any time in any State. It is nothing short of astounding to find it within the sixteenth-century State.

That is not all. I have already noted how the nobility, when they joined the movement, naturally took over the protection of congregations. During the turbulent years 1560 and 1561 most of the individual churches placed themselves under a noble protector. Consistories and Synods encouraged this, and the nobility took their place, by right of birth, on the governing bodies of the churches they protected.

The dangerous possibilities of this development were soon evident. The French nobility still retained the old feudal traditions which grouped the lesser nobles under the leadership of greater noblemen, and these in turn under still greater, until the few greatest noblemen in the land were reached—a feudal pyramid. Obviously, this grouping of the nobility fitted perfectly into the pyramid organization of the Huguenot Church, with its district, provincial, and national bodies. And so the Church was able and indeed tempted to create a military organization coinciding with its ecclesiastical organization. The individual church had its captain, the Colloquy its colonel, and the Province its general (chef-général). This was the military organization devised in November 1561 for the provinces of Bordeaux and Toulouse.

At this point I can, for the moment, leave my story, for I am verging on the political problem of the age—the subject of my next chapter. I would merely ask you to consider the amazing character and terrifying possibilities of this organized heretical party; consider also the passions that its growth had aroused in France. And I know no better way to secure an imaginative grasp of the situation than to reflect on the turbulent history of the ideological movements in our own days—the history of the Fascist movement in Italy, and better still of the Nazi movement in Germany. Governments have collapsed before them.

PIETER GEYL

THE DUTCH REVOLT: A REVISIONIST VIEW

The following selection from the writings of the eminent Dutch historian Pieter Geyl represents a radical departure from the general thesis we have been examining in this section. He reviews the conventional interpretation, i.e. that it was the Calvinist temper of the Dutch that led them to rebel against Spain, strengthened them in their heroic resistance, and finally led them to the formation of their independent and staunchly Protestant state. And then he examines the facts: there was a long tradition of Dutch language and culture, predating by centuries the formation of a Dutch state; there was, moreover, a long tradition of self-government which was offended by "the relentless policy of centralization and autocracy pursued by the royal government"; in the early and crucial years of the rebellion the Protestants were a minority everywhere, not only in the Catholic south but in the allegedly Protestant north; and finally, the most significant fact was the course of military action in the war itself and the military advantage represented by the natural defensive lines of the great rivers. The result is that "the true explanation, then, of the division of the Netherlands into a Protestant north and a Catholic south is the exact opposite of the current one. . . ." Thus cause and effect are reversed and rather than Calvinism causing the revolt, the triumph of Calvinism is the result of a revolt which was successful on other than religious grounds.

Of course Geyl is dealing with only a part of the general thesis—its application to the Dutch revolt—and he claims nothing more. He does indicate that the whole thesis "would bear discussion of a more general theoretical character." The student should attempt such a discussion for himself. He should note the revisionist methodology, so well demonstrated by Geyl, of testing a plausible theory against hard fact and see if he can apply this methodology to the other parts of our theory and to those other regions of Europe where Calvinism is said to have been the prime cause in making revolution.

The problem I shall here discuss—the problem of the modern State and my own Netherlands history—is one that posed itself before me very early in my career. It is a problem that would bear discussion of a more general theoretical character than I shall venture upon. I shall write as a practicing historian—which is what I am—who has come up against a problem that required some thinking out, some grappling with theory.

The Dutch State resulted from revolution and war in the closing decades of the sixteenth century; but there had been a long history in the Low Countries before it came into existence—a long history when the Dutch language was spoken and Dutch literature flourished, when people felt and thought about religion in ways which still have a meaning today, when churches were built which still dominate our towns and villages, and pictures painted in which we can still recognize ourselves.

If there was no Dutch State, there had been, ever since the migrations and settlement of the Franks in

the sixth century after Christ, a Dutch linguistic area. The extent of this linguistic area has remained extraordinarily constant throughout the centuries. The linguistic boundary separating Dutch from French still runs where it ran when the Frankish colonization was completed some thirteen centuries ago. Expressed in present-day political terms it runs right through Belgium, so that the Dutch linguistic area now embraces Holland (or the Kingdom of the Netherlands, to use the official description) and the northern half of Belgium, commonly called Flanders. (Let me say in passing that this name *Flanders,* historically speaking, belongs only to the western part, the ancient County of Flanders. Flanders in the modern sense of the Dutch-speaking region of Belgium, extends also over the ancient Duchy of Brabant and other districts still further East. Similarly *Holland* is originally no more than the northwestern part of the Kingdom which is now commonly so called. The ancient county was later on only one of the seven provinces constituting the Dutch Republic.)

Now the point that needs stressing is that this ancient

From Pieter Geyl, *Debates with Historians* (New York, 1958), pp. 179–93. Reprinted by permission of World Publishing Company and William Collins Sons & Co. Ltd. Copyright © 1958 by the World Publishing Co. All rights reserved.

The Eve of the Modern World

(and still modern) Dutch linguistic area is not co-terminous with the Dutch State as it suddenly sprang into existence in the course of the sixteenth-century revolt against Philip II of Spain. It is much larger. The Dutch State comprises not quite two thirds of the Dutch-speaking people in the Low Countries and the region which remained outside at the critical moment in the last quarter of the sixteenth century was the region in which the Middle Ages—with towns like Ghent and Bruges, Antwerp and Brussels—Dutch literature and civilization had had their earliest and most significant development.

It is a fact deserving careful attention that the linguistic area had never been the basis of any political formation. In the late Carolingian times part of it owed allegiance to the French Kingdom, another part to the German Kingdom; but, as time went on, in both cases this allegiance came to mean less and less. The reality were the feudal principalities—duchies, counties, bishoprics; and these gradually became completely independent. At last, in the fifteenth and early sixteenth centuries, a union was brought about by an outside power, the French Dukes of Burgundy, and their successors the Hapsburg rulers. But in this union the French-speaking provinces—as the old principalities now came to be called—Hainaut, Namur, Artois, and the rest—were combined with the Dutch-speaking provinces, Holland, Gelderland, Groningen, Brabant, Flanders and the rest; and the whole of the Netherlands came, moreover, to be connected with the extensive Hapsburg Empire, and in the end more especially with Spain. The Burgundian-Hapsburg rulers had meanwhile brought the beginnings of a central administration to the Low Countries; the governor and his councils resided at Brussels.

Within the framework thus created it was a natural development for a national sentiment, a sentiment of belonging together, to grow up. But the Burgundian-Hapsburg rule had at the same time introduced subjection to a foreign system, and it was in opposition to this domination, in opposition particularly to the purely Spanish tendencies of the rule of Philip II, that the national sentiment became more keenly aware of itself. It was fully awakened in the revolt in which all the seventeen provinces, with the single exception of Luxemburg, participated from 1576 on, under a States General meeting in a revolutionary fashion at Brussels.

Everybody knows that this union was broken up in the course of the resulting war and that only a group of Northern provinces achieved independence, becoming the Protestant Republic of the Seven United Provinces, while the Southern provinces were reduced to obedience and became, under the sovereignty of Spain, an advanced post of the great Counter-Reformation movement. Today the Dutch Kingdom is still preponderantly Protestant, or at least non-Catholic, and the Kingdom of Belgium homogeneously Catholic. The great question is: how did this separation, and how did this divergence in religion, come about?

There is one answer to this question which I am afraid is the one which will occur spontaneously to most of you. It is that it must have been because Protestantism steeled the Northern rebels—the Dutch—to a successful resistance, while the Southern rebels—the Belgians—being Catholics, did not have the heart to persevere in the struggle. It is the answer that is still to be found in innumerable English and American textbooks and that indeed until fairly recently used to be given, in various disguises, or to a greater or lesser extent attenuated or qualified, by both Dutch and Belgian historians. But it never agreed with the facts.

You should note, first of all, that at the outset, before opposition had developed into revolt and war had altered the face of things, the Protestants were not more numerous in the North than they were in the South (and everywhere they constituted no more than a small minority). When in 1576 all the provinces united against the King of Spain—by the so-called Pacification of Ghent—it was not long before in all of them, in the provinces of Flanders and Brabant no less than in the Northern provinces, the Protestant minority managed to get hold of the positions of power and actually were in command of the rebellion. How was this possible? For one thing, because the only armed force which was from the start at the disposal of the Prince of Orange, the Sea Beggars, had helped the Protestants into the saddle four years earlier in the Northwestern provinces of Holland and Zeeland. If they managed in 1572 to revolutionize those two provinces alone it was not because their inhabitants were so much readier to welcome them, but because their geographical position invited attack from oversea and their soil offered special advantages for defence against Spanish attempts at reconquest. These partisan bands were composed of the exiles of the abortive rebellious movement of 1566–7; they were drawn from all the provinces; and they were Protestants to a man. The rebellious spirit in the country, however, was by no means exclusively caused by the new religion. It was primarily due to the irritation of a people wedded to their medieval tradition of self-government at the relentless policy of centralization and autocracy pursued by the royal government. But the Protestant minority, placed in a position of power by the armed invaders in 1572, were the most determined, in fact irreconcilable, enemies of the King, and that was in itself another reason why they came to occupy the leading positions everywhere. Revolutions are always led by minorities, and so it was here. It had been so in Holland and Zeeland from 1572 on, and soon after 1576 in Brabant and Flanders as well the Protestants came to the top.

But now the Spanish Government had got another army ready, which under the Duke of Parma, from 1578 onward, set about conquering the rebellious Netherlands. This army started from the outlying province of Luxemburg and in the course of not very many years managed to reduce to obedience a considerable part of the country. The fall of Antwerp (the great commercial metropolis of the Netherlands at that time) in 1585 completed the conquest of Flanders and Brabant. But Parma also took the whole East, up to the extreme North; Groningen made its submission as early as 1580. In 1590 Parma's advance was definitely halted, and the rebels, reduced now to a small group of Northwestern provinces clustered round Holland, set in a counteroffensive, by which they recovered part of the ground lost.

The religious convictions of the populations had little to do with these movements of conquest and reconquest. One glance at the map will show you that Parma's farthest advance, about 1590, was bounded by the strong strategic barrier of the rivers traversing the Netherlands from East to West (the Rhine and the Maas) and by the river Ysel. How strong this barrier is we learned to our cost in September 1944, when Montgomery was held up at Arnhem and the liberation of exactly the same portion of the Netherlands—all the country north of the great rivers and west of the Ysel—was delayed by a terrible eight months. If Parma was never able to cross that barrier, if the rebels on the contrary were able to take the offensive and push him back, it was because he was ordered by Philip to intervene in the French civil war and had to divide his forces. The counteroffensive, led by Maurice of Orange, Wil-

liam the Silent's son, was again conditioned by the geographic factor. It was easy to recover the country east of the river Ysel, but not because the population there were in sympathy with their "deliverers." On the contrary they were overwhelmingly Catholic —much more so than Flanders and Brabant had been, although today that region, Groningen for instance, is solidly Protestant. But in those years the Groningers clung to the Spaniards as their protectors from the heretics. If they were "delivered," and then Protestantized, it was because the region was too far removed from the base of Spanish power in the South. To push on south of the great rivers, on the contrary, was a task beyond the power of Maurice. It would have meant a head-on attack on the main strength of the Spanish position.

Meanwhile, these military events were deciding the fates of the two religions contending for mastery. As soon as Parma and his Spaniards had recovered their hold on a district, Protestantism was strictly suppressed; most of the Protestants in fact emigrated —the majority settling in the provinces which were still holding out, in the North, that is, where they strengthened the Protestant element. The rebels, on their part, were all the time carrying on a reverse process of Protestantization, in which all means of pressure were used. This was a process, however, for which time was needed, and only where the rebellion survived for a generation or longer could the majority of the population be brought over to the new church.

The true explanation, then, of the division of the Netherlands into a Protestant North and a Catholic South is the exact opposite of the current one. It is not because the South was Catholic and the North Protestant that the rebellion failed here and succeeded there: it is because the rivers enabled the rebellion to entrench itself in the North, while Spain recovered the provinces situated on the wrong side of the strategic barrier, that in course of time there sprang into existence this dual system of the Protestant Northern Republic and the Catholic Southern Netherlands, of Protestant Holland and Catholic Belgium.

I have now given you, reduced to its simplest form, and somewhat dogmatically, an argument which I adumbrated for the first time more than thirty years ago and which I have since set out on many occasions, elaborating certain aspects of it or indicating its implications in connection with a variety of topics. Here I shall discuss something of the historiographical background to the conflicting views on this matter. I never discovered any new facts. The relevant facts were not unknown nor are they in dispute. Is it not remarkable, then, that historians both in Holland and Belgium either completely overlooked them, or at least gave them little attention, failed to draw the obvious conclusion, and commonly wrote as if the separation had been a perfectly natural event and the emergence of a Holland and a Belgium, the one Protestant and the other Catholic, was the consummation of divergent tendencies inherent in the history and character or civilization of the populations?

Seeley, in his little book on *The Growth of English Policy*, refers to "that curious sort of optimistic fatalism to which historians are liable" and which in England caused them to argue (as he puts it) "that the loss of our American colonies was not only inevitable, but was even a fortunate thing for us." It is in that spirit exactly that Simon Stijl, about 1770, in a popular one-volume *History of the United Netherlands*, wrote that "one of the principal causes to which our Republic owes its durability resides in its *correct size*. Had it been smaller, its neighbours would have despised it. Had it been larger, it would have become unmanageable." Remember that this "correct size" of the Republic of the Seven Provinces was less than one third of that of the single state of Pennsylvania. Remember also that this paean to its durability was written twenty-five years before it was overthrown for good and all by the armies of the French Revolutionary Republic. And in fact this was not the first occasion, nor was it to be the last, on which the break-up of the old seventeen Netherlands into two unrelated small states left both helpless in the face of foreign invasion.

Here is another example of the way in which historians dealt with the problem. In 1860 Fruin wrote: "It was no passing misunderstanding that brought about the separation; it was a profound difference between the northern and the southern provinces, in origin, in national character, . . . in religion. . . ."

Now, Fruin is a historian of a very different stamp from Stijl. He is the acknowledged master of the modern, methodical school in Holland, and his work is still very highly regarded. There is no glamour about Fruin. He is pre-eminently critical. He does not paint, he tries to explain. When he was a rising scholar, the reading public in Holland as well as in the rest of the world was captivated by the moving and colorful work of Motley. Fruin devoted to Motley's *The Rise of the Dutch Republic,* and later on to its sequel, two very long essays, small books really, very deferential in tone; but the effect of the story as told anew by the critic is to make the reader realize that Motley had sacrificed everything to his sense of the dramatic and that he had no real understanding of the problems of Dutch history. Today nobody—among Dutch or Belgian historians at least—will take Motley's views and explanations seriously any longer, but everybody will study Fruin's magisterial essays. It is all the more amazing, then, that a scholar of this calibre could go so utterly wrong in discussing the causes of the Netherlands split.

He says that it was due to *difference in origin*. Apparently he was thinking of the difference between the Dutch-speaking section and the Walloons. But the line of political separation did not follow the linguistic boundary. The fact that requires explanation on the contrary is the splitting-up of the Dutch-speaking population.

He says that it was due to *difference in religion*. But, as he knew very well, Protestantism was no less strong in the South than it was in the North. The homogeneous Catholicism of present-day Belgium and the preponderance of Protestantism in present-day Holland cannot have caused a sixteenth-century event.

He says that the separation was due to *difference in national character*. No more is needed to answer this than to quote another English historian, Maitland, who once described national character as "a wonder-working spirit, at the beck and call of every embarrassed historian, a sort of *deus ex machina,* which is invoked to settle any problem which cannot readily be solved by ordinary methods of rational investigation."

In the present case "rational investigation" will yield the solution readily enough, if only it is resorted to. But the most surprising thing of all is that Fruin never once mentions the Spaniards when enumerating the causes of the split. Antwerp held out for a year when Parma laid siege to it in 1584, and yet we find Fruin and a host of writers, both Dutch and Belgian, speaking as if the separation were due to mutual misunderstanding or incompatibility. . . .

The revolt and the separation in the late sixteenth

century form critical points in the debate outlined; and if time permitted it could be shown from Belgian writers as well as Dutch how other details came to be misrepresented under the influence of contemporary preoccupations. But it is obvious that the whole course of Netherlands history *before* the separation must present difficulties to anyone placing himself on the modern State point of view.

Yet this was generally done, and the first author to do it systematically and with really brilliant synthetic power, was Henri Pirenne, the first volume of whose *Histoire de Belgique* appeared in 1900. Here the past was uncompromisingly subjected to a conception inspired by the modern State. In his preface Pirenne announces quite plainly that it is his aim to bring out "the character of unity presented by the older history of Belgium." Of Belgium? He means, of course, of the regions which were at one time, many centuries later, to constitute Belgium. For in the days of Caesar or of Charlemagne, or even of Philip the Good or Charles V, Belgium really was still far to seek. But Pirenne sees it coming all the time. He does not for a moment conceal the fact that we are in the presence here of an unusual phenomenon: the exchange of influence between, the gradual growing together into one nation of, Germanic and Romance populations, Flemings and Walloons. But he is all the time out to show how criss-cross connections, economic, political, social and cultural, led to a similarity of conditions and bound together the regions on either side of the linguistic boundary.

It is clear to me that there is a large element of artificiality in this conception of Pirenne's. Given the unmistakable present-day political inspiration, one would on general grounds expect this to be the case; but the imposing work actually abounds in passages, as well as in omissions, where the constructive intention can be seen to have done violence to the unruly multiplicity of historic reality. . . .

The most striking expression of these views is to be found in a little book, *Nederland en België*, published in 1905 by a young historian, Colenbrander, who was to be one of the leading men of his generation. It was inspired entirely by Pirenne. The Flemings, by Pirenne's theory, had been skillfully and unostentatiously detached from the Dutch, and had been safely, and to all outward seeming honorably, incorporated in a mystic Belgian unity stretching back into the remotest ages. It now remained for Dutch historiography to show that a similar unity had from ancient times embraced the regions which in the late sixteenth century came to constitute the Protestant Republic, forerunner of the contemporary Kingdom. What the argument required particularly was a demonstration of the original and innate difference that had caused Dutch and Flemings to diverge. Colenbrander found evidence in religious movements, in schools of painting, in architecture. The method has been applied many times since, by writers on art, on literature and on religion, and also by the political historians, to prove that a Dutch nation existed in the midst of the feudal confusion, or in a corner of the Burgundian-Hapsburg State, before ever a Dutch State had been born—a nation already complete with all the virtues which present-day Dutchmen love to regard as being their own: soberness and simplicity, a strong spiritual awareness under a reserved exterior, a nation, in short, of regular little Calvinists before ever Calvinism had been thought of.

How easy a game it is! The civilization of the medieval Netherlands was a rich one and richly diversified; features to suit a particular argument can always be discovered and, if isolated and arranged in a certain way, can be used to produce the desired impression. How easy a game, but how unprofitable! These ingenious speculations might have some interest if the separation of the sixteenth century had indeed been a voluntary one. The assumption that this is so underlies the whole argument of Colenbrander, just as it did that amazing passage of Fruin. Like Fruin, Colenbrander seems to forget about Parma and his Spanish army; and although I have always been ready to meet the speculators on their own ground, the recollection of the way in which things actually came to pass in the sixteenth-century war of liberation and reconquest is enough to brush their fallacies aside as so many cobwebs.

CHRISTOPHER HILL

THE "PURITAN REVOLUTION":
A SUMMARY OF REVISION

The politico-religious doctrines of Calvinism came to the British Isles largely through the agency of John Knox who brought Presbyterianism to Scotland by way of Geneva and the Marian exiles, those English Protestants who had fled their country during the brief Catholic revival of Mary Tudor's reign, who had been deeply affected by Calvinist influences during the exile, and who returned to England under Elizabeth as the Puritans, the most familiar label for the English Calvinists. Their strength and their explosive religious doctrines grew through the long reign of Elizabeth to become the major force in the civil war which came under her Stuart successors, which took the life of a king, which for a generation established a Protestant "Rule of Saints," and which ended in the Stuart restoration.

The above is a sketch of the conventional thesis that the English civil war was a "Puritan Revolution." Its greatest exponent was the nineteenth century English historian Samuel R. Gardiner whose many books—including a ten-volume *History of England from the Accession of James I to the Outbreak of the Civil War*—and whose awesome archival research gave to his position a seemingly unassailable orthodoxy. But the forces of historical revision are irreverent and twentieth-century scholars have assailed the unassailable. Of all the facets of the general problem we have dealt with, none has been more besieged by revision than that of the English Puritan Revolution. And in no area has the revision been more subtle and sophisticated. In view of the complexity of the interpretations the following selection has been chosen, the chapter entitled "Recent Interpretations of the Civil War," from *Puritanism and Revolution* by Christopher Hill. It is precisely what its title claims, a summary statement of recent scholarship on the problem written by one of the most eminent authorities on the subject.

The student should not only follow these arguments with reference to their specific subject but should attempt to apply them, where they are applicable, to the parallel problems of continental Calvinism and revolution.

In 1913 R. G. Usher wrote: "The English Revolution of 1640 is as much an enigma today as it was to Charles. It is a riddle which has to be solved. No one has tried to solve it because all assumed it was solved by repeating the Grand Remonstrance. Every Englishman born since 1800 has . . . been born into a view of English history."[1]

Anyone who has studied the pages of the *Economic History Review* recently will agree that the English Revolution is still an enigma, though not now be-

[1] R. G. Usher, *The Historical Method of S. R. Gardiner*, p. 156.

cause historians repeat the Grand Remonstrance. One school of thought appears to believe (roughly) that the revolution was caused by the rise of the gentry during the century before 1640. Another school believes (roughly) that it was caused by that section of the gentry which was declining during the same period. The subscriber pays his guinea and takes his choice. The object of this essay is to take stock of the present state of the controversy over the causes of the civil war.

We have to start with Gardiner. His eighteen volumes on the history of England between 1603 and 1656, supplemented by Firth's *Last Years of the Protectorate*, established fifty years ago an interpretation of the civil war as "the Puritan Revolution," a struggle for religious and constitutional liberty. Gardiner's immense learning and mastery of the then available sources, his narrative gifts and his knack of hitting on the telling quotation—all this has made his authority very difficult to overthrow.

Yet Usher long ago pointed out Gardiner's bewildering eclecticism of method; and the case against Gardiner has been reinforced by much detailed research published since he wrote, especially in the field of economic history. A. P. Newton's *Colonizing Activities of the Early Puritans* showed that Pym and many of the Long Parliament's leaders had important trading connections. J. U. Nef's *Rise of the British Coal Industry*, and other works by Nef himself, Wadsworth and Mann, Ramsay, Dobb, Court and others have established the existence of something like an industrial revolution in the century before 1640. Professor Tawney's *The Agrarian Problem of the Sixteenth Century*, Professor Arkhangelsky's two volumes on *The Agrarian Legislation of the English Revolution* (in Russian) and Mrs. Thirsk's articles[2] have revealed agrarian problems whose depth Gardiner does not seem to have suspected. All these works—and many more could be cited—suggest that far more importance should be given to economic developments in preparing for civil war than Gardiner allowed. Moreover, Professor Tawney's *Religion and the Rise of Capitalism*, popularizing a great deal of German work on that sub-

ject, stated a connection between Puritanism and the rise of capitalism which most historians would now accept, even if they differed about which was cause and which effect. It is difficult to go on speaking about "the Puritan Revolution" *tout court*.

Finally, since the publication of Professor Namier's great works on eighteenth-century politics, historians have got into the habit of asking new questions. They have become more interested in the "connections," whether of patronage or economic interest, of historical characters, than in their proclaimed political principles. The "Namier method" has already been extended forward to analyse nineteenth-century parliaments and back to the fifteenth century. The witenagemot still awaits Namierization: not so the Long Parliament.

Today, then, the "Puritan Revolution" is in eclipse, though many of its assumptions still haunt our thinking. The view which explains the civil war as a struggle for liberty is little more acceptable to historians trained to ask "liberty for whom to do what?" It is a question to which many answers can be given. Liberty for witch-hunters to burn witches, and liberty for wicked capitalists to grind the faces of the poor, have been two of the simpler and least convincing, which I shall not be discussing.

In many ways the reaction against Gardiner has been healthy. "The Puritan Revolution" was a nineteenth-century invention: there is virtue in going back to explanations current in the seventeenth and eighteenth centuries. Men so diverse in their political outlook as Winstanley, Harrington, Hobbes, Baxter, Clarendon, all explained the civil war in terms of social forces which we are today less likely to dismiss than Gardiner was.[3] We hardly need to be reminded, in this ideological age, that there were more reasons than religious conviction for supporting a "protestant" foreign policy which expressed itself in war to open up the Spanish empire to English trade; that a greedy citizen of London might object to paying tithes no less than a pious Quaker; we observe remarks like that of the servant giving notice: "I would have the liberty of my conscience, not to be catechized in the principles of religion,"[4] because we now realize that the liberating effects of

---

[2] Mrs. Thirsk has shown that large numbers of royalists regained their confiscated estates even before 1660 ("The Sales of Royalist Land during the Interregnum," *Economic History Review, Second Series*, V, pp. 188–207; "The Restoration Land Settlement," *Journal of Modern History*, XXVI, pp. 315–28). Space has not permitted a discussion of this very important contribution, which must modify our view of the Restoration.

[3] But Gardiner had his moments of insight. Cf. his excellent analysis of the social function of Scottish Presbyterianism in his *History of the Great Civil War* (1901), I, pp. 226–8.

[4] T. Edwards, *Gangraena* (1646), p. 138.

toleration extended beyond the purely religious sphere.

But many of the reactions against Gardiner have so far been rather negative. To be told that many of those whom we call "Presbyterians" opposed the establishment of a Presbyterian church in England, and that many of those whom we call "Independents" were Presbyterian elders,[5] is helpful in so far as it stops us thinking of the two great parties as primarily religious groupings. But that is only half our problem. Gardiner's interpretation of the English Revolution will no longer do: yet no alternative interpretation has yet acquired general acceptance, and none has been put forward, in this country, which can compare with Gardiner's in scope and solidity.[6] It is noteworthy that in the *Oxford* and the *Penguin Histories of England* the volumes dealing with this period are among the least satisfactory in the series. They have not escaped from Gardiner, though they supply the evidence for showing that his (and their) interpretation is no longer convincing.

II

Professor Tawney came nearest to establishing a new orthodoxy, especially in his still unpublished Ford Lectures of 1936, and in "The Rise of the Gentry" (*Economic History Review*, XI, No. 1) and *Harrington's Interpretation of his Age* (*Raleigh Lecture*, 1941). Professor Tawney's views are familiar and easily accessible, so I shall not attempt to summarize them: they amount to an adaptation of Harrington's theory that the civil war was fought to redress the balance of property which had been upset by the redistribution of land in the century before 1640. This position seemed to be strengthened by an article by Mr. Stone, "An Anatomy of the Elizabethan Aristocracy," which suggested that a majority of the peerage was heavily indebted by the end of Elizabeth's reign, and was saved only by subsidies from her successor. Mr. Stone's figures, however, were criticized by Professor Trevor-Roper, and Mr. Stone himself modified some of his original statements, though he did not abandon his general argument.[7]

In 1953 Professor Trevor-Roper produced his own rival interpretation. Criticizing Professor Tawney's use of the concept "gentry," he argued that the civil war was caused not by the rise but by the decline of a section of the gentry. The really big profits in the century before 1640 were made not by farming but by holding court office, by the practice of the law, or by taking part in industry or trade. The "mere gentry," those who enjoyed none of these alternative sources of income, inevitably got into financial difficulties.[8] They struggled to get positions at court. Essex's revolt in 1601, and Gunpowder Plot in 1605, are to be seen as desperate attempts by the "outs" to get "in."[9] So apparently is the civil war. Professor Trevor-Roper explains that as a gentleman became impoverished, he retired to his estates and set about economic reorganization. For this he needed "an ideology of economy, of retrenchment." Such an ideology he found either in Roman Catholicism or in extreme Puritanism. His adherence to either of these beliefs would complete his isolation from the Court and strengthen the bonds between himself and others of his like who had been through similar experiences. Independency and Roman Catholicism are both creeds of the declining gentry.[10]

A summary so bald cannot do justice to the vigour and cogency with which Professor Trevor-Roper argues his case. He has certainly established the need for more, and more reliable, statistics before we can safely generalize about "the gentry" in this period. He has performed a useful service in emphasizing the importance of court office as a source of windfall profits for the fortunate few. Nevertheless, on balance, I do not myself feel happy about the thesis as a whole. . . .

Even if we could accept the equation of Independents with declining gentlemen, it would not help us to explain the civil war. For when the war began the men in control at Westminster were not those whom we call Independents, and certainly not declining gentlemen; they were great peers like Warwick, Essex, Manchester (the last named a *court* peer who had bought out the declining *Royalist* Cromwell); Hampden, the richest commoner in England; Pym,

[5] J. H. Hexter, "The Problem of the Presbyterian Independents," *American Historical Review*, XLIV, pp. 29–49.

[6] The only one known to me is a two-volume collective work published in the U.S.S.R. in 1954 entitled *The English Bourgeois Revolution of the 17th century*, whose 800 large pages interpret the revolution in Marxist terms as "one of the most important turning-points in English, European, and world history."

[7] *Econ. H. R.*, XVIII, Nos. 1 and 2; *Second Series*, III, No. 3; IV, No. 3.

[8] H. R. Trevor-Roper, *The Gentry, 1540–1640* (*Econ. H. R. Supplement*), pp. 24–31.

[9] *Ibid.*, pp. 32, 38–42.

[10] *Ibid.*, p. 31.

government employee and treasurer of a City company; Holles, son of a gentleman rich enough to buy an earldom. When the Five Members escaped from the King's attempt to arrest them in January 1642, they did not flee to the backwoods: they retired to the City of London, where they were warmly welcomed. The civil war might not have been won without the Independents, but they did not start it. Professor Trevor-Roper speaks always of Presbyterians and Royalists as though they were "on the same side,"[11] which is absurd in the years before 1647.

But the point at which Professor Trevor-Roper's analysis seems to me least satisfactory of all is his attitude to religion. For him the economic needs of a declining gentleman might be expressed either by Roman Catholicism or by Independency, and it seems to have been of no significance which of the two he happened to take up. For the declining gentry were behind all the political upheavals of the early seventeenth century—Essex's revolt, Gunpowder Plot, 1642. Even if this thesis fitted the English facts (which it does not), it would still be intolerably provincial. For over a century before 1640 men all over Europe had been suffering, dying, and killing for what they held to be high ideals; from the sixteen-twenties a great war was being waged on the Continent over ideological issues which aroused the intensest excitement in England and created a profound cleavage of opinon about questions of foreign policy. Professor Trevor-Roper asks us to see in all this only a reflection of the financial difficulties of a section of the English gentry. The spiritual wrestlings of a Milton, a Vane, a Roger Williams are nothing but the epiphenomena of economic decline. The idea is difficult to discuss seriously. Only three brief points may be made. First, if we are to look for causal connections between recusancy and economic decline, it is surely less likely that a gentleman turned Catholic because of poverty than that his poverty was caused by recusancy fines. Secondly, radical Puritanism is specifically associated by contemporaries with the towns, as indeed similar creeds had been all over Europe since Calvin's day. Thirdly, one of the few generalizations we can make about the civil war is that Catholics and Independents were on opposite sides. So if they were both declining gentlemen fighting to get back to the spoils of office, both "outs" trying to become "ins," on which side were the "ins"? Perhaps they were the Clubmen, the only neutralist party?

[11] Op. cit., pp. 33–4, 42–3, 53.

III

Professor Trevor-Roper has had second thoughts on the Independents, published in a brilliantly argued essay on "Oliver Cromwell and his Parliaments."[12] In this "the Independents" are divided into two sharply contrasted categories. The first is "the Whigs" —men like Hesilrige, Scot, Bradshaw, Slingsby Bethel. These are in fact those whom most of us regard as the main parliamentary leaders of the Independents, though for Professor Trevor-Roper they have now become "the republican usurpers." The second category comprises "those ordinary Independent gentry whom Cromwell represented," the back-benchers and the officers.[13] This distinction has validity: but what remains now of the thesis that it was the Independents, the declining gentry, "who made the revolution"? To define the Independents proper in such a way as to exclude the majority in the Rump, and simultaneously to attribute the making of the revolution to them, is like saying that the French Revolution was "made" by those Jacobins who were to support Napoleon after 1802. How many of those now claimed as the real Independents even sat in Parliament before 1645? It surprises Professor Trevor-Roper, but need surprise no one else, that those who sought to create "an Independent political caucus" for Cromwell in the Parliaments after the expulsion of the Rump "were not real Independents but, all of them, ex-royalists"—Ashley-Cooper, Wolseley, Broghill.[14] A "real" Independent is clearly a rare bird. It seems to me that in refining and improving his definition to suit his argument Professor Trevor-Roper has destroyed his own thesis about the causes of the civil war. . . .

IV

Another recent work which discusses the line-up in the civil war is that of Messrs. Brunton and Pennington, *Members of the Long Parliament*. This book has been rightly praised by many reviewers, and it contains a wealth of valuable information. If I dwell on what seem to me its less satisfactory aspects it is, first, because I believe some reviewers have claimed

[12] In *Essays Presented to Sir Lewis Namier* (ed. R. Pares and A. J. P. Taylor), pp. 1–48. On p. 28 Professor Trevor-Roper is mistaken in saying that the Instrument of Government preserved the old property qualifications.

[13] *Ibid.*, pp. 16, 20, 45–6; cf. Professor Trevor-Roper in *Annales* (1956), p. 493.

[14] *Ibid.*, pp. 18, 46–7. Wolseley was born in 1630.

The Eve of the Modern World

too much for it (indeed, more than its authors would); secondly, because I believe harm may be done if it is too easily assumed that its negative conclusions are irrefutable; and thirdly because I believe methodological considerations of some importance for future work on the subject are involved.[15]

The authors analysed the personnel of the Long Parliament, and asked themselves whether this analysis threw light on the causes of the civil war. Their conclusions were entirely negative. Gentlemen, lawyers, and merchants were found among M.P.s on either side. The only significant difference was that the average age of Royalist M.P.s was thirty-six, that of their opponents forty-seven. Therefore, the authors concluded, attempts to explain the civil war in terms of class divisions are unfounded.

This conclusion may be criticized on two grounds. First, I believe the facts have in certain important respects been incorrectly interpreted; secondly, even if the interpretation were correct, the conclusion would not follow.

(I) Even on Messrs. Brunton and Pennington's own analysis, significant differences between the two groups of M.P.s can be seen. Though there were merchants on either side, they were not equally divided. Of the London merchants elected to the House of Commons, the twelve monopolists were expelled; in the civil war they naturally supported the court through which their profits had come. Of the remaining nineteen London merchants, eighteen were Parliamentarians. The one exception, George Lowe, held estates in Wiltshire and was connected by marriage with Edward Hyde.[16] Provincial merchants were more equally divided. But in the Eastern Association merchants were solidly Parliamentarian, and even in the Royalist-occupied areas a small majority among the merchant M.P.s had the courage to declare for Parliament.[17] The authors did not ask how many of the Royalist merchants were royal officials like the customs farmer and Duchy of Lancaster official who were returned for the borough of Lancaster, presumably thanks to Duchy pressure. Nor did they ask how many were members of urban governing oligarchies maintained in their privileged

position by the royal charters which the Levellers and Diggers wanted to abolish. The Royalist M.P.s Hooke and Long "represented actually the merchant oligarchy of Bristol,"[18] a city in which, Sir Samuel Luke was told in 1643, "they are all Roundheads . . . except the major and 2 or 3 aldermen."[19]

Similarly, to say that the numbers of gentlemen on either side were roughly equal does not get us very far. The authors warn against the dangers of dividing the landed from the mercantile interest, especially in the clothing counties.[20] But should we not attempt to divide *within* the landed interest? The economic life of most gentlemen in Cumberland or Wales was very different from that of gentlemen in Norfolk or Surrey. Messrs. Brunton and Pennington brush aside altogether too lightly the distinction between the economically-advanced south and east of the country, which was Parliamentarian, and the economically-backward north and west, which was Royalist. Mr. Pennington admits that "a study of how the estates of landed members were managed might reveal an economic line of cleavage corresponding to the political one."[21] Until this question has been investigated it is premature to tell us what the answer to it is.

The authors also note that

among county families it is easier to find Parliamentarian than Royalist members who were exploiting local assets and opportunities. More characteristic of the Royalists are the supplementary sources of income that could be picked up through connections at the court and in the capital.[22]

This contrast between local economic activity (whether in industry or agriculture) and the economic parasitism of the Court would be a profitable field of research for those looking for divisions between M.P.s (and among the gentry as a whole). And were such activities only local? Mrs. Keeler notes some 60 M.P.s known to have been members of trading companies, and there were no doubt many more:

[15] See a review of *Members of the Long Parliament* by B. Manning in *Past and Present*, No. 5 (1954) and a discussion between Messrs. Manning and Pennington in *ibid.*, No. 6.

[16] Keeler, *op. cit.*, pp. 257–8.

[17] Brunton and Pennington, *op. cit.*, p. 62.

[18] Keeler, *op. cit.*, pp. 47, 53.

[19] Ed. I. G. Philip, *Journal of Sir Samuel Luke* (Oxfordshire Record Society), p. 218; cf. the similar remarks in John Corbet's *Historical Relation of the Military Government of Gloucester* (1645), in *Bibliotheca Gloucestrensis* (1823), I, p. 14.

[20] Brunton and Pennington, *op. cit.*, p. 73.

[21] *Past and Present*, No. 6, p. 88. This most important reservation was mentioned in the last dozen lines of *Members of the Long Parliament*.

[22] Brunton and Pennington, *op. cit.*, pp. 166–7.

most of them seem to have been Parliamentarians.[23] A thorough exploration of all these business activities, central and local, might even help us towards answering Messrs. Brunton and Pennington's rhetorical question: "What is it that makes one great grandson of a Tudor copyholder or a Tudor judge a progressive bourgeois and another a feudal aristocrat?"[24] We are at least more likely to find the answer here than in even the most exhaustive examination of members' pedigrees. Independency, the authors note, was strong among M.P.s from the clothing counties: it was weakest in the north and west.[25]

Further, to divide members of the House of Commons into two parties, labelled "Royalist" and "Parliamentarian," and then to treat all members of the two groups as statistically equivalent, is misleading. Side by side with men prepared to sacrifice property to principle, like Henry Marten or Sir Bevil Grenville, our authors perforce list the marginal turncoat on either side who had no principles at all. They were aware of the dangers here, and they may be right in arguing that no other division was possible. But statistics so compiled are of highly dubious value. Mr. Pennington recognizes that "the crucial problem" is the M.P.s who were firm opponents of Strafford (and, we might add, continued to oppose the Court throughout 1641) and yet fought for the King.[26] Mrs. Keeler's book shows the very large number of M.P.s who no doubt owed their place in the Commons to their opposition to the government and yet ultimately changed sides. Nineteen Cornish M.P.s swung over to the King between the summer of 1642 and the end of 1643.[27]

There might be many reasons for this: fear of the consequences of treason;[28] fear for the safety of one's estates; alarm at social disorder (anti-enclosure riots, refusal of rents, pressure of London citizens on M.P.s, "mechanick preachers"). . . .

Another reason for changing sides might be the possession of estates in areas occupied by the royal forces. Something approaching 100 M.P.s who

transferred their support to the King after 1642 came from areas controlled by Royalist armies in the early stages of the war. . . .

As in dealing with Professor Trevor-Roper's views about management of the Commons, so here we are faced with the larger question of the applicability of "the Namier method" to periods of acute political crisis. The method was originally devised to illuminate English politics at the accession of George III. It would be difficult to find a period in the whole of English history when the political nation was more "at one in all fundamental matters." It was therefore legitimate to apply a technique of analysis which ignored political principles, or treated them as rationalizations of economic or other interests. But if we go even a few years forward—to the Wilkes question—or a few years back—to the Jacobites, to 1688—principles begin to rear their inconvenient heads.[29] Here the Namier method is of more limited value, as its author specifically warned. Messrs. Brunton and Pennington analyse their M.P.s into family groupings, local groupings, economic groupings, patronage groupings, age groupings. (It may reasonably be argued that family and regional groupings were also economic groupings more often than Messrs. Brunton and Pennington recognize.[30]) But none of their groups are united by ideas. Yet there was in the House of Commons a group of republicans; perhaps some M.P.s even took their religion seriously enough to work together with men of like convictions?[31]

About the relation of M.P.s to the electorate questions must also be asked which would have been less relevant in 1760. Politics then was what went on at Westminster. But a civil war by definition transcends the limits of the old governmental institutions. The war was maintained not so much by the 500 M.P.s as by the citizens of London, Hull, Gloucester, Plymouth; by the freeholders of Buckinghamshire riding up to London to defend John Hampden; by the russet-coated captains of Cromwell's Ironsides; by the members of the sectarian congregations. Even if Messrs. Brunton and Pennington had established (as they have not) that there

[23] Keeler, op. cit., pp. 25, 30; Brunton and Pennington, op. cit., pp. 162–4.

[24] Ibid., p. 178

[25] Ibid., pp. 43–4.

[26] Past and Present, No. 6, p. 87.

[27] R. N. Worth, Buller Papers, p. viii.

[28] See a discussion of this point between the Oxinden cousins in The Oxinden Letters, 1607–43 (ed. D. Gardiner), pp. 308–9.

[29] I owe this point, as so much more, to discussions with Professor Richard Pares.

[30] Keeler, op. cit., p. 30; Manning, Past and Present, No. 5, p. 72.

[31] "Mr. Pennington finds it difficult to understand the division into the parties in the Commons because he ignores the ideas that underlie it" (Manning, Past and Present, No. 6, p. 90.)

were no significant economic divisions between M.P.s on the two sides, they would have proved very little about the division in the country. The House of Commons was elected on the same franchise as had prevailed since 1430: naturally men of the same social types as in previous Parliaments were returned. Parliament contained a cross-section of the ruling class. The two houses were divided because the ruling class was divided. What needs analysis, if we are to understand the civil war, is the exact nature of this division; and, secondly, its relation to division in the country at large and in the electorate.

How did any particular M.P. get into Parliament? The contestants at Great Marlow were all gentlemen, but they represented such different interests that we need different categories to place them in. Whitelocke and Hoby "stood for the liberty of the commons in the election," with the support of shopkeepers and labourers as well as of the burgesses and "the ordinary sort of townsmen"; their opponent John Borlace, son-in-law of Attorney-General Bankes, was a great local landowner. Men feared that "if they left Mr. Borlace out . . . he would not let them buy any wood of him, but do them many ill turns." Bankes had to give Borlace the seat for his borough of Corfe Castle, vacated by the expulsion of Windebanke from the Commons.[32] In Essex "it was said amongst the people that if Nevill [the royalist candidate] had the day they would tear the gentlemen to pieces." The victorious candidates were of course also gentlemen: but gentlemen clearly with a difference. The defeated candidate thought that the 40s. freehold qualifications should be raised to £20. "Then gentlemen would be looked up to."[33] The only Royalist returned from Northamptonshire was M.P. for Higham Ferrers, a borough in the Queen's jointure.[34] In general it was a Royalist commonplace that corporations were "nurseries of schism and rebellion." Messrs. Brunton and Pennington give away a larger point than they appear to realize when they admit that, at the time of Pride's Purge, "in the country generally there were undoubtedly the beginnings of a resistance by the small men, the propertyless and the oppressed," but "little sign of a class division" in Parliament.[35] This means either that Pride's Purge bore no relation to events in the country, or that Messrs. Brunton and Pennington are looking for the wrong sort of connections.

V

Fortunately Mr. Pennington too has had second thoughts, or rather has pressed his investigations beyond Westminster into the depths of the country. The simultaneous publication in 1957 of excellent studies of the county committees of Staffordshire and Kent has very sensibly added to our understanding of social divisions in the provinces.[36] In each county two parties appeared in the course of the civil war. The compromise-peace party drew its main strength from the old ruling families, concerned primarily with the preservation of their property and dominant influence. The win-the-war party, in each county, was led by members of leading families who were directly engaged in military operations, but in general its members were of markedly lower social origin. Inevitably it looked to London for a national lead and a national military organization. Religious radicals gravitated towards this group, but the conflict within county committees, which corresponds to the national rivalry between Presbyterians and Independents, was not primarily religious. Originally a dispute about military tactics, it soon revealed itself as also a social quarrel. The old ruling families were ousted from control of both counties in the middle sixteen-forties. . . .

The civil war, then, cannot be explained merely by looking at M.P.s. Men did not die and kill one another for four years over issues which can be satisfactorily analysed by a method evolved for a period in which there were no serious political disagreements. The civil war was fought about issues of principle which roused large numbers of men to heroic activity and sacrifice. To say that account should be taken of these issues need not lead us back to Gardiner's conception of "the Puritan Revolution."

The methods, the techniques of analysis employed by Messrs. Brunton and Pennington, and by Mr.

---

[32] M. R. Frear, "The Election at Great Marlow in 1640," Journal of Modern History, XIV, No. 4, pp. 437–45; Brunton and Pennington, op. cit., p. 167.

[33] C.S.P. Dom., 1639–40, pp. 608–9. The writer added that raising the franchise "would save the ministers a great deal of pains in preaching [away] from their own churches"—an interesting side-light on the political role of the pulpit.

[34] Keeler, op. cit., p. 57; cf. p. 64.

[35] Brunton and Pennington, op. cit., p. 182.

[36] Ed. D. H. Pennington and I. A. Roots, The Committee at Stafford, 1643–5; A. M. Everitt, The County Committee of Kent in the Civil War.

Stone and Professor Trevor-Roper, seem to me in danger of giving a false emphasis which, unless very great care is taken to guard against it, would render their interpretations as lop-sided as Gardiner's, though on the opposite side. By their exclusive concentration on interests, whether economic, geographical, or those of patronage, the impression is given that all politics is a dirty game, struggles for the spoils of office, the "ins"*versus* the "outs," that principles are merely rationalizations. I do not believe that material conflicts are the only ones deserving serious analysis. This approach indeed brings its own refutation. The civil war did, after all, take place, but Messrs. Brunton and Pennington supply no adequate explanation of that fact. Professor Trevor-Roper has to dismiss as "futile" the deliberate waging of war for trade, colonies and markets by the Commonwealth and Protectorate.[37] Yet these policies were to be followed by successive governments for the next 175 years. The men of undeniable political principle, whose theories of democracy inspired the American revolutionaries, the Radicals and Chartists, and are still alive today, he dismisses as "the lunatic fringe," who were able to become vocal only because of the degeneration of politics after 1643. This is not dealing very seriously with history.

VI

An earnest evangelical once expostulated with Baring-Gould about the chorus of "Onward Christian Soldiers." Dangerous concessions to ritualism, he thought, were made in the words

With the cross of Jesus/Going on before.

Baring-Gould accepted the criticism with due solemnity, and suggested that the low church gentleman might prefer to sing

With the cross of Jesus/Left behind the door.

"The Puritan Revolution" is dead and buried, and I do not want to resurrect it; but need Puritanism be left altogether behind the door? The importance of economic issues has been established; but we still have to find a synthesis which will take cognizance of this and yet give some explanation of why in 1640 not only M.P.s but a large number of other people thought bishops the main enemy; why there were so many conflicts before 1640 over the

appointment of lecturers in town corporations; why, when the troops got drunk of a Saturday night in 1640, their animal spirits were worked off in the destruction of altar rails; why Cromwell's Army marched into battle singing psalms.

The following points, I would suggest, will have to be included in our ultimate synthesis:

(i) A much more serious study needs to be made of the political effects of the "industrial revolution" of the century before 1640. Professor Nef's valuable suggestions in his *Rise of the British Coal Industry* have not been properly followed up. The struggle over monopolies was not only of financial and constitutional importance; it was also of the greatest consequence for the future of capitalism in industry that there should be freedom of economic development. Further knowledge here might help us to a clearer understanding of the support which towns (except sometimes their ruling oligarches) and the rural industrial areas gave to the parliamentary cause.

(ii) When Dr. Valerie Pearl's eagerly awaited thesis on the City of London is published, we shall have a clearer picture of politics there in the crucial years 1640–3. We shall know more about the links between the ruling oligarchy of aldermen and the Court, which made the City government Royalist, and isolated it from the majority of the Common Council and of City voters, who were radical Parliamentarians: and about the fierce conflicts which led to the violent overthrow of the royalist clique in the winter of 1641, just in time to make the City a safe refuge for the Five Members. But more work is still needed on London politics after 1643, and on political struggles in other towns.

(iii) We should also, I believe, look more closely at colonial and imperial policies. Since Newton's book we all recognize the crucial importance of the Providence Island Company, but this was after all one of the smaller companies. The full political effect of disputes over colonial questions on the origin and progress of the revolution has never been fully worked out.[38] But when we find the Witney blanket-makers asking the House of Lords in 1641 to protect the rights and privileges of the Royal

---

[37] Trevor-Roper, *The Gentry*, p. 43.

[38] Cf. Manning, *Past and Present*, No. 5, p. 71. There are some valuable chapters on this subject in the Russian work quoted on p. 6, n. 2 above.

The Eve of the Modern World

Africa Company, we can image how many people's lives were already affected by freedom of export.[39]

(iv) Professor Campbell and Dr. Hoskins have directed our attention to the rising yeoman;[40] but there has been no full analysis of his economic problems in relation to government policy, nor of those of the small clothiers and artisans generally. Yet traditionally these classes are believed to have formed the backbone of the New Model Army, and most contemporaries agree in putting them solidly on the parliamentary side, at least in the south and east. There is a danger that in riveting our attention on the gentry we may underestimate social groups which were at least of equal importance once the old stable social structure began to crumble, and whose grievances helped to make it crumble.

(v) This brings us to a subject one mentions with diffidence—the people of England. Gardiner and the Whigs often assumed too lightly that Parliament represented "the people," that it is easy to know what "the people" wanted. But the modern tendency is again to throw the baby out with the bath water, and to leave out of account those who actually fought the civil war. Tenants no doubt often turned out to fight as their landlords told them, London demonstrations could be organized, the rank and file of the New Model Army were not all as politically sophisticated as the Agitators. Granting this, the evidence still suggests that in 1640 there was a real popular hostility to the old régime whose depth and intensity needs analysis and explanation, and whose influence on the course of events after 1640 we almost certainly tend to underestimate. The consumers and craftsmen who suffered from the high prices caused by monopolies, the peasants whom Laud's good intentions failed to protect,[41] and who thought the time had come to throw down enclosures in 1640–1; the ordinary citizens who resisted the Laudian attempt to increase tithe pay-

ments; the small men for whom the parson of the established church (any established church) was "Public Enemy No. 1"; the members of the sectarian congregations of the sixteen-forties and -fifties whose naïve but daring speculations have still to be properly studied in their social setting[42]—it was these men, not M.P.s or "the gentry," rising or declining, who bore the brunt of the civil war. It would also be interesting to have studies of those who fought for the King. But I suspect that in the Royalist areas the traditional "feudal" machinery still worked, landlords brought out their tenants, the militia was officered by the gentry of the county. The New Model was an army of a new type.

(vi) On the gentry, let us admit that we still do not know enough. I personally believe that the contemporary analyses of Winstanley, Harrington, Hobbes, Baxter, and Clarendon are still the safest guides, and that Professor Tawney is more right than Professor Trevor-Roper. But we should stop generalizing about "the gentry." Professor Trevor-Roper himself points out the regional differences which made a gentleman with £150 a year in Devon comparable with one who had far more in the home counties.[43] We also need to know more about different types of estate management and leasing policies, about investments in trade and industry, before we can begin to see the way in which the rise of capitalism was dividing the gentry into different economic classes. We need more studies of individual families like Dr. M. Finch's admirable The Wealth of Five Northamptonshire Families, 1540–1640;[44] more documents like those of the Herbert and Percy families edited respectively by Dr. Kerridge and Mr. James.[45] We also need more regional inquiries like those of Professor Dodd and Messrs. Everitt and Pennington and Roots, and local documents like the minutebook of Bedford Corporation. Such local studies will divert us from exclusive attention to the small group of men at Westminster, and help us to see the deeper social currents on which the politicians were floating.

[39] Victoria County History of Oxfordshire, II, pp. 247–8. Viscount Wenman, whose family had risen to a peerage through the Witney wool trade, represented Oxfordshire in the Long Parliament.

[40] M. Campbell, The English Yeoman; W. G. Hoskins, Essays in Leicestershire History.

[41] It is significant that when the Levellers, the party of the small men, were using every stick to beat the Parliamentarian leaders, even going so far as to say that England used to be merrier before the Reformation, they never, to the best of my knowledge, argued that things had been better under Laud and Charles I. If the prosperity and "social justice" of the sixteen-thirties had had any reality for the small men, it is very unlikely that they would not have used this argument.

[42] But cf. P. Zagorin, A History of Political Thought in the English Revolution.

[43] The Gentry, p. 52.

[44] Publications of the Northhamptonshire Record Society, Vol. XIX (1956).

[45] Ed. E. Kerridge, Surveys of the Manors of Philip, First Earl of Pembroke and Montgomery, 1631–2 (Wilts. Archaeological and Natural History Society, Records Branch, Vol. IX, 1953); ed. M. E. James, Estate Accounts of the Earls of Northumberland, 1562–1637 (Surtees Society, Vol. CLXIII, 1955).

(vii) Professor Trevor-Roper has done a great service in drawing our attention to the significance of control of the state. But this was not important merely as a source of spoils, of windfall wealth for individuals. The state was an instrument of economic power, maintaining monopolists and customs farmers, fining enclosers, endangering property by arbitrary taxation; in different hands the same instrument was used to confiscate and sell land, to pass the Navigation Act which challenged the Dutch to fight for the trade of the world, to conquer Ireland and grab Spanish colonies. Yet the relation of individuals and groups to the state power still needs fuller investigation.

(viii) We also need far more understanding of ideas, especially at the point where they interact with economics. Over twenty years ago Mr. Wagner wrote a fascinating article on "Coke and the Rise of Economic Liberalism."[46] This line of thought needs fuller working out; it may prove as important as that summarized in Professor Tawney's *Religion and the Rise of Capitalism*. Contemporaries were influenced by legal theories little less than by religion: Lilburne held the Bible in one hand, Coke in the other. It is therefore important to take legal history out of the hands of the lawyers, as religious history has been taken away from the theologians, and to relate both to social development. Law deals with property relations, and liberty and property were the two things most strongly and consistently emphasized in the Long Parliament in 1640–1. The fact that after 1640 (and after 1660) Sir Edward Coke was regarded as *the* legal authority, whereas before 1640 his writings were suppressed by the government, shows the importance of clarity about the exact relation of his legal doctrine to the social and economic changes of the seventeenth century.

(ix) Finally, questions of religion and church govern-

[46] *Economic History Review*, VI, No. 1.

ment should not be "left behind the door." We must have a better explanation of their importance for contemporaries than the theory that Puritanism helps landowners to balance their income and expenditure, or encourages the bourgeoisie to grind the faces of the poor. Professor Haller has shown us how the Puritan ministers acted as organizers of something approaching a political party;[47] and the ministers were more interested in religion than economics. Puritanism means Vane and Milton and Bunyan as well as Alderman Fowke, who was "not much noted for religion, but a countenancer of good ministers" and who was "deeply engaged in Bishops' lands."[48] We are in no danger today of forgetting those who fought well because they thought they were fighting God's battles. We must remember too the vision of Bacon and George Hakewill and John Preston, of a freer humanity glorifying God by abolishing evil through profounder knowledge of the world in which men live. Bacon's influence in inspiring revolt against the past became widespread only after the political revolution of the sixteen-forties:[49] modern science entered Oxford behind the New Model Army. The connections of religion, science, politics, and economics are infinite and infinitely subtle. Religion was the idiom in which the men of the seventeenth century thought. One does not need to accept the idiom, or to take it at its face value, to see that it cannot be ignored or rejected as a simple reflex of economic needs. Any adequate interpretation of the English Revolution must give full place to questions of religion and church government, must help us to grasp the political and social implications of theological heresy. . . .

[47] W. Haller, *The Rise of Puritanism, passim*.

[48] Quoted in J. Stoughton, *History of Religion in England*, III, p. 148.

[49] Cf. R. F. Jones, *Ancients and Moderns*, pp. 48–69, 122. For Preston, see pp. 239–74 below.

5

THE THIRTY YEARS' WAR

It has been claimed that not one year of the seventeenth century was free of major war somewhere in Western Europe. The claim is almost true. Thus the century that has come to mark the birth of the modern world saw to it that that world should be born in conflict.

Because general wars were so typical of the century and because the results of these wars were of such importance to the shaping of modern Europe, the Thirty Years' War was chosen as the topic of this problem. This struggle was certainly the most important war of that century. It was also chosen for another reason: as we shall see in the first selection following, there is not a single major assertion of the traditional interpretation of the Thirty Years' War which has not come under attack in recent critical scholarship. Indeed the revision has been so complete that even the concept of the Thirty Years' War as a special, separable topic is virtually lost. In approaching the subject, on the one extreme scholars have gone back along the chain of causation well beyond the events which are traditionally alleged as the immediate causes of the war—the disputed succession to the throne of Bohemia and the Bohemian insurrection of 1618. At the other extreme they have tended to see the Peace of Westphalia, the general settlement which traditionally marks the end of the war, as the conclusion of only a limited portion of the war and to make the Peace of the Pyrenees (1659) the breaking point of the century. They have lengthened the focus of their interpretations to take in not simply Germany and central Europe, but a sphere of interconnected conflicts reaching from Poland and the Baltic to the Spanish New World and the Dutch East Indies; and in temporal terms reaching back to the so-called Wars of Religion in the previous century.

There is substantial disagreement as to the relationship between the cycle of religious wars in the sixteenth century and the greater wars of the seventeenth. Some scholars still insist that the Thirty Years' War was essentially a war of religion and, while their construction is more sophisticated than that of many writers of earlier generations, the earlier assertion remains. There are more scholars who tend to reduce the element of religious causation not only in the Thirty Years' War but even in the earlier religious wars. They see a sequence of two or three rounds of war beginning with the Habsburg-Valois conflict of the early sixteenth century, then expanding to the wars in France, the Low Countries, and off the channel coast in the later sixteenth century—but still tied fundamentally to the same string of cause, the European menace of Habsburg hegemony. They tend to view the Thirty Years' War and the Franco-Spanish conflict of the seventeenth century as a major expansion and extension of this same causal theme. And, to project the subject a bit beyond the limits of this problem, they then show that the ascendancy of France in the second half of the century and the wars that flowed from the policies of Louis XIV represented only a shift in the center of power from Spain to France and the emergence of a new threat of French hegemony.

As the student studies the revisionist selections that deal with this problem, he should keep in mind this larger politico-military context. And he should ask himself the question whether with such wholesale revision of a traditional subject we may see emerging not so much a new orthodoxy as a new controversy. But regardless of the specific interpretations of the Thirty Years' War and whether one accepts or rejects one or another of them, we can see in the early seventeenth century the thread of the major theme which runs through western history from the "first Europe" of the High Middle Ages to the mid-seventeenth century, the rise of the modern state.

S. H. STEINBERG

THE THIRTY YEARS' WAR: A GENERAL REVISION

The following selection, while perhaps not entirely "A New Interpretation," as the author claims, may still be taken as one of the best examples of this generation's almost total revision of the traditional picture of the Thirty Years' War. That traditional picture may be sketched in the following terms. The war began with the Bohemian uprising of 1618; the Bohemian phase was followed in 1625 by the phase of Danish intervention; in 1630 began the Swedish phase; and the last was the French phase which ended in 1648 with the general peace settlement of Westphalia which conclusively redrew the map of Europe. Each of these standard periods of the war was dominated by its identifying personalities—Ferdinand V, Frederick V, Christian IV, Wallenstein, Gustavus Adolphus, and Richelieu. The causes of the war were seen as German constitutional and religious issues held over from the later Middle Ages and the Reformation and which were gradually broadened as non-German powers entered the war and complicated it with dynastic politics until the war which had begun as "the last war of religion" ended in being the first war of modern political issues. Finally, the Thirty Years' War has been traditionally viewed as one of the most brutal and destructive of conflicts and writers have dwelt in horrified fascination upon this theme.

There is not a single element of the foregoing picture that Steinberg and other revisionist scholars have not challenged. Steinberg, in this selection, points out that the war did not arise from German causes—either constitutional or religious—but was from the beginning part of the larger dynastic conflict of Bourbon and Habsburg and that "seen against this European background, German affairs are of minor importance." Moreover, he claims, "the conception of the Thirty Years' War as a 'war of religion' has been abandoned to a large extent," or has at least been demoted from cause to pretext. Even the time-honored theme of the brutal destructiveness of the war has been questioned.

The author of the most recent book on the "Thirty Years' War" sums up its causes and results as follows.[1] "The larger issue was that between the

[1] C. V. Wedgewood, *The Thirty Years War* (1938), p. 31, 65, 526.

dynasties of Hapsburg and Bourbon. . . . But . . . the geography and politics of Germany alone give the key to the problem. The signal for war was given . . . in May, 1618, by revolt in Bohemia. There was no compulsion towards a conflict.

. . . The war solved no problem. Its effects, both immediate and indirect, were either negative or disastrous. Morally subversive, economically destructive, socially degrading, confused in its causes, devious in its course, futile in its result, it is the outstanding example in European history of meaningless conflict."

Apart from the first dozen words quoted here almost every word of this statement is debatable. However, Miss Wedgwood only voices what may be called the *consensus gentium;* and it will take time and patience to uproot the prejudices and misconceptions of historians which have been strongly backed by playwrights, novelists and poets.[2] To Miss Wedgwood's version the following may be opposed. The various European wars fought between 1609 and 1660 decided the issue between the dynasties of Hapsburg and Bourbon. France's need to break her encirclement gives the key to the problem. Open warfare ensued over the Hapsburg effort to strengthen their grip on France to the north and north-east (truce with the Netherlands and attempted seizure of Jülich-Cleve, April, 1609). The only alternative to armed conflict was tame submission to Hapsburg domination. The series of wars ending with the peace of the Pyrenees (1659) solved the outstanding problem of Europe: the final overthrow of the Hapsburg hegemony established the principle of the balance of power, which henceforth would militate against every attempt to set up a single-state rule over Europe. The immediate effects of most of the wars were negligible; cumulatively and indirectly, they were momentous. Morally, the age of rationalism affirmed the equality of the Christian denominations and, implicitly, the freedom of worship and thought; economically, the age of mercantilism rid Europe from the curse of the American gold which had wrecked the economics of the sixteenth century; socially, the age of absolutism dissolved the feudal structure of society. It is the outstanding example in European history of an intrinsically successful settlement.

The traditional concept of the Thirty Years' War is based on two main groups of sources: deliberate official propaganda and unwittingly one-sided private records. The first reflect the opinions of the victorious powers—France, Sweden, the Netherlands, Brandenburg; the second, those of the educated middle class which was hit hardest by the economic upheaval of the time. That these distortions should have gained credence may perhaps be ascribed to two failings of the nineteenth-century schools of German historians: they consciously or unconsciously made the political interests of the Prussian monarchy the criterion by which they judged the course of German history; and they preferred narrative sources and dispositive documents to administrative and business records.

Now of the two German powers which gained most by the peace of Westphalia—Brandenburg and Bavaria—the latter lapsed into a state of indolence and complacency after the death of Maximilian I (1651), whereas in the former, Frederick William I, the Great Elector, pursued a vigorous policy of aggrandizement. He was a master of political propaganda, the first to put over the identification of Hohenzollern and German interests; and he laid the foundations of the Prussian monarchy in the ideological sphere as well as in that of power politics. In Samuel von Pufendorf (1632–94) he secured as court historiographer a scholar and pamphleteer of European reputation who had already served the Dutch, Swedish and Palatine governments. Pufendorf's interpretation of the Thirty Years' War was taken up by Frederick the Great in his *Mémoires pour servir à l'histoire de la maison de Brandebourg,* and has become part and parcel of the national-liberal historiography of the nineteenth century.

The original "atrocity" propaganda emanating from Berlin had a double aim: for home consumption it was meant to accentuate the magnitude of the political, economic and cultural successes, real or alleged, of the Great Elector by painting the background as black as possible; while at the same time the darker aspects of his policy—the abandonment of the peasantry to the tender mercies of the Junkers, the oppressive taxation of the poorer classes in general and of the townspeople in particular, the tax exemption of the Junkers, and the inordinate expenses for the standing army—could, to the more

---

[2] There can be no doubt that Schiller's *Geschichte des Dreissigjährigen Krieges,* first published in 1792, and his dramatic trilogy *Wallenstein* (1799) have crystallized and popularized the main features of the traditional concept.

From S. H. Steinberg, "The Thirty Years' War: A New Interpretation," *History,* XXXII (1947), 89–102. Reprinted by permission of the editor of *History.*

gullible, be justified as unavoidable consequences of the war. As an instrument of foreign policy, the Brandenburg version of the Thirty Years' War—Brandenburg as the defender of the protestant religion and of the "German liberties" against Hapsburg interference and foreign aggression in general—was meant to serve the shifts and vagaries of the Great Elector's policy: one aspect or another of this picture could always be turned against his *pro tempore* enemy—the emperor, Sweden, Poland, France, Denmark—and incidentally win for him the moral support of the German and Dutch Protestants or of the anti-Hapsburg German Catholic princes, or the latent German patriotism of the liberal professions.

This picture of the Thirty Years' War, born of the needs of the Brandenburg propaganda of 1650–90, more or less coincided with the historical preconceptions of nineteenth-century national liberalism. The current version of the Thirty Years' War therefore largely reflects the Prusso-German attitude of Bismarck's fight against the German middle states, Austria and France, the *Kulturkampf* against the Roman Church, and the cultural and economic expansionism of the Hohenzollern Empire.

While the official records reflect the light in which the victorious party wished the nexus and causality of events to be seen, the private sources—chronicles, annals, diaries, letters—chiefly show the results of the war as experienced by those who lost most. These documents have been used to fill in the lurid details of famine and starvation, epidemics and cannibalism, ruin of town and country, decline of civilization, extinction of large sections of the population and complete pauperization of the remainder. It is not the purpose of the present paper to glorify the Thirty Years' War; and much misery, brutality, cruelty and suffering no doubt added to the terror and slaughter of purely military actions. But nothing is gained by putting the Thirty Years' War in a class by itself: its destructive aspects are common to every war—and were in any case smaller than those of "total war" in the twentieth century—and an impartial assessment of the facts will lead to the conclusion that some of the features most commonly attributed to it are unconnected with the war itself, while others have been generalized and exaggerated. The generalization of isolated events, the exaggeration of facts and, above all, figures, the special pleading for a particular cause, lay the contemporary chroniclers and diarists less open to crit-

icism than modern historians who have failed to recognise the distorted perspective from which these accounts have been written: for the compilers of town chronicles, parish registers, family albums and personal diaries, all belonged to the same class of educated, professional men—clerks, priests, officials, lawyers—who were hit by every vicissitude of the times, and always hit hardest. Whenever circumstances forced upon the treasury a cut in expenditure, it was the educational and cultural departments which were the first victims.[3]

The very term "Thirty Years' War" is fraught with misunderstanding. Seventeenth-century authors speak of the military events of the first half of the century as "wars," *"bella"* in the plural and clearly distinguish between the *"bellum Bohemicum," "bellum Suecicum"* and so forth. The figure "thirty" and the singular "war" seems to occur for the first time in Pufendorf's *De statu imperii Germanici* (1667). One of the liveliest and still most readable pamphlets of seventeenth-century political science, its success was immediate and far-reaching: German, French, English and Dutch translations, popular adaptations and polemical treatises secured the rapid spread of its arguments throughout Europe. Here we have already all the well-known theses of later historians: the Bohemian revolt of 1618 as the beginning, the peace of Wesphalia as the end of the war; its character as a religious conflict; its extension over the whole of Germany; the omission of its European setting; the economic ruin and exhaustion; and the insinuation that Austria is a foreign power like France and Turkey.

From the political point of view the Thirty Years' War offers two aspects: the general European, and the particular German one. Both issues can be traced to the foreign and home policies of the emperors Maximilian I and Charles V. In the European field, Maximilian started the antagonism between the houses of Hapsburg and Valois by claiming the inheritance of Charles the Bold of Burgundy, and made it permanent by marrying his only son to the daughter and heiress of the Spanish world-monarchy. He thereby welded a ring of Hapsburg possessions round France which every French statesman was bound to try his utmost to break.

[3]To give an illustration: as a result of a general change in financial policy, the imperial city of Goslar, from 1625 to 1630, reduced its expenditure from 221,744 guilders to 54,342 guilders; expenditure on defence dropped from 590 to 460 guilders, on schools from 102 to 4 guilders.

The Eve of the Modern World

In Germany, Maximilian deliberately wrecked the last prospect of equitable settlement of the constitutional dispute between centralism and federalism. As at the same time the imperial crown became hereditary in the house of Hapsburg, in all but legal prescription, he made this dynasty the permanent champion of that centralism which had become unattainable and was therefore by force of circumstances reactionary; so that any combination of forces, which for different reasons might be opposed to the Hapsburgs or the empire or centralisation, might appear as fighting for progress.

Charles V, Maximilian's grandson, intensified this development. He completed the total encirclement of France by acquiring the duchy of Milan, subduing the papacy, and drawing Portugal, England, Denmark and Poland into the Hapsburg orbit. The very greatness of his successes made a reaction inevitable. The exploits of Elizabethan England, the secession of the Spanish Netherlands, the alliance between France and the German Protestants (1552), the pacification of France by the edict of Nantes (1598)—are all signs of the growing restiveness against Hapsburg universalism. In fact, during the fifty years following the death of Charles V (1558) all European powers were jockeying for position.

France was obviously the rallying point of every opponent of Hapsburg domination throughout the whole of western Europe and the New World. The aggressive and expansionist policies of Louis XIV and Napoleon I have obliterated the fact that up to the death of Mazarin (1661) it was France which was the protagonist of the European balance of power against the domination of the continent by a single power.

The political struggle was accompanied by an ideological struggle. The antagonism between the old and the new faith made itself felt in the early stages of the conflict, and religious catchwords and propaganda were meant as sincerely or insincerely as were in more recent times the slogans of democracy and totalitarianism. The Hapsburgs, it is true, represented all the life-forces and the spirit of the reformed church of Rome; and the defeat of the Hapsburgs undoubtedly benefited the Protestant powers of Sweden, the Netherlands, England and Brandenburg. But the victory was chiefly a victory of Catholic France, which during the war was successively led by two cardinals of the Roman church; and the papacy itself had from 1523 to 1644 consistently opposed the Hapsburgs and even lent its support to the Protestant hero, Gustavus Adolphus of Sweden.

France could become the ideological leader of Europe as well as its political protagonist as she herself had solved the fight between Protestantism and Catholicism in a *tertium quid* which transcended both these sixteenth-century points of argument. Because the French leaders—the Protestants Henry IV and Sully and the Catholics Richelieu and Mazarin alike—recognized that the absolute claims inherent in every religious system were irreconcilable, they replaced religious standards, by the criterion of the *raison d'état*. This enabled France to destroy Protestantism within her own frontiers and to save Protestantism in Germany, Sweden and the Low Countries, to secure religious unity at home, and to perpetuate the split of western Christendom abroad. Catholic apologists tried in vain to counter this onslaught of secularism by elaborating a *ragione della chiesa*; it has never been a serious challenge to the *raison d'état*.

Seen against this European background, German affairs are of minor importance. Germany, as such, i.e. the "German section of the Holy Roman Empire," was not at all involved in any of the European wars of the period. The individual German states entered and left one war or another as partisans of the European antagonists; only the emperor was engaged in every conflict, not, however, as German king, but as the head of the Austrian branch of the house of Hapsburg. The German wars started in 1609 with the war of the Jülich-Cleve succession and ended in 1648 with the treaties of Münster and Osnabrück. They decided the political future of the empire, in that the last attempt to set up a centralistic government was defeated in favour of a loose confederation of virtually independent states. The concerted action by which the electors forced the emperor to dismiss his generalissimo Wallenstein in 1630 was their last achievement as a corporate body. They, too, who for centuries had represented the federal principle of the German constitution, henceforth showed an ever diminishing concern with the affairs of the empire and were content to look after their own interests. However, the constitution agreed upon in 1648 proved its soundness in that it lasted for more than 200 years, until 1866, with the short interval of the Napoleonic settlement. The wars also decided the dynastic rivalries within the leading German houses—curiously, every time in favour of the younger branch: the Palatine Wittelsbachs, the Thuringian Wettiners and the Wolfenbüttel Guelphs had to give way to their cousins of Bavaria, Saxony and Hanover, who henceforth formed the leading group of German powers. The most far-reaching result, however, was the rise of the electorate of Brandenburg, before 1609 the least important of the bigger principalities; it came to equal Bavaria and Saxony and was to outstrip them in the following century.

The conception of the Thirty Years' War as a "war of religion" has been abandoned to a large extent since it has been recognized that religious divisions coincided largely with political, constitutional and economic ones. It will always remain a matter of dispute which of these motives was decisive at a given moment. It does, however, seem that rational considerations of political and economic gains determined the policies of the cabinets to the same extent to which religious emotions held a strong sway over the masses, sufficient to whip up their passions in battle and to make them endure with fortitude their plight in adversity. The Swedes, under Gustavus, fought for the pure gospel, caring little for the *"dominium maris Baltici"* and knowing nothing of the French subsidies on which they subsisted; while Tilly's men were fired by an equal zeal for the Holy Virgin, with no stake in the power politics of the Wittelsbachs and ignorant of the pope's support of the heretic Swede.

Political and dynastic, religious and personal motives are inextricably mixed in the actions of the champions of the Protestant and Catholic causes. Both Gustavus Adolphus of Sweden and Maximilian of Bavaria were fervent devotees of their creeds. At the same time, the Lutheran establishment was also Gustavus's strongest bulwark against the claims to the Swedish throne, made by his Catholic cousin, Sigismund of Poland; and as the Palatine Wittelsbachs had assumed the leadership of the Protestant estates of the empire, the head of the Bavarian branch found safety and prospect of gain in rallying the Catholic princes under his standard. The struggle for the *"dominium maris Baltici"* set Gustavus in opposition to Protestant Denmark, Catholic Poland and Orthodox Russia. The occupation of the Hartz mines by the imperial forces (1624) endangered the Swedish copper market; Wallenstein's appointment as "General of the Atlantic and Baltic Seas" (1628) threatened Sweden's maritime position: her vital interests demanded armed intervention against the Catholic Hapsburgs and alliance with Catholic France, and the edict of restitution (1629) only added religious zeal to the dictates of power politics. Likewise, political considerations brought Maximilian into conflict with the Lutheran imperial cities of Swabia and Franconia, Catholic Austria and Spain, and the Calvinistic Netherlands and Palatinate; but after he had overawed the cities and, in alliance with Austria and Spain, crushed the elector Palatine, his interests as a prince of the empire and member of the college of electors made him turn against the Hapsburgs as his chief opponents. The reduction of the dominant position of the emperor and the removal of the Spaniards from the empire were from 1627 onward his overriding aims which, in co-operation with the pope, Catholic France and Lutheran Saxony, were brought to a successful consummation.

The ruinous effect of the war years on German economic and cultural life has been very much exaggerated. War is by its very nature destructive, and the wars of the seventeenth century are no exceptions. But all the campaigns of the period 1609–1648 were of short duration and the armies themselves of a very small size.[4] It was only the districts of primary strategic importance which had to bear the brunt of successive invasions in the seventeenth century, as they have been the focal points of every fight in central Europe, from Caesar's to Eisenhower's campaigns: the Rhine crossings of Breisach and Wesel, the Leipzig plain, the passes across the Black Forest and the roads to Regensburg and the Danube Valley. Other tracts of Germany were hardly affected at all, some only for a few weeks; the majority of towns never saw an enemy inside their walls.

From the middle of the thirteenth century the towns were the undisputed masters of German economics. Even agriculture, if not brought under direct control of city financiers, was at least completely dependent upon the town markets for home consumption as well as exportation (with the notable exception of

[4] The Catholic League had an effective strength of about 15,000 men; Gustavus Adolphus landed in Germany with 15,000 men; the imperial army under Wallenstein may have exceeded 20,000 men; Bernhard of Weimar received French subsidies for 18,000 men—Richelieu had originally only bargained for 14,000; Condé's army in 1645, the strongest French contingent to be employed in Germany, numbered 12,000 men. The numbers of "regiments," "squadrons," "standards" etc. are meaningless in themselves: for instance, in the battle of Breitenfeld, the 15,000 troops of the League were organized in 10 regiments, the 15,000 imperialists in 28 regiments.

the Teutonic Order in Prussia, whose totalitarian economy comprised production as well as commerce and excluded the citizen middlemen). This whole system of German economics was breaking down in a series of disastrous events from the middle of the sixteenth century: the south German cities were ruined by the repeated bankruptcies of the Spanish crown (1557, 1575, 1596, 1607), in which they lost every financial gain accumulated in the preceding century. The Hanse towns of North Germany were equally hit by the sack of Antwerp (1585) and the closing of the London Steelyard (1598) which deprived them of the two western pillars of their trading system; and even more by the separation of the Netherlands from Spain. The new republic vigorously asserted its independence in the economic sphere, intruding into the Baltic trade, hitherto the jealously-guarded monopoly of the Hanse.

About 1620 the German towns still presented an outward picture of opulence and solidity—very much emphasized to the casual observer by the splendour of their architectural achievements, as shown in Mathias Merian's topographical engravings published from 1640. Yet the foundations of their prosperity had gone, and the big inflation of the years 1619–23 only set the seal upon the utter ruin of German economics which had started some fifty years earlier. . . .

The part of the economic structure which was hit hardest by the immediate effects of the war was agriculture, especially for medium-sized and small farmers. To big land-owners, on the other hand, the war itself, the maintenance of troops over wide distances and the new methods of logistics and commissariat as introduced by Wallenstein and Gustavus Adolphus, offered fresh possibilities of enrichment. In fact, the seventeenth century is the period of the growth of the big *latifundia* of the Junkers at the smallholders' expense. The eviction of peasants, and the sequestration of peasant land by the lord of the manor had started at the end of the sixteenth century, caused by the steady rise of corn prices which made large-scale farming and bulk selling more profitable. The depopulation of the countryside and the disappearance of whole villages were in full swing before the first shot of the "Thirty Years' War" was fired, and went on long after the conclusion of the peace of Westphalia.

On the other hand, the improved organization of the

commissariat resulted in increasing the apparent burdens of occupied countries. Indiscriminate pillaging by a band of marauders may have done greater damage, but it appeared as a natural phenomenon, whereas the methodical requisitioning by quartermasters was felt the more irksome as it was planned and therefore rigid, thorough and therefore inescapable, fixed in writing and therefore long remembered and resented.

Ignorance of scientific demography and inability to visualize large figures account for the legend of the enormous loss of population, which is variously given as ranging from a third to half or more of the total. All these figures are purely imaginary. Such statistical surveys as were occasionally made were always designed to support some special pleading: to obtain a grant in aid, a reduction of payments, or an alleviation of services.[5] The main sources, however, are contemporary reports and, rarely, records of deaths, to the virtual exclusion of registers of births. In view of the huge birthrate this neglect amounts to thirty to fifty per cent[6]; in other words, exactly that third or half by which the population is said to have been reduced. It is, of course, indisputable that the irregular movements of troops, especially of ill-disciplined mercenaries, and the migration of refugees greatly contributed to the spreading of epidemics, such as the various kinds of typhoid (the greatest terror of the seventeenth century) or, to a lesser degree, of the plague and syphilis. On the other hand, the mortality of the urban population shows a surprising likeness in a place which was far remote from the European battlefields, and one which was right in their midst: it has been computed at seventy *per mille* for London in 1620–43, and at sixty-eight *per mille* for Frankfurt in 1600–50.

What actually happened was an extensive inner migration chiefly from the agrarian countryside into the industrial town, and from the economically retrograde town to the prosperous one. As with the ownership of movable and immovable property, so with regard to the population it is more appropriate to speak of redistribution than of destruction.

[5] For example, the district of Militsch in Silesia in 1619 furnished the government in Breslau with a list of 976 men available for military service; whereas at the actual census, 1,527 men had been recorded in this category.

[6] These percentages are based on eighteenth-century statistics (when the birthrate was already beginning to decline) for Prussia and Saxony where the surplus of births over deaths was 30 per cent. and 50 per cent. respectively.

The net result is that of an all-round, though very limited increase. This almost imperceptible rise, and over long periods, virtual stagnation, is characteristic of every community of a predominantly agricultural type. Keeping in mind the vagueness of the term "Germany," it seems safe to assume a population of fifteen to seventeen million in 1600. A loss of five to eight million by 1650 could not possibly have been made good by 1700, for which year a population of seventeen to twenty million is fairly well documented. . . .

The Thirty Years' War, put in its proper perspective, was therefore not such a catastrophe as popular historians have made out. Perhaps the one irreparable damage Germany sustained in the first half of the seventeenth century was that German civilization and German politics parted company. This separation may be the greatest misfortune of German history.

H. R. TREVOR-ROPER

THE LARGER PATTERN OF CAUSE

In the following selection the eminent British historian of the seventeenth century, H. R. Trevor-Roper, is concerned to argue by analogy from the instance of the Thirty Years' War to the general question, "Why do Great Wars Begin?" But in the process he adopts a point of view with reference to the causes of the Thirty Years' War which is at considerable variance with the traditional picture of those causes and in agreement with one of the several recent reinterpretations. To Trevor-Roper the causes of the war are no longer to be seen in terms of Germany or the empire but rather in terms of the complexity of European international relations. He treats the Bohemian revolt of 1618—the immediate cause of the war in the traditional view—as only one in a string of incidents (and not an especially important one at that) any of which might have set off general war. But, in the larger argument, Trevor-Roper holds that it is never incidents that cause great wars but rather the policy decisions of great powers. And, in the instance of the Thirty Years' War, he argues that the great power whose deliberate policy decision caused the war was Spain. He argues that the Thirty Years' War did not really break out in 1618 in Bohemia but in 1621 with the Spanish declaration of war. He argues that it was not the issues of religion or the imperial constitution that caused its outbreak but the decision of Habsburg Spain to take the offensive once more in her two-centuries-old attempt to gain the hegemony of Europe. And we may extend his argument to presume that he would mark the end of the war not with the Peace of Westphalia in 1648 but the Peace of the Pyrenees in 1659. In this analysis we lose even the concept of the Thirty Years' War: it becomes part of a larger whole rather than an entity in itself. We turn now to the question of why it began.

Why, indeed? Several times in history the pattern has recurred, we see a general peace, apparently welcome to all powers, but beneath this peace we see fear and suspicion constantly threatening it. No

From H. R. Trevor-Roper, "Why Do Great Wars Begin?," *Horizon*, V (Nov. 1962), pp. 32–41. Reprinted by permission of American Heritage Publishing Co., Inc.

power wants war, but each fears that some incident will create war. The atmosphere is combustible and therefore a spark may set the world ablaze. Consequently when a spark does fly, there is a rush to isolate or stifle it. Even those who might profit by a fire in that quarter are too frightened to exploit it; for it might spread. And so the peace is kept; the various danger spots are guarded; even their dangers are preserved, not eliminated, for to eliminate them is to touch them and to touch them is to set them off. And then, suddenly a spark flies which is not isolated; the complex system of insurance suddenly fails; the wind blows, and all the danger spots are simultaneously alight: it is general war. . . .

On such occasions it is customary to say that the incidents lead to the war: they generate a fear whose pressure is irresistible, and cause men to build up armaments which must be used. In other words, the war is inevitable: it is only a question of time. This may be so, but since the question is open, perhaps it is worthwhile to look back at the outbreak of the greatest, most destructive war in preindustrial Europe: the Thirty Years' War, which is customarily dated from the last of a series of such incidents, the Bohemian Revolt of 1618. . . .

Obviously there were opportunities for incidents everywhere. But if we wish to find a pattern in these incidents, we must always look to Spain. After all, it was Spain that had made the peace of the great powers: in 1598, in 1604, in 1609 the Spanish monarchy, bankrupt but still powerful, had wound up the wars of Philip II with France, England, and Holland. It was Spain that kept the peace; and it was Spain that, in the end, broke it. The Thirty Years' War is generally thought of as a German war; but it was the Spanish Hapsburgs who dominated their cousins in Vienna and Prague, and it was the Spanish declaration of war in 1621 that made the local German war into a European war. . . .

The Spanish empire in Europe consisted of Flanders and Italy. Since its chief problem was the revolt of the Netherlands, its most essential communications were between Spain and Flanders, across or around the huge intervening body of France. In the old days the regular route had been by sea, from Laredo or Coruna to Flushing. But now the Dutch held Flushing and with the English commanded the sea lanes, so that Spanish forces — men, munitions, money — all had to reach Flanders by land. They sailed from Barcelona or Naples to Genoa (nominally free but in fact a Spanish protectorate) and assembled in Milan. Then they marched north, over the Alps, along the Rhine to the Low Countries. On this route there was one solid Spanish steppingstone: Franche-Comté, on the borders of France and Switzerland. There were also imperial fiefs, like Alsace, held by the Austrian Hapsburgs. Then there were theoretically independent states that, in fact, were safely Spaniolized, like the prince-bishoprics of Cologne or Liège: no trouble came from them. And there were allied states like the Catholic cantons of Switzerland which, by treaty, allowed free passage to Spanish (but only Spanish) troops. As long as Spanish power was firm, all these could be managed.

But there were other spots which were more difficult. There was Savoy: its duke had a mountainous terrain and an army and could be very troublesome, especially if supported by France. Then there was the Palatinate on the middle Rhine. The Elector Palatine was a dangerous enemy: he was a Calvinist, the titular leader of the activists among the German Protestants, and he had a vote in the making of emperors. It was most inconvenient that his castle of Heidelberg should overlook a sector of the Spanish route. And finally there were other petty German principalities which the chance of election or heredity might place in the wrong hands.

Moreover there was another vital area. To the Spanish Hapsburgs it was essential that their Austrian cousins rule the Holy Roman Empire: the emperor was overlord of the German princes on the Rhine; he ruled over Alsace; he also held legal rights over a number of princes in Italy. But the Austrian Hapsburgs in 1609 were inconveniently weak; they were also childless and there was no agreed heir. For those reasons it was necessary to Spain to have means of communicating with Austria and means of influencing imperial elections. These necessities raised two other areas to the status of danger spots. To communicate with Austria, Spain needed to control the land route from Milan to the Tirol; to influence elections it needed to control the otherwise irrelevant kingdom of Bohemia.

The land route from Milan to the Tirol ran through the Valtelline passes to the south of Switzerland. The inhabitants of the Valtelline were Catholics, but they were subject to the Swiss Grisons, who were Protestants. This made matters difficult. To secure the pass, the Spanish governor of Milan had built a fort near Lake Como. This provoked the Grisons, who looked round for sympathy. They found it in France. They also found it in Venice, the last of the independent republics of Italy, conscious of its historic greatness. Venice also felt itself strangled by the Hapsburgs. By land, the Austrian Hapsburgs overhung it from north and east, the Spanish Hapsburgs from the west. By sea, the Austrians encouraged the Bosnian pirates, its enemies in the Adriatic, and the Spaniards dominated the outlet of the Adriatic at Apulia. The Venetians had no desire to see the Valtelline closed and the two enemies joining hands to encircle them.

As for the kingdom of Bohemia, its claim to be a danger spot was purely political, not strategic. The king of Bohemia was an elector to the Empire, and in the present balance of power he might even control the deciding vote. It was therefore essential to Spain that the Bohemian Diet should elect the Spanish candidate to the Bohemian crown. This candidate was the Archduke Ferdinand of Styria, who would then, according to the Spanish plan, help to elect himself emperor. In 1609 this plan was not yet complete, least of all in Madrid, but the Spanish ambassador had built up a solid party in Prague by lavish distribution of favors, honors, promises, and pensions, and was prepared for the future.

Thus all the danger spots name themselves: the Rhineland, the Palatinate, Savoy, Venice, the Valtelline, Bohemia. Incidents that occurred elsewhere could be settled locally, but incidents in these places invariably endangered the peace.

The first trouble came in the Rhineland. Scarcely had the truce between Spain and Holland been signed, and the last great war wound up, when a disputed succession in Jülich-Cleves, on the lower Rhine, lauched a general crisis. The Duke of Cleves who had died had been a Catholic, but two rivals now claimed the throne, both Protestants. A Protestant prince on the lower Rhine! To Spain such a thought was impossible, and one of the claimants, to ensure Spanish support, promptly turned papist. But the dispute remained and soon engaged all Europe. Henri IV of France allied himself with the German Protestants and with the Duke of Savoy. There was general mobilization. Savoy prepared to pounce on Milan. Henri IV had his queen crowned as his regent in his stead and set out to the Rhineland front. Then, quite suddenly, all was over: in the streets of Paris an assassin sprang into the royal coach, stabbed and killed Henri IV. With that sudden coup

the course of history was stayed. The anti-Spanish alliance collapsed.

But other crises soon followed. In 1613 there was another disputed succession. This time it was in Montferrat, an exposed enclave lying between Milan and Savoy. The Duke of Savoy claimed control over it, refused mediation, occupied it, defied Spain, expelled the Spanish ambassador, sent back his Spanish decorations. Successive Spanish governors of Milan made war against him. He was defeated in the field, forced to submit, but bobbed up again with foreign support, unofficial but valuable.

While Savoy was fighting against Spain by land, Venice was engaged in a fierce struggle by sea against the Bosnian pirates who enjoyed the protection of the Archduke Ferdinand. Before long Venice found itself at war with the Archduke himself on land, and a Dutch fleet brought Dutch soldiers through the Straits of Gibraltar to fight for Venice. And then another force entered the ever-widening fight. The Spanish viceroy of Naples, the Duke of Osuna, was a man of wild visions and ruthless methods. He sent troops by land through a protesting Italy to assist Milan against Savoy, and he sent a fleet—his own fleet, flying his own personal flag—into the Adriatic to destroy the ships of Venice, with which Spain was not even at war. He had an ally in Venice in the Spanish ambassador there, the Marquis of Bedmar, who was equally self-willed and independent. There can be no doubt that Osuna and Bedmar were determined to destroy Venice.

And yet in fact the Italian crisis came to nothing just as the Rhineland crisis had done. The great powers were never engaged. The governor of Dauphiné might make war, but the government of France was still. The Archduke Ferdinand might be at war, but the Emperor, his sovereign, did not stir. The governors of Milan and Naples might act, but Madrid remained uncommitted. Dutch soldiers fought in Italy, but the Dutch government remained at peace. It seemed as if the great powers would only fight through agents. The second crisis had passed.

Immediately it was followed by a third, a fourth, a fifth: 1618 was a year of crises. On May 18 there was one in Venice. On that morning the inhabitants of the city awoke to see two corpses hanging upside down from the public gibbet. Their legs were broken, a sign that they were guilty of treason. Five days later a third corpse joined them, mutilated by torture. No explanation was given: the Venetian Inquisitors of State never explained; they acted, and left the public to guess. But all agreed that there had been a deep plot against the independence of the city. Osuna and Bedmar had planned a sudden coup: Bedmar had organized the fifth column within, Osuna had his fleet ready to strike without. But Venice had struck first. Osuna and Bedmar of course protested their innocence; but whereas the cautious Bedmar continued his diplomatic career and was made a cardinal of the Church, the impetuous Osuna was afterward recalled, accused of seeking to make himself king of Naples, and died in prison. On all sides the matter was dropped.

In Bohemia, meanwhile, the Spaniards had won a great victory. The old Emperor, who was also the king of Bohemia, persuaded the Bohemian Diet to pre-elect the Spanish candidate, the Archduke Ferdinand, as next king when the Emperor should die. That guaranteed the crown of Bohemia. Indirectly, it ensured that the imperial election should go as the Spaniards wished. And further, by a secret treaty signed with the Archduke, the Spaniards agreed that he should be the next emperor. The King of Spain himself had claims, but by this treaty he renounced them. He renounced them in exchange for solid assets: for Alsace, an essential stage on the route to Flanders; for the Tirol, which linked Italy with Germany; and for the imperial fiefs in Italy. Thus at one blow Spain had secured Bohemia and the Empire for the most dependable of its allies and fastened its own hold over its European communications. At least it had been done so on paper.

In fact it had not. In fact, on May 23, 1618, three days after the ruin of the Spanish conspiracy in Venice, the Spanish conspiracy was ruined in Prague also. On that day the Protestant nobility of Bohemia revolted, threw the Hispanophile Catholic ministers out of the window of the Hradčany Castle, and set up a revolutionary government. The first act of this government was to expel those constant allies of Spain, the Jesuits. The second was to look round for a Protestant heir to replace the pre-elected Archduke. Only a radical prince would accept such a revolutionary throne, and therefore their eyes lit on the most radical of German princes: the Calvinist Elector Palatine, whose own capital of Heidelberg was such a nuisance on the Spanish Rhineland route.

The revolution in Prague, coinciding with the delivery of Venice, sent a thrill of excitement through all Protestant Europe. All the enemies of Spain were roused. Two months later the Protestant party in the Valtelline murdered their Catholic enemies, whom they accused of "Hispanismus," seized control of the pass, and so cut Milan off from the Tirol. At the same time Savoy and Venice made a formal alliance against future aggression. The following year Venice and Holland made a defensive alliance against Spain, and on the death of the Emperor the members of the Bohemian Diet formally elected the Elector Palatine as their king.

From this point on, historians say, general war was certain. Of course it is easy to say this because in fact war did break out: the Thirty Years' War is conventionally dated from the Bohemian revolt. But let us look a little more closely at the course of events after that revolt. We may find that the easy answer is not necessarily the true or only answer. The causes of war are so important that we ought to take nothing for granted.

The first fact to notice is that the Bohemian revolt was far less fatal than might appear. It did not in fact lead to the loss of the Empire. In 1619, while the Bohemian Diet was electing its new Protestant king in Prague, the Archduke, as legal king of Bohemia, was in Frankfort helping to elect himself emperor. Therefore the major part of Spanish policy was undamaged. The Empire was safe. All that was lost was Bohemia. Moreover, it seemed that Bohemia could be isolated. The Archduke had been legally elected, and his election could not be superseded. The election of the new king was illegal; even his own father-in-law, the king of England, refused to support him, and a French envoy succeeded in persuading the two German leagues—the Catholic League and the Evangelical Union—to remain neutral. The Bohemian rebels had overplayed their hand. They had even given a moral advantage to Spain.

It was an advantage which Spain was quick to seize. In 1620 a Spanish army under Spinola marched from the Netherlands and occupied the Palatinate. The Elector could hardly complain: he had deserted his own country to usurp a crown elsewhere and, in the general view, deserved what he got. In the same year the Spanish governor of Milan carried out a successful coup in the Valtelline. Under his patronage the Catholics in the valley suddenly rose and in the "Holy Butchery" massacred their Protestant rulers and placed the vital corridor under Spanish protection. A few months later a Bavarian army acting for the Hapsburgs totally defeated the usurping king of Bohemia and drove him headlong from Prague. By the spring of 1621 all, it seemed, was over; the *status quo* had been restored; the danger of general war was past.

Thus when we look closely at the facts we see that the last of the "incidents" did not, of itself, precipitate a general war. The revolt in Prague no more created the war than the conspiracy in Venice had done, or the war in the Adriatic, or the war over Montferrat, or the affair of Jülich-Cleves, or the Palatinate, or the Valtelline. And yet, later, in 1621, real war broke out, bringing devastation and revolution to Europe for the next three decades. How then did this happen? To seek an answer to this question we must turn away from the facile assumption that war rises spontaneously out of "incidents" and look instead at the men who create incidents and are the real makers of history.

The European war that broke out in 1621 was caused not by accumulated accidents but by human decisions. Those decisions were taken in Madrid. The questions we must ask are: Who were the men who made those decisions and why did they make them? I believe that it is perfectly possible to answer these questions. The men were a party of Spanish officials who came to power in Madrid in 1621, and they made war deliberately because, unlike their predecessors, they believed that war would be more profitable to Spain than peace. . . .

And who were these men? Essentially they were two. First there was Baltasar de Zúñiga, the advocate of a forward policy throughout Europe. He had been ambassador to the Archduke Albert and then to the Emperor, and had always opposed the truce in the North and argued action in Bohemia. He was now the most powerful figure in Madrid. Secondly there was the new King's young tutor, Gaspar de Guzmán, Zúñiga's nephew, who would dominate Spain for the next twenty-two years as the Count-Duke of Olivares. Behind them stood the whole party: the party of the pushing, powerful, uncontrolled governors and ambassadors throughout the Empire who had long been openly impatient of the restraining peace which all the great powers were conspiring to keep. For years these men had fretted at the weakness of politicians in Madrid. They had longed to throw into action the armies they commanded and maintained, the fifth columns they had created and nursed. With the change of government, they found politicians who shared their views.

But why should anyone want war in 1621? . . .

The answer is not difficult to find. It is to be found in their own statements. These men believed that, in spite of appearances, Spain was losing the peace. This loss was not a loss of territory (Spanish territory had been constantly increasing), nor even merely a loss of trade (Spanish trade had never been much). It was something far greater than this. Beneath the surface of spectacular peaceful triumphs the whole Spanish "way of life" was being undermined by a more successful rival ideology that had its headquarters in Amsterdam, the capital of those insubordinate, invincible, unpardonable heretics and rebels, the Dutch.

For the Spanish peace had, in some respects, represented the victory and spread of a way of life. It was the triumph of princely bureaucracy, of an official class in a monarchical society, living to a large extent on taxes which grew as it grew. This official class had by now an official ideology, an ideology of the court: an ideology shared even by the great merchants, who farmed the taxes and felt themselves half courtiers; and consecrated by the Church, which was a court-Church, and particularly by the religious orders—most of all by the courtliest of all orders, the Jesuits, who at this time were the invariable allies of Spain. Such a system had its outward charm, of course. The bureaucracy patronized official art and architecture; it advertised itself and its solidity through magnificent buildings, which we admire today, and magnificent shows and pageants, which dissolved overnight. But it also had its weakness. Though it created a form of state-capitalism, it discouraged private trade and industry. Everywhere we see the same spectacle: industry and commerce crushed under bureaucracy; merchants shifting their capital into the purchase of land, titles, or offices; peasants oppressed by taxes; craftsmen fleeing to other lands.

This "Spanish" way of life was not confined to the Spanish empire, or even to Catholic countries. Wherever Spanish influence was felt, it was encouraged. We see it in France, the France of Marie de Médicis; we see it in England, the England of James I and the Duke of Buckingham. But over against it there was another way of life, the ideology of the country opposed to the court: of country landlords opposed to court magnates, of lesser merchants opposed to the great monopolists of the court, of taxpayers opposed to taxeaters. This ideology was conservative: it was nationalistic, for it opposed an international system; it was anti-Spanish, and anticlerical, for that system was operated by Spain and Rome; and against the ostentatious consumption of the court, it was "puritan." This ideology had been suppressed—indeed could hardly exist—in Spain and Spanish Italy; it seethed below the surface in England and France; but in Venice and Holland, in different forms, it ruled. Against Venice and Holland, therefore, all the hatred of Spanish officialdom was directed.

Of course, if the Spanish peace had really been consolidating Spanish power in Europe, there would have been no need for action: Spain could have waited till the dwindling "puritan" generation had died out. But the Spanish officials were convinced that time was not on Spain's side. They believed that the purpose of peace was to recover from the bankruptcy of war, to renew military strength, to create new resources for final victory. And that, it was only too clear, had not been done. Behind the façade of its wealth and strength, Spain had sunk deeper into bankruptcy, deeper into feebleness. Meanwhile its old enemies were using the peace to grow in power and prosperity. The courtly clerical, aristocratic system of Spain might be magnificent, but it did not work. The ideology of the Dutch might be heretical, rebellious, vulgar, but it worked. Time therefore was on their side. Fortunately, said the Spanish officials, the balance of power was still on the side of Spain, provided Spain struck, and struck now. . . .

In Madrid [these] arguments were driven home by Baltasar de Zúñiga himself. It seemed to him as if the Spaniards had shed their blood only to fill the veins of subject nations: "We have left our own country deserted and sterile in order to people and fertilize the lands we have conquered." Therefore, the Carthage on the Zuider Zee must be destroyed: the treasure of Spain that had been secretly drained away to the north must be brought back by force. Was it not for this day that Zúñiga himself and his fellow imperialists had worked so hard, throughout the Spanish Peace, to secure the vital corridors—the Valtelline, Alsace, the Palatinate? Now they had secured them all. Were they then not to strike?

When these arguments were first advanced in Madrid, there was resistance. How, men asked, could Spain face the cost of war? With his dying voice, the Archduke in Brussels urged that the truce be prolonged. "We must suppose," he protested, "that even if all Europe is destined to be subject to one monarch, that time is not yet." But as the old rulers died off, the new prevailed; and besides, they had other allies. The Councils of Portugal and the Indies, representing the East and West India trades, agreed with Zúñiga and Coloma. Those men had long suffered from the Dutch. In the years of the war the Dutch had seized half the East Indies from Portugal; in the years of peace they had stolen the trade of the West Indies. It was vain to hope of defeating them at sea, but a well-aimed blow by land would solve the problem. Struck in the heart, the octopus would loosen its distant tentacles. Thanks to this argument, and this support, the party of war prevailed. The truce was denounced. The half-settled troubles of Germany were swept up into a general war.

Thus we can answer our question. The Thirty Years' War, as a general war, was not created by the Bohemian and German incidents which officially began it. These could have been settled, or at least localized, as so many other such incidents had been. Perhaps no general war ever arises out of mere incidents. General wars arise because the governments of great powers, or the men behind such governments, want war and exploit incidents. . . .

CARL J. FRIEDRICH

"THIS GREATEST OF THE RELIGIOUS WARS"

One of the traditional assumptions about the Thirty Years' War was that it was a war of religion. Now, as we have seen, most modern revisionist scholars tend either to reject this assumption or move it to a much lower priority position in the list of causes. Yet is it possible to separate religion from politics—or from anything else—in the early seventeenth century? This is essentially the question that Carl J. Friedrich poses in his treatment of the Thirty Years' War in his influential book, *The Age of the Baroque,* from which the following selection is taken. He flatly calls it "this greatest of the religious wars," and states that "without a full appreciation of the close links between secular and religious issues, it becomes impossible to comprehend the Thirty Years' War."

Such a position is itself a form of revision in that it is a sophisticated restatement of an older thesis but within a new framework. Friedrich is as well aware of the play of dynastic power politics in this age as is Steinberg or Trevor-Roper. Indeed he holds that the war was a transition between the age of religious war and the age of political war and that the reason why the forces of the counterreformation won most of the battles and yet lost the war was "that the forces of the modern state were predominantly on the other side." He feels that the new framework within which we must understand this play of religious and secular forces is the concept of the baroque in which religion and politics, faith and power are mixed, in spite of contradiction; and that contradiction itself is an essential part of the baroque that modern men easily misunderstand.

It has been the fashion to minimize the religious aspect of the great wars which raged in the heart of Europe, over the territory of the Holy Roman Empire of the German Nation. Not only the calculating statecraft of Richelieu and Mazarin, but even Pope Urban VIII's own insistence lent support to such a view in a later age which had come to look upon religion and politics as fairly well separated fields of thought and action. Liberal historians found it difficult to perceive that for baroque man religion and politics were cut from the same cloth, indeed that the most intensely political issues were precisely the religious ones. Gone was the neopaganism of the renaissance, with its preoccupation with self-fulfillment here and now. Once again, and for the last time, life was seen as meaningful in religious, even theological, terms, and the greater insight into power which the renaissance had brought served merely to deepen the political passion brought to the struggle over religious faiths.

Without a full appreciation of the close links between secular and religious issues, it becomes impossible to comprehend the Thirty Years' War. Frederick, the unlucky Palatine, as well as Ferdinand, Tilly and Gustavus Adolphus, Maximilian of Bavaria and John George of Saxony, they all must be considered fools unless their religious motivation is understood as the quintessential core of their politics. Time and again, they appear to have done the "wrong thing," if their actions are viewed in a strictly secular perspective. To be sure, men became increasingly sophisticated as the war dragged on; but even after peace was finally concluded in 1648, the religious controversies continued. Ever since the Diet of Augsburg (1555) had adopted the callous position that a man must confess the religion of those who had authority over the territory he lived in—a view which came to be known under the slogan of *"cujus regio, ejus religio"*—the intimate tie of religion and government had been the basis of the Holy Empire's tenuous peace. Born of the spirit of its time—Lutheran otherworldliness combining with Humanistic indifferentism—this doctrine was no more than an unstable compromise between Catholics and Lutherans, the Calvinists being entirely outside its protective sphere. But in the seventeenth century not only the Calvinists, who by 1618 had become the fighting protagonists of Protestantism, but likewise the more ardent Catholics, inspired by the Council of Trent, by the Jesuits and Capuchins, backed by the power of Spain and filled with the ardor of the Counter Reformation, had come to look upon this doctrine as wicked and contrary to their deepest convictions.

When Ferdinand, after claiming the crown of Bohemia by heredity, proceeded to push the work of counter reformation, his strongest motivation was religious; so was the resistance offered by the Bohemian people, as well as Frederick's acceptance of the crown of Bohemia on the basis of an election. Dynastic and national sentiments played their part, surely, but they reinforced the basic religious urge. The same concurrence of religious with dynastic, political, even economic motives persisted throughout the protracted struggle, but the religious did not cease to be the all-pervasive feeling; baroque man, far from being bothered by the contradictions, experienced these polarities as inescapable.

If religion played a vital role in persuading Ferdinand II to dismiss his victorious general, it was even more decisive in inspiring Gustavus Adolphus to enter the war against both the emperor and the League. The nineteenth century, incapable of feeling the religious passions which stirred baroque humanity and much impressed with the solidified national states which the seventeenth century bequeathed to posterity, was prone to magnify the dynastic and often Machiavellian policies adopted by rulers who professed to be deeply religious, and the twentieth century has largely followed suit in denying the religious character of these wars. But it is precisely this capacity to regard the statesman as the champion of religion, to live and act the drama of man's dual dependence upon faith and power that constituted the quintessence of the baroque. The Jesuits, sponsors of the baroque style in architecture all over central and southern Europe, advised Catholic rulers, but more especially Ferdinand II, concerning their dual duties. The somber and passionate driving force behind so much unscrupulousness was religious pathos in all its depth. What the Catholics did, elicited a corresponding pattern of thought and action in the Protestant world: Maurice of Nassau and James I, Gustavus Adolphus and Cromwell, as well as many minor figures of the European theater, conceived of themselves as guardians of the "secrets of rule," the *arcana imperii*, to be employed for the greater glory of God and the Christian religion. ... .

The five battles of the White Mountain, Lutter am Barenberge, Breitenfeld, Lützen and Nördlingen, were the decisive ones of the great war; after Nördlingen many a bloody engagement was fought, but none turned the scale as these battles had done. It is a startling testimony to the inner weakness of the cause of the Counter Reformation that in spite of losing only one of these great encounters, it could not win the war in the end. The deeper reason was that the forces of the modern state were predominantly on the other side.

In any case, the battle of Nördlingen had sufficiently reduced the power of Sweden and with it the prospects of a sweeping Protestant predominance, to strengthen negotiations begun earlier in 1634 for an all-round compromise. In contrast to the French cardinal, who protested a desire for a general peace while fanning the flames of war, the German emperor and his estates proceeded to treat of peace among themselves and eventually arrived at a settlement which acknowledged the existing state of affairs. The peace of Prague (1635), the third of the peace treaties by which the great war was punctuated, might have brought the conflict to an end thirteen years earlier than the peace of Westphalia, had it not been for Swedish and French determination to reduce the Hapsburg power further and to secure extensive compensations for their sanguinary and financial efforts up to that time. The peace of Prague expressly challenged such pretensions by providing that any lands lost to either the emperor or one of the states, like Lorraine and Mecklenburg, should be restored to them, if necessary by force of arms. An army for the entire Empire was provided, and the liberation of German territories from foreign armies was made the express purpose of this army. As for the problem of religious peace, the doctrine of "cujus regio, ejus religio" was by implication reaffirmed, and the Edict of Restitution by similar implication set aside. Instead, it was provided that the ecclesiastical domains, foundations, monasteries and the like should be divided on the basis of actual possession at the time of the peace of Passau and, for those acquired after Passau, the date of November 12, 1627 should serve, but for a forty-year period only. There was a certain number of exceptions, and since Ferdinand was unwilling to grant religious toleration in his crownlands, especially Bohemia, in spite of strong Saxon representations, it was agreed that this matter might be further negotiated.

As a whole, the peace of Prague constituted an attempt to rally all German estates behind the ancient constitution and unite them against the foreign invaders, especially Sweden and France. . . . Obviously this settlement was bound to look to France and Sweden more like a defensive alliance than like a peace treaty. Estates threatened by either French or Swedish forces could not but look upon the document in a similar light, since adherence to its terms entailed joining forces with the emperor and hence might bring about conquest by his enemies. As a result, its conclusion did not bring peace, but an intensification of the war.

The historian may well be pardoned for not reviewing the sorry tale of this long-drawn-out disaster. Largely it was the story of a Swedish-French-Spanish struggle. In 1637, Emperor Ferdinand passed away, unsuccessful and a victim of his bigotry and his delusions. Recurrently responsible for the continuation of the great war which he had himself allowed to get under way, he could look upon his crown lands, as well as upon the larger Empire, for which he was in his own conception of rulership the God-appointed shepherd, as not only devastated and exhausted, but also as no more Christian in the Catholic way than when he ascended his throne.

In 1635 Richelieu had finally *declared* war upon the Austrian Hapsburgs—France would never admit it meant the Empire—after having *participated* in it certainly since the entrance of Gustavus Adolphus. This step was in a sense the result of the battle of Nördlingen, in which the Spanish Hapsburgs had combined with their Austrian kinsmen to defeat the

Protestants and Swedes. French intervention was also intended to counteract the peace of Prague. Since this peace had all but reunited the Empire, Richelieu was determined to split it again. He believed that the time had come to launch the final assault upon Hapsburg power, and if not utterly to destroy it, in any case to reduce it to the point where it could no longer threaten the imperial ambitions of France. If in the course of this, France secured Alsace and reached the Rhine, so much the better; but such was not a primary or initial goal of French policy. More important by far was the prospect of wresting control of Franche-Comté and the Spanish Netherlands from the Hapsburgs, since these territories constituted the eastern prong of the vise in which the Hapsburgs had held France for generations. If it meant the continuation of the war in Germany for another thirteen years, this was a regrettable incident to the more important goal of securing France against Hapsburg power.

The French aggression, though seemingly well supported by Sweden, the Netherlands, and the German Protestants, did not at first work out well. The Spanish, invading from the Netherlands, all but captured Paris; elsewhere, too, the French met defeat, due to incompetent commanders and lack of logistic support for badly organized armies. But in the face of these reverses, Richelieu showed his accustomed fortitude and perseverance, as told in another chapter. In due course, the internal weakness of Spain, highlighted by the successful revolt of Portugal in 1640, was revealed in the crushing defeat at Rocroy (1643), which ended the legend of the invincibility of the Spanish infantry. The emperor thereupon authorized peace negotiations. Spain lost almost fifteen thousand men and never recovered from the disaster. . . .

After Rocroy, the Bavarian army had once again become the mainstay of the imperial position. It had successfully defended Württemberg against Turenne and Condé. But its dominance was due in part to General Piccolomini's being needed in the Netherlands, while General Gallas, through incompetence, wrecked the imperial forces in a vain attempt to check a Swedish attack upon Denmark (1644). Fortunately Queen Christina, now eighteen, mounted the throne of Gustavus Adolphus in that year. Determined to help secure peace, she insisted that the Swedish plenipotentiaries actively promote the negotiations. Furthermore, the Dutch, after Rocroy, had finally decided that France had become a greater danger than Spain, and were therefore quite willing to help further the peace which they more than others had ever been prepared to welcome. Finally, Pope Urban VIII, often the champion of the French cause, while at the same time keenly concerned over his own power, had died. In his place, the weaker and unaggressive Innocent X had mounted St. Peter's throne; by merely failing to support Mazarin and the French position with the energy of his predecessor, Innocent enhanced the chances of peace.

Actually, beginning about 1641, the preliminaries of a peace had for a number of years been under negotiation. They took definite shape after Rocroy when the emperor decided to go ahead. Crosscurrents of policy had previously caused the negotiations to be divided into halves. At Münster the treaty between the Austrian Hapsburgs, their allies and France was being negotiated, while at Osnabrück, some miles away, the Swedes negotiated with the Empire and its estates. There were endless wrangles over etiquette and protocol, but these disputes were often baroque designs, hiding deeper policy conflicts. Thus the refusal of the French ambassador to meet the Spaniard presumably served Mazarin's desire to avoid a peace settlement with Spain; seemingly senseless insistence upon forms for the furtherance of concrete policy was frequent.

The real difficulties arose from the complexity of the situation. France and Sweden both insisted that they were at war with the Hapsburgs, rather than the Empire, since part of the estates were on their side. The estates on their part insisted upon participation, not only to protect their territorial rights, but also to settle the constitutional and other internal issues from which the war had originated; for under the constitution of the Empire these were issues of immediate concern to them. . . .

Unfortunately, two other factors besides the resulting clumsy procedure contributed to the extreme slowness of the negotiations. One was the fact that a number of other powers were brought into the negotiations. Richelieu's aspiration to make France the arbiter of Christianity favored this extension, but so did a variety of other ambitions, including the Holy See's similar desire. Thus Spain and the United Provinces, Portugal and Venice, Denmark, Poland and a number of others appeared on the scene. And while no peace was agreed upon between France

and Spain, such a peace was worked out between Spain and the United Provinces.

The other, and perhaps the more serious difficulty, resulted from the failure to arrange for a cessation of hostilities, while the congress met. For not only was the course of negotiations continually being affected by the shifting fortunes of the battlefield, but some of the negotiating powers, notably Sweden and France, were thereby induced to intensify their war activities, in order to force a decision or effect an alliance. A striking illustration was the frightful devastation of Bavaria by French troops, undertaken in order to force the elector to abandon his connection with the emperor, May to October, 1648. At that point, fortunately, the peace was concluded, and the outrages came to an end. There can be little doubt that this would have happened much sooner if there had been a cease-fire agreement at the start, but the parties were too far apart at the outset to make this kind of agreement possible. So for five years they wrangled, maneuvered and shifted at Münster and Osnabrück, living in plenty while the surrounding countryside starved, and while terrible destruction was wrought upon the helpless mass of the people, not only in Germany, but in Italy, eastern France and elsewhere.

The main political and territorial provisions of the treaty, now generally known as the Treaty of Westphalia of 1648, were as follows: (1) Each German principality was declared a sovereign member of the body known as the Empire, and hence could declare war and make peace at its own discretion. (2) Alsace, with the exception of the free imperial city of Strassburg, was ceded to France, and the forcible acquisition of the bishoprics of Metz, Toul and Verdun by France was confirmed. (3) Sweden acquired the western parts of Pomerania (including Stettin) and the bishoprics of Bremen and Verden, thereby securing control of the mouths of three great German rivers: the Weser, the Elbe and the Oder. (4) Brandenburg, starting on its career of expansion, added most of eastern Pomerania to its possessions, along with the contested lands of the former bishoprics of Magdeburg, Halberstadt and Minden. (5) Saxony was confirmed in the possession of Lusatia. (6) Both France and Sweden, through their territorial acquisitions, were placed in a position to interfere in the affairs of the Empire at any time; since the treaties reaffirmed the constitution (Articles 8 of Osnabrück, 62–66 of Münster), any breach of the constitution was made a concern of France and

Sweden; besides, Sweden was given the status of an estate of the Empire for Bremen, etc. (Article 10 of Osnabrück). France's full sovereignty over Alsace[10] precluded this status. (7) The vexatious question of the electorate and Palatinate, which had been so largely involved in the continuation of the war after 1622, was resolved by creating a new electoral office, so that both the duke of Bavaria and the son of Frederick could become electors; at the same time the Lower Palatinate along the Rhine was given back to the Elector Palatine, while the Upper Palatinate remained with Bavaria. (8) Status of full sovereignty was formally accorded to the United Provinces and Switzerland, which had hitherto been bound to the Empire by a shadowy dependence. (9) Calvinists, at the insistence of Brandenburg, were given equal status with Lutherans, and the year 1624 was chosen for determining ecclesiastical control, while the terms of the religious peace of Augsburg were relaxed and greater toleration enjoined upon rulers. (10) On the imperial courts, the number of Catholic and Protestant judges was to be equal thereafter. The terms of treaty precluded objections by the church; consequently, Pope Innocent X forthwith condemned the treaty as unacceptable. While this ban was never lifted, the treaty remained as a symbol of the emergence of the modern state and of the system of many such states, facing each other as strictly secular sovereigns. The Counter Reformation's long-drawn-out struggle to recapture the unity of Christendom by force of arms had ended in failure.

The negotiations for the Treaty of Westphalia initiated what became a standing operating procedure of the new diplomacy; congresses of ambassadors at the end of a war to try to negotiate a peace settlement on the basis of the sovereign equality of victor and vanquished. This method with all its faults seems in retrospect superior to the more recent practice of dictating peace terms: its often elaborate compromises resulted in a greater degree of genuine pacification. But not always. The vague and in important respects contradictory provisions of the Treaty of Westphalia concerning Alsace served as a welcome pretext for Louis XIV when he decided to challenge them in the next generation. It is interesting that French opposition opinion—rather paradoxically, considering the substantial French gains under the settlement—attacked the treaty savagely and delayed its signing by France until 1651. Indignation was leveled at Mazarin because he had failed to establish peace with Spain at the same time. The anger of the public over this was an important in-

gredient of the commotion which led to the Fronde.

But throughout Germany the announcement of the conclusion of peace was greeted with such joy as the utterly exhausted populace could still muster. There were celebrations upon celebrations, and all the baroque poets burst into heavily ornate song to welcome the dove of peace. . . .

In spite of the tendency of historical scholarship to tone down the doleful tales which are traditionally associated with the Thirty Years' War, there can be little doubt that its effects were not only disastrous in terms of the immediate future, but that the aftereffects of this war thwarted German life for a hundred years. It was only in the period of Goethe and Schiller that the German people seemed to shake off the pallor that had hung over the nation's cultural life. To be sure, there were noble exceptions, such as Leibniz and Bach, but on the whole the loss in human creative talent as well as the material devastation in town and country could not be overcome until after a long convalescence. Even worse, in the long run, was the institutional confusion which the war brought about. The perpetuation of a vast array of principalities large and small could only serve to prevent the growth of a healthy national spirit related to a suitable government and constitution. For a system of social order and government which had served well enough within the context of the medieval unity of church and empire could in the age of the sovereign state and nation lead only to endless frustrations and eventual violence in the search for a solution. It may be a bit far-fetched to trace an explanation of the violence of Fascist nationalism in Germany back to the Thirty Years' War. But that the "monstrosity" which the young Pufendorf saw in the German constitution had something to do with the rise of Prussia few will deny. In any case, the Thirty Years' War marked the effective end of the medieval dream of universal empire, until the revolutionary first Napoleon revived it on a novel basis. . . .

All in all, the toll in human suffering resulting from this greatest of the religious wars was staggering, the results in terms of the religious objectives practically nil. The high hopes of Ferdinand II and his Counter Reformation associates were finished, as were the Calvinists' projects for a predominantly Protestant Empire. The activities on both sides had merely succeeded in demonstrating that rather than surrendering their religious convictions, Germans would divide permanently into many principalities, each governed according to the formula of the religious peace of Augsburg: *"Cujus regio, ejus religio."* A vicious doctrine on the face of it, it nonetheless provided a tolerable compromise for the Germans as a people; a man could remove from one "sovereignty" to another, if compelled by religious scruples. Thus religion triumphed, in a negative sense, over the political requirements of building a modern national state. The outcome of the Thirty Years' War in this sense permanently shaped the course of German history, in contrast with England and France, where the religious wars led, eventually, to a consolidation of religious views, favoring Protestant predominance in one, Catholic in the other. To modify the "forcing of conscience" inherent in such unity, religious toleration—the willingness to let the individual decide for himself—served as the pathmaker for a later more pronounced individualism. In Germany, each "state" patriarchally protected the individual's conscience, while the nation remained a cultural community without firm political framework. Protestant Prussia and Saxony, Catholic Austria and Bavaria, not to mention the dozens of lesser princes, nobles and "free" cities, could proceed to develop a political absolutism, untempered by cultural aspirations. The fatal split in German thought and action between the realm of the spirit and the realm of material power had been started. The modern state emerged from the Treaty of Westphalia in all the kingdoms, duchies and principalities, but it was a crippled, barebones "state," a mere apparatus—a bureaucracy serving princely aspirations for power and aggrandizement. The nation remained outside.

ROBERT ERGANG

THE ALL-DESTRUCTIVE WAR?

One of the commonplaces of the traditional view of the Thirty Years' War is that it was the very exemplification of brutality, devastation, and suffering. It is as if historians, looking back through the horror of modern general war, had taken the Thirty Years' War not only as the first such conflict in its scope and duration but as the terrible forecast of the cost of modern war in misery, loss of life, and destruction of property. And yet, modern scholars have begun to call even this venerable tradition of the Thirty Years' War into question. Steinberg, in the first selection of this section, speaks of the "atrocity propaganda" to which he attributes so much of the tradition. Carl J. Friedrich, in the selection just past, speaks of "the tendency of historical scholarship to tone down the doleful tales which are traditionally associated with the Thirty Years' War"—even though he disagrees with the tendency. One of the modern scholars who subscribes to this revisionist view is Robert Ergang from whose monograph, *The Myth of the All-destructive Fury of the Thirty Years' War,* the following selection is taken.

The student should note in particular the author's use of what might be called historical perspective as a basic tool. With reference, for example, to the destruction of villages, he points not to the immediate effects of the war but to long-term economic changes which can be traced back to the Middle Ages. With reference to the reputed loss of population, he points to the fairly uniform incidence of epidemic disease before, after, and during the war and to the fact that the loss of population was more apparent than real owing to the large number of displaced persons.

The student should also test Ergang's answers (and those of Steinberg) to the question, why did contemporary records present so unrelieved a picture of disaster? Are their answers persuasive?

In their eagerness to disprove the myth of the all-destructive fury of the Thirty Years' War certain revisionist historians have gone too far in the other direction. Thus some have contended that affairs in Germany took a turn for the better as early as 1617 as a result of the adoption of a more vigorous policy by the Habsburgs. The wide differences of opinion must be ascribed not only to the personal prejudices of the historians but also to the nature of the "evidence" upon which the opinions rest. Before we can arrive at a definitive answer regarding the destructive effects of the war the documents, chronicles, reports, and parish records must be critically re-examined and many monographs must be written. Even then certain lacunae will remain because so many essential materials were destroyed during and since the Thirty Years' War. Many special studies by German scholars have already appeared. The best we can do at the present time is to consider briefly the conclusions revisionist scholars have reached, so that from them we may derive a more authentic view of the general effects of the war.

The revisionist trumpet was sounded soon after the middle of the nineteenth century. As early as 1857 G. Brückner requested a thorough-going critical re-examination of the primary sources for the purpose of ascertaining if the destruction of the war had been exaggerated. "Historical truth no less than national feeling demand it," he stated. The call seems to have fallen on deaf ears. Other historians also advocated a re-examination of the evidence with no better results. Indeed, during the succeeding years the trend was rather in the direction of greater exaggeration. In the decade of the nineties, however, a number of historians sharply questioned the myth. Thus R. Wuttke stated:

It is an exaggeration if the decline of Germany, the loss of its trade position is ascribed to the effects of the war. Contemporary reports take pleasure in dwelling on the special horrors, and in summarily making the war responsible for the lack of moral backbone and spirit of enterprise which characterized the seventeenth century.

The real impetus, however, for a re-examination of the question came from B. Erdmannsdörffer's *Deutsche Geschichte vom westfälischen Frieden bis zum Regierungsantritt Friedrichs des Grossen*, in which he discussed the problem at some length. Soon a number of German scholars turned their attention to some phase or other of the problem.

After a careful re-examination of the evidence revisionist historians have concluded that practically all the reports of cannibalism have no foundation in fact. O. Meinardus took it upon himself to trace to its sources the story which has Melchior der Schütz and his band of men kill and devour 500 human beings. "After careful and thorough-going research in the printed literature of Silesian history as well as in the Silesian archives," he found no mention whatever of cannibalism or the hunt for human beings. He did, however, find mention of Melchior der Schütz. In the Royal Archives at Breslau he found the record of a criminal case which was tried in the winter of 1653–1654 with Melchior Hedloff, also known as "Schütze Melchior," as the defendant. Melchior was accused of having murdered 251 people while committing robberies over a period of eleven years. The court record states that he buried his victims in various places. The only reference to cannibalism is in the accusation that on one occasion he had killed a pregnant woman and eaten the heart of her unborn child. His purpose in doing this, the record states, was "to make him more fierce, so he could rage with greater fury and be more respected." Thus, in so far as cannibalism was involved, it was based on superstition and not motivated by hunger. As the author states in the title of his study, the story of Melchior's cannibalism is "an historical fable."

A broader study of reports of cannibalism was made by F. Julian who reminds us that such stories are not peculiar to the Thirty Years' War, but are "typical of longer periods of war and famine." He takes eight stories of cannibalism and shows how they were borrowed from past history as far back as ancient times. Some of the other stories, he says, are the products "of unbounded exaggeration of individual occurrences for purposes of propaganda." Hearsay also played an important part in the creation and

From Robert Ergang, *The Myth of the All-destructive Fury of the Thirty Years' War* (Pocono Pines, Pa.: Craftsmen Press, 1956), pp. 16–22, 24–27. Reprinted by permission of the author; available through Richard S. Barnes, Bookseller, 1628 North Welles St., Chicago 14, Ill.

The Eve of the Modern World

circulation of such stories. "Many a clergyman," he states, "wrote down in his parish records what he heard as a proof of the gravity of the times." A number of these stories, he believes, were "typical inventions which were put into circulation only after the Thirty Years' War." Julian further shows how rumors of cannibalism in the vicinity of Zweibrücken were started by the writer of a *Kollektenbrief*[1] who, in an effort to excite sympathy, stated, "The dearth of food is so great that the dead are no longer safe in their graves." When this device proved successful others adopted it and before long a goodly number of cannibalist stories were in circulation. "There is," Julian writes in summing up his studies, "no credible confirmation of these extreme incidents in the source materials that have been examined up to this time." The only exception he is ready to make is in regard to reports of cannibalism during the siege of Breisach (1638). "In the besieged Breisach," he writes, "an exceptional case of cannibalism turned up which probably can be accepted as an actual happening."

Revisionist historians have also presented evidence to show that barbarities were the exception rather than the rule. Historians of the old school give the impression that plundering and burning, rape of children and old women, cannibalism, and perversions of all kinds were ordinary every-day occurrences. In most of the stories the soldiers are the perpetrators of the horrible deeds. Armies are depicted as "great bands of robbers, held together solely by their lust for murder and their inordinate desire for plunder." The soldiers, almost without exception, are painted in the darkest colors. Thus one historian wrote, "The soldiers were nothing but highway robbers, who maimed and tortured the country people to make them give up their last remaining property." Another stated, "Nowhere in the armies, as regards both officers and common soldiers, was there order and discipline." Undoubtedly some of the troops did at times commit terrible cruelties and were guilty of senseless slaughter, rapine, arson, destruction, and plundering. It was, in a sense, an age of inhumanity in the rest of Europe as well as in Germany. Many of the reports must, however, be ascribed to exaggeration and atrocity propaganda. The latter is, of course, not limited to the Thirty Years' War. . . .

[1] A letter asking religious brethren living in other parts of Germany or in Holland, England, France and Switzerland, to relieve the need of those in the war area by taking up collections.

Actually most of the soldiers who participated in the Thirty Years' War were not permitted to disobey military regulations with impunity. Both Tilly and Gustavus Adolphus enforced a rather strict discipline. In Wallenstein's armies the discipline was less strict, but only because he permitted it. Even Wallenstein had no intention of destroying villages and towns and devastating districts, for he preferred to collect "contributions" from them. His correspondence frequently expresses concern for the civilian population. The distinguished German historian Leopold von Ranke wrote that when Wallenstein's armies marched into a district "there was no lack of violence, as is recorded with a righteous indignation in the local chronicles and in correspondence. At the same time it is clear that a certain order was preserved." Another historian writes that in the records of Wismar there are many reports of thefts and burglaries supposedly committed by Wallenstein's soldiers stationed in and about that city. One report states the conditions were so bad that "shrouds were being stolen out of coffins in broad daylight," a characteristic exaggeration of the period. The historian adds, however, "The most drastic punishments were meted out as a means of maintaining discipline among these troops. According to the records gallows were erected during the night of September 9, 1628, and at dawn, by the personal order of Wallenstein, fourteen men were hanged for refusing to obey orders." According to the regulations of all armies the soldiers were to pay for the food they consumed. The districts in which they were quartered were to furnish them only lodging, salt and vinegar, light and wood, and hay and straw for their horses. E. von Frauenholz states that the average pay for cavalrymen was fifteen gulden per month and for foot soldiers from six to ten. This, he feels, was adequate for the purchase of food and necessaries, if the stipend was paid. Vast sums were sent into Germany for this purpose from Sweden, France, Holland, Spain and England. On occasion cities reported a considerable increase in business from armies that passed their way. Oxenstierna, the Swedish general, succeeded in getting a raise in pay for the Swedish soldiers on the plea that German merchants and artisans had raised their prices so high that the pay of the soldiers no longer sufficed to purchase the necessaries of life.

Not until the middle period of the war did the discipline become less strict with the result that plundering and barbarism increased. Even then the authorities did not cease their efforts to enforce order and discipline. A general order, issued from imperial headquarters on August 1, 1641, reads in part:

Swearing will be punished the first time according to the discretion of the authorities; thereafter it is punishable with death. Stealing a cow or horse, secretly or by force, will without judgment and investigation, and without mercy, be punished by hanging. If one is in possession of a stolen horse and cannot show from whom it was purchased, he will be punished as if he were the thief. Whoever mistreats or tortures a civilian or attacks anyone on the highway will pay with his life.

Although the prohibitions were clear, they were at times openly flouted, particularly when the troops did not receive the stipend they had been promised. The fact that they were not paid gave the troops an excuse for demanding food from peasants and townspeople. Such a search for food and fodder often resulted in other things being taken. At no time did the high command condone plundering of friendly districts, but at such times as the military authorities failed to pay their troops they could hardly enforce their prohibitions. Strict enforcement would have caused troops to desert to the enemy. Nevertheless, on occasion, to curb the worst excesses, the authorities summarily hanged those apprehended in the act of plundering or maltreating civilians. The perpetrators of most of the misdeeds, it appears, were small marauding bands, the members of which were often deserters from the large armies. If the marauding force was not too large the peasants often defended their property vigorously, and at times successfully. When reports about such bands reached the larger army camps detachments of troops were usually sent out to capture the marauders and hang them on the nearest trees. At times, of course, enemy forces deliberately devasted certain areas to weaken the opposition. But this was not a common occurrence.

Pillage and theft did not necessarily mean complete disappearance of wealth, as some historians have contended. Most of the salable articles were quickly sold and the money was put into circulation. F. Kaphahn states that the soldiers "spent their money with subtler-women, tavern keepers, merchants and tradesmen." Thus many of the valuables which the marauders took from the peasants and townspeople were not lost to the country.

But there is a brighter side to the picture. In the contemporary records there are laudatory as well as critical comments. Many chronicles of the decade of

the thirties and forties report that such veteran troops as those of the French general Turenne were well-behaved. Ranke approvingly quoted Count Khevenhueller (1588–1650) who in the *Annales Ferdinandei* praises the conduct of the soldiers, stating that the country was not devastated and burned, that the people were not driven from home and manor, that everything was well-cultivated and harvested, and that soldier and peasant got along well together.

Revisionist historians have also shown that such statements as "thousands of villages disappeared completely from the map" are not based on fact. This is not to gainsay that many villages were completely destroyed and for a time deserted by their inhabitants. Most of them, however, were soon rebuilt. W. Zahn writes regarding Brandenburg, "A large percentage of the villages were burned during the course of the war, but they were all rebuilt; hence the assumption is unfounded that the numerous deserted villages are attributable to the Thirty Years' War." J. Gebauer states emphatically, "Let one thing be finally and clearly established: In Brandenburg's narrower or wider precincts not one single village was permanently destroyed by the great war; the devastated and deserted villages of the countryside were one and all laid waste in the last centuries of the Middle Ages." O. Kius asserts that in Thuringia "no village was permitted to lie in ruins." Regarding Saxony R. Wuttke writes, "In Saxony there can be no question of the destruction of entire villages, as has been reported from other parts of Germany." W. Arnold states that in Hesse individual farms were deserted, but that there is no evidence to show that a single village disappeared. G. Mehring states that in Württemberg no large villages disappeared completely "only individual estates and smaller hamlets." "There is no doubt," another historian writes regarding Württemberg, "that parts of our country suffered terribly . . . but only in very rare instances was the devastation permanent. Even during the war years many who had sought refuge in the cities dared to return to their villages and to rebuild them if they had been destroyed." In Austria, A. Grund states, no villages were abandoned during the period from 1500 to 1683. On the contrary, fourteen villages were repeopled during this period.

This does not mean, however, that there were no deserted villages or ruins of villages in Germany after the war. W. Beschorner shows that many of the villages which were supposed to have disappeared during the Thirty Years' War actually disappeared

The Eve of the Modern World

long before that time. "In numerous instances," he wrote, "it has been proved by the records, often right down to the day and year, that villages which, according to folk tradition were burned or deserted by their inhabitants during the Thirty Years' War, had vanished from the earth much earlier, some as early as the thirteenth, fourteenth, and fifteenth centuries." Finally, F. Kaphahn states, "As it has been proved ever more clearly, the war had no part, or no considerable part, in causing the permanent desertion of villages. This took place almost exclusively in the thirteenth and fourteenth centuries." The reason for leaving the villages was that the soil was too poor for intensive cultivation.

In general, devastation in the agricultural districts was not as widespread and as permanent as historians of the old school have pictured it. The war undoubtedly interfered with the cultivation of the land in many places and in some the tilling of the soil was suspended entirely for some years. But the war did not ruin the fertility of the soil; on the contrary, the fact that the soil was uncultivated for a time may have helped to restore its fertility. Cultivation was resumed at the earliest possible time where the soil was fertile. E. Gothein asserts that "dwellings rose on the land surprisingly quickly and the arable land was soon put under the plow." In 1649 the Cistercian Mauritz Vogt wrote regarding Bohemia and Moravia: "In this year the subjects who had previously lived in the woods again became good cultivators, and cities, castles, markets and villages shook the sad ashes from their ruins and all will within a short time be resplendent with new roofs. In 1657 Cardinal Harrach wrote, "There is no doubt that Bohemia suffered tremendous damage and devastation during the war . . . but now everything hereabouts has been rebuilt." The French Field Marshal Grammont who had been in Westphalia in 1646 said when he visited it again in 1658 that all traces of the war had disappeared. K. Schmidt in his *Geschichte des dreissigjährigen Krieges* (1848) describes the destruction and devastation in superlatives, but then adds:

As a result of the newly awakened activity cultivation of the soil was restored so quickly that it would be difficult to find a better example of German industry. Soon the fields were blooming and better towns and villages were arising from the ashes. Trade and commerce revived on the highroads and in the markets, and science and art rose to higher levels than ever before.

Ilse Hoffman made a careful study of the diaries and reports of English travelers who visited Germany during the two decades after the Peace of Westphalia. She found that what they saw in most parts of Germany was not devastation, but thriving villages, well-cultivated fields, and plentiful crops. "Where one expected," she wrote, "to find descriptions of neglected acres, uncultivated vineyards or deserted stretches . . . one hears only a few years after the Peace of Westphalia the old song of the rich fertility of the German countryside." Schiller described a parallel situation in his *Jungfrau von Orleans* when he has Thibaut say:

Unworried can we view the desolation,
For steadfast stand the acres which we till.
The flames consume our villages, our corn
Is trampled 'neath the tread of warrior steeds;
With the new spring new harvests reappear,
And our light huts are quickly reared again.

Livestock was not replaced so quickly, but in this respect, too, the loss has been greatly exaggerated. The heavy losses in certain districts cannot be used as a norm for Germany as a whole. If at all possible the peasants would hide their cattle in woods, swamps, and caves at the approach of armies and marauding bands. E. Brückner shows that in some parts of Germany the number of sheep, pigs, and cattle increased during the war. On the other hand, the number of horses declined sharply, causing more and more peasants to use oxen to cultivate their fields. One reason for the decline of the number of horses was that so many were "used up" by the cavalry regiments of the time. We find that even near the end of the war many districts were able to furnish large numbers of sheep, pigs, and cattle. Thus in 1646 the Duchy of Laubach sent 600 cattle into the imperial camp in Bavaria and in the fall of 1647 General Montecucculi was able to obtain 1000 sheep, 150 steers and 160 pigs on a raid in the vicinity of Cassel. F. Beyhoff writes regarding the city of Giessen, "Despite the chaos of the war there were still many cattle in Giessen in 1648: 76 horses, 12 yoke oxen, 600 young and old steers, and 2900 sheep." . . .

Most controversial is the question of the loss of population. Since no general census was taken in Germany there are no reliable figures either for 1618 or for 1648 on which to base an estimate. Members of the old school gave such varying estimates for the decline of the population as from thirty to twelve million, from thirty to eighteen million, from twenty-one to thirteen million, from sixteen to six million, from sixteen to four million. In no instance are we told how the losses were computed. Neither are we informed whether the decline takes into account the population of the territories formally separated from the Holy Roman Empire by the peace, i.e., Switzerland and the Dutch Netherlands. In one respect there is almost unanimity. Most historians agree with the statistician who in the second half of the seventeenth century estimated the number of those killed in battle at 325,000. The number of civilians killed by soldiers was, according to the parish records, very small. Furthermore, there is little evidence to show that famine was a great destroyer. The greatest loss of life resulted from epidemics, epidemics of dystentery, typhus, and bubonic plague. The fact is often overlooked that there were epidemics before and after the war. From the fourteenth to the eighteenth centuries they were recurring phenomena. On the eve of the Thirty Years' War a series of epidemics claimed many lives in different parts of Germany and in neighboring countries. After the war epidemics caused loss of life on a large scale in the Rhine region (1665–1670), Austria (1678–1681), and Silesia and Saxony (1681). During the war they raged first in one, then in another part of Germany at various times. Cities far removed from the fighting suffered equally with those near the battlefields. Hence the war must not be held primarily responsible for the epidemics, although the dearth of the necessities of life in certain districts, caused by the devastations of the war, probably weakened the resistance of the inhabitants to disease. Even if epidemics did claim many times as many lives as warfare the decline of the population would still have been small.

In endeavoring to arrive at an estimate of the loss of life one must take into account the fact that there was a large floating population in Germany during the period of the Thirty Years' War. Consequently what was often regarded as destruction of the population was only dislocation of the population. Smaller or larger groups, composed of servants, the families of soldiers, dispossessed peasants, and rabble, usually moved along in the wake of the armies. There is little agreement among historians as to the size of these groups. While some believe the numbers were large, others argue that they were not. Furthermore, it was not uncommon for the entire population of a village to leave at the approach of an army. Often the local parson or priest would then note in the parish records that the village was depopulated. Later, after the army or armies had passed,

some peasants would return, while others remained in the fortified cities. "The cities," one historian wrote, "which were surrounded with earthworks and walls with substantial gates and whose citizens were well trained in defense were certainly able to defend themselves, particularly during the first years of the war." Many cities were able to obtain *Schutzbriefe* (letters of protection) from the commanding generals through payment of large sums of money.

To such cities the inhabitants of neighboring villages often fled in considerable numbers. In Weimar, for example, the number of "strangers" was fifty per cent larger than that of native citizens. During the period from 1634 to 1648 some 2000 peasants from neighboring villages lived in the city of Heilbronn where crude shelters were put up for them in every available space. "It is well known," another historian writes, "that the city of Lübeck was spared by the war. It was neither besieged nor surrounded and was therefore a safe refuge for many fugitives, especially for the Holstein nobility." Even W. Menzel whose writings helped to give the myth a wider circulation stated that the principal reason for the rapid growth of the population in Württemberg, one of the hardest hit sections of Germany, immediately after the war was "the return of a large part of the many who had left the fatherland after the battle of Nördlingen in 1634 to take refuge in Switzerland." G. Brückner states that in Germany generally the gradual return after the war of scattered peasants to the villages in which they had originally lived "explains in part the fact that the population appeared to increase so rapidly from 1649 to 1659." F. Beyhoff sums up the situation in the words:

It is an altogether erroneous procedure to attempt to assess the decline of the population by trying to ascertain the size of the population immediately after the war. At this time the population was still in a fluctuating movement started by the war and had not returned to a quiet state. Certainly during the war a great shift of population had taken place from territory to territory. Many thousands had fled from their homes to seek safety at a distance. Only gradually did they return.

To be sure, certain parts of Germany did suffer heavy population losses, but the sharp decline in some districts was offset at least in part by gains in others. The population of Saxony, for example, increased from 25,965 in 1608 to 46,317 in 1659. The population of many cities, including Würzburg, Strassburg, Hamburg and Bremen, increased during

The Eve of the Modern World

the war. Moreover, such figures as are available in specialized studies show that in many cities the population decline was not as drastic as had been stated. In contrast to the statement that at the end of the war "the city of Berlin contained but 300 citizens," F. Faden has shown that the population of Berlin numbered about 7,500 in 1643 and was even larger in 1648. F. Riegler, after reexamining the parish records, asserts that the population of the free city of Schwäbisch-Hall was 1279 in 1618, 1326 in 1631 and 1106 in 1650. "One would think," he comments, "that the misery of the last war years would have resulted in an even greater depopulation of the city, in a sharp decline in the number of inhabitants. This was not the case." K. Weiss takes issue with Schiller for stating that "Nuremberg buried more than ten thousand of its inhabitants." "The figures given by Schiller," he says, "are too high."

Revisionists have also shown that the so-called Franconian decree is spurious. Among the earlier historians who cited it was M. Menzel, and since that time it has been cited again and again as proof of the calamitous decline of the population. The "decree," supposedly issued "with the assent of the spiritual princes" by the diet of Franconia meeting at Nuremberg on February 15, 1650, forbids all males under sixty to become monks during the succeeding ten years, gives the Catholic clergy the right to marry, and permits each layman to take two wives. F. Julian, after careful investigation, calls it "the bigamy swindle," asserting that no meeting of the Franconian diet was held on the date cited. He further states that the story first made its appearance early in the eighteenth century and is patently the work of a practical joker. G. Wolf, too, labels it "an invention."

As to actual figures for the whole of Germany revisionists differ widely among themselves. R. Hoeniger states, "According to my estimate the total population of Germany at the end of the war was only two or three million less than it had been in 1618. In the decade of the forties the population resumed its growth, so that at the end of the war the loss may have been as low as one or two million." This estimate has been vigorously denounced as being too low. Hoeniger undoubtedly went too far in his reaction, but his statements did stimulate a wide interest in the subject. Special studies which appeared during the succeeding two decades presented revised figures for the losses in specific localities. But the figures for other localities and dis-

tricts still stand in need of critical reexamination. Although many historians disagreed with Hoeniger regarding the total losses, some joined him to form "the left wing" of the revisionist group. W. Windelband, who remained conservative in other respects, writes, "The assertion that the total losses were as high as a third of the population is to be regarded with a healthy skepticism. In some places, however, a decline of as much as a fifth can be established with considerable certainty."

The right wing of the revisionist group is far more conservative. Günther Franz, for example, estimates the population decline for Germany as a whole at one third. In doing so he still accepts the old figures which set the population loss in some districts as high as 60 to 70 per cent. More cautious are the conclusions of G. Oestreich who finds it impossible to arrive at "an accurate estimate" until historians have marshalled more facts. "The figures quoted in the reports and records of the time," he writes, "are exaggerated beyond all bounds."

The present writer agrees that it will be impossible to arrive at a reliable figure until more records have been critically reexamined and correlated. The estimates of the conservative revisionists are largely based on figures collected by members of the old school who were trying to paint the picture as black as possible. Even though the decline of the population was as large for certain localities as stated, emigration and dislocation have not been adequately considered as factors in the decline. It is the opinion of this writer that when more local figures are carefully reexamined they will show that the total decline of the population in the Holy Roman Empire from 1618 to 1648 was considerably less than the one-third estimated by the conservative revisionists. Johann Peter Süssmilch (1707–1767), whom the German economist Wilhelm Roscher regards as the outstanding population expert of the eighteenth century, asserted long before the myth of the all-destructive fury of the Thirty Years' War was created that by the early eighteenth century "the population losses had not only been recovered, but many sections of Germany were so thickly populated that they could send, nay were almost forced to send, colonists to America and other parts of the world." More than a century later Karl Biedermann, before he was influenced by Freytag's *Bilder aus der deutschen Vergangenheit*, denounced those who stated that it required more than a century to restore the population of Germany to the size it had been in

The All-Destructive War?

1618. He was willing to agree that the population of certain districts, as, for example, parts of Franconia and Thuringia, had suffered a sharp decline, but "for the whole of Germany, and even for larger sections of Germany, this has been denied by the most scrupulous statisticians of the last century."

4472 52

1234567890

The Eve of the Modern World